Historic American Towns along the Atlantic Coast

*Published in cooperation with
the* Center for American Places
*Santa Fe, New Mexico, and
Harrisonburg, Virginia*

Historic
along the

WARREN BOESCHENSTEIN

American Towns
Atlantic Coast

The Johns Hopkins University Press
BALTIMORE AND LONDON

© 1999 The Johns Hopkins University Press
All rights reserved. Published 1999
Printed in the United States of America on acid-free paper
9 8 7 6 5 4 3 2 1

The Johns Hopkins University Press
2715 North Charles Street
Baltimore, Maryland 21218-4363
www.press.jhu.edu

Library of Congress Cataloging-in-Publication Data will be found
at the end of this book.
A catalog record for this book is available from the British Library.

ISBN 0-8018-6144-6

For Karen, Anna, and Nell

Contents

For twenty-five years, my family and I have returned once or twice a year to Kennebunkport, that quintessential summer colony and seafaring village on the southern coast of Maine. At first these visits were for me desultory, somewhat aimless occasions during which I visited with relatives, downed an obligatory lobster, admired both the view and the newly arrived babies, and lamented the days "wasted" in this so-called geographic and cultural backwater. I was, after all, a St. Louis native, a city chauvinist, an architect whose training emphasized the primacy of large-scale urban buildings in the professional hierarchy of prestigious achievements. Small towns, even those I conceded were attractive, had scant instructional value. I wanted to return to the city and to my meaningful work. Gradually, as the allure of metropolitan areas waned just enough for me to take stock of my occasional coastal home, its significance and pleasures began to interest me, first as an appreciative visitor and then as a student of the lessons in livable community design it presented.

Then I began teaching in the School of Architecture at the University of Virginia in Charlottesville, equidistant from many of the cities I had studied and from the coastal areas I was beginning to notice. Now I had time for more research and exploration, and Kennebunkport seemed a convenient spot for sustained writing, if not for the actual research. So our visits grew in length, as did my appreciation for the variety of building types, delicacy of scale, range of landscapes, and quality of life in that remarkable village. I also became increasingly aware of, and alarmed by, the negative impact that rapid growth, traffic congestion, inconsistent zoning, and a heavy influx of tourists were having on the area. The very qualities that had attracted the admiring crowds were in danger of being overwhelmed and destroyed by them.

At the same time, in my larger professional world, I was hearing frequent and anxious complaints about the quality of the constructed environment that my immediate predecessors and my contemporaries and I had proposed and, in some cases, built. All too often, we, as professionals, produced homogenized landscapes, ones that had little identity and even questionable humanity. We emphasized isolated buildings rather than the matrixes that could sustain community life. Couldn't we do better? And, if so, where could we gain insights? America's varied Atlantic coastline seems to reflect an inherent diversity, certainly in the geography but also in the ethnic settlement patterns. Kennebunk-port seems to command an extraordinary allegiance from those who frequent it. Surely, I thought, there remain a few other historic coastal towns that also reveal the richness of our past and offer possibilities for the future. And so I set about finding them.

Selection of Towns

On my periodic trips between Charlottesville and Kennebunkport, I began to explore the coast, avoiding—with a sense of guilt at first—the great metropolitan centers I had previously frequented. I now looked forward to overnight stays in places such as New Castle, Delaware, Ocean Grove, New Jersey, or Stonington, Connecticut, as opportunities to study the qualities that made each of these towns desirable and unique. Eventually, spurred by my growing conviction that such communities could be valuable examples of town planning, I systematically drove the Atlantic coast from northern Maine to southern Florida, searching for those coastal towns and villages with significant histories, coherent plans, and intact identities. I became fascinated with the coast, as the meeting place of the two great realms of land and water, and with the prospects of that boundary experience.

The New England coast has an oft-noted majesty, with its jagged rocks acting as ramparts against the pounding sea. The Mid-Atlantic coast is a more measured, placid, and civilized mingling of flat land, beach, and ocean. The South Atlantic coast conveys great antiquity, with its luxuriant vegetation and edges worn smooth over the millennia. I selected towns from each of these regions for their livable qualities, their respect for their pasts, and their conscious decisions to anticipate their futures in the present. I found I could best understand the general by first understanding the specific features, and so, I thought, could other professionals.

I compiled a list of towns that had a range of site topographies, town patterns, and contemporary pressures. After subsequent visits, I winnowed this list to nine. In New England I selected the village of Castine, which lies at the head of Maine's Penobscot Bay and tiers up a slope to overlook an island-protected harbor. In southern Maine, where curving, rocky shores alternate with shallow coves, crescent beaches, and river mouths, the familiar Kennebunks' Port clusters upstream on either side of the Kennebunk River, sheltered from, but convenient to, the nearby ocean.[1] The flexed arm of Cape Cod separates waters warmed by the Gulf Stream, which sweeps up the coast, from the colder Gulf of Maine, to the north. Here in southern New England, glaciers have left terminal moraines as offshore islands, and Edgartown on Martha's Vineyard, one such island, arcs around a protected bay. Farther south, the retreating glaciers have raked the Connecticut coast to leave an intricate shoreline. These glaciers, wearing back weaker landforms, once cut coves and bays, but they yielded to the rocky headlands that today protrude into the water. Stonington sits on one of the resulting peninsulas at a point where Long Island Sound opens to the Atlantic.

All four New England towns share common Puritan origins, prosperous maritime years during the nineteenth century, Victorian summer visitors, and contemporary pressures for gentrification. Yet they differ in their proximity to metropolitan centers and the impact tourism is having on each town. Retirees and yachtsmen favor Castine, the most removed of these towns. Castine also hosts the Maine Maritime Academy, a major institution for a town its size. The Kennebunks are a convenient commute from Portland and a popular weekend excursion for Boston residents. Edgartown, once isolated on its island, is now accessible by plane and boat to the heavily populated Northeast. Stonington has become an exclusive residential enclave, largely unvisited by the tourists and travelers who stream along the Connecticut coast.

South of New England in the Mid-Atlantic region, where the flat coastal plain extends into the ocean as the continental shelf, the shoreline meanders across this broad geologic margin. Here I found two exemplary communities. The first, Ocean Grove, is situated on the New Jersey shore where it faces the open ocean. Its Methodist founders wisely located on high ground, using coastal ponds to mark boundaries for their community, but the town is nevertheless subject to brutal storms and unrelenting erosion. Among the towns in this study, it is the only one that was established primarily as a summer resort. It is also the town that has changed least in appearance since its founding, even though it is now a secular, not a religious, community.

New Castle, Delaware, lies along the broad estuary of the Delaware River on low, poorly drained land. Built on a bend in the river for strategic purposes, it controlled the approach up the river valley to Wilmington and Philadelphia. Over its long history, New Castle has seen a succession of cultural and physical transformations. The Dutch, Swedes, Scots, Irish, and Welsh Baptists disembarked here to settle the town and surrounding region.[2] Once a major port, state capital, and market center, New Castle is now a sedate suburb of Wilmington and stands in contrast to the gigantic twentieth-century industrial and chemical installations that dominate its region.

Although the three southern towns selected are all on the flat coastal plain, each one enjoys a unique site. Off the mainland of North Carolina, long and continuous barrier islands stretch up and down the coast to shield large inland bodies of water from ocean storms. Edenton lies on the northwestern side of Albemarle Sound, bracketed by streams that drain the swampy terrain. Along the South Carolina coast, rivers and ebb tides snake through broad deltas. Beaufort rests on a point of land encircled by tidal flats, salt marshes, and meandering water channels. To the south the town overlooks one of the best deepwater harbors on the Atlantic coast. Both of these towns were settled by the English, both had strong cultural ties with Barbados, and both developed under oligarchies of landed gentry who controlled populations of workers, including slaves.[3]

Florida has no streams draining its land mass by carrying away alluvium. Instead, waves have driven sediment shoreward to shape beach ridges and sandy barrier islands. Saint Augustine lies on a low peninsula sheltered behind one of these islands. The Spanish established Saint Augustine in the sixteenth century as an outpost to protect their treasure fleets as they sailed from New Spain to Europe through the narrow channel west of the Bahamas.[4] Later, Saint Augustine became the introduction to Floridian pleasure for Americans seeking escape from cold northern winters. It remains the nation's oldest continuously inhabited mainland community.

With the exception of Ocean Grove, New Jersey, which dates from 1867, all of these towns are at least 250 years old. All have experienced the inevitable economic cycles, population shifts, technological revolutions, political changes, human disasters, and natural calamities that communities of this age have faced. With populations of, for the most part, fewer than 12,000 people, these towns are comparatively small, although several do call themselves cities. Ocean access, tidal locations, and maritime conditions define them. And even though locations vary, from those directly on the open sea, such as Ocean Grove, to those sheltered miles up an estuary, such as New Castle, coastal environments and economies continue to shape each town. Intimacy is a part of everyday life in all these communities—it is continually fostered by the human scale of the town fabric, the pedestrian orientation, and the proximity of people to institutions and commerce and to other people.

These nine towns form the heart of my study. In my research, however, I visited many others and the regions in which they lie. I describe some of these additional towns in the text and note still others to suggest the extraordinary richness of this tradition. Of course, many more historic settlements have been irrevocably lost, ravaged by natural disasters, tawdry development, and neglect, or incorporated into larger cities in which they have lost their identities. I have arranged the towns in this book in geographical order from north to south, also noting their populations using the 1990 census figures, the most recent ones available.

The experiences of these towns continue, as should our discussions of them. New events are unfolding to add to their rich histories. Inevitably, however, more problems will arise to threaten their legacies. I hope that, in the future, new solutions to common problems might be shared more easily among historic coastal towns, helping to ensure their continuity.

I wish to thank a number of people who helped me in this most enjoyable of undertakings. In innumerable ways these people offered information, shared insights, provided hospitality, and commented on earlier versions, and, in so doing, they encouraged me to continue. I list them not geographically but alphabetically, because their influences permeate the entire book, reaching beyond the specific locations or issues they may have addressed.

These people are Marie Ahern, Eugene Angers, Timothy Beatley, Wayne T. Bell, Jr., Peter Bettencourt, Thomas E. Bradbury, Christina Brown, Mary Bryant, Troy Bunch, Thomas R. Butchko, Joyce Butler, James Cato, Henry C. Chambers, Charles Clifford, Mr. and Mrs. William Crichton, Ellenore W. Doudiet, Ben Douglas, John Dowd, Arch Edwards, Phillip W. Evans, Ronald Lee Fleming, D. H. Gould, Rick Griffin, Cathryn G. Harding, Edward R. Heite, Phillip C. Herr II, Jeanette Gentry Husted, Mr. and Mrs. Ross Inglis, Cynthia Cole Jenkins, Buckley C. Jeppson, Robert Jones, Ray Juizenga, Harry Kaiserian, Frank Keane, John Klingmeyer, Ruth Landon, Robert E. Marvin, Timothy J. Mullin, Earl Newton, Gary Okerlund, Phillip Perkins, Louise Pittaway, Marty Rakita, William Rauch, William Rawn, Gerald Rowland, Daphne Spain, Joel Stein, George F. Thompson, Craig Thorn, Charles Tingley, Jean Trapido-Rosenthal, John Trask, Frank Usina, Celestia Ward, Fred Washington, Jr., Ken and Jean White, and Richard Guy Wilson.

Most appreciatively, I thank my wife, Karen, who, having grown up on the coast of Maine, introduced me to the traditions of that area and encouraged me to visit others. She provided me with wise counsel and help throughout the writing of this book.

Historic American Towns along the Atlantic Coast

CHAPTER ONE

Lessons from the Towns Left Behind

In the tentative early settlements along the Atlantic coast, the ocean determined life, offering ties to the outside world and yielding an abundance that allowed colonists to gain footholds on land and establish communities. Unlike European cities, which often developed as civil and religious centers, North American seaports typically grew as places of commercial exchange, transferring the raw materials of the New World to European and West Indian markets and, in return, importing prized European manufactures to colonists on the expanding frontiers. As settlement succeeded, certain towns prospered through strategic advantages such as larger hinterlands, shorter distances to trade with foreign markets, and the physical capacity to accommodate growing trade. As industrialization progressed during the nineteenth century, some of these towns became significant cities and totally transformed themselves in the process. Other settlements—including those that are the focus of this book—stagnated in relative isolation. Bypassed by the transportation and industrial revolutions, these towns grew slowly and nurtured, by necessity if not willfully, another set of community design qualities that today provides a commentary on those of the great cities which have otherwise dominated American life.

The Growth of Coastal Towns

Until the early nineteenth century, urbanization remained relatively insignificant along the Atlantic coast. Colonial America was overwhelmingly rural, characterized by small towns, villages, and farms. Coastal towns formed a network of trade with one another and with European and West Indian sources. North of the Chesapeake Bay, towns dotted the coast and spread inland along the incipient road network. In the South, town settlers favored the extensive rivers that penetrated far inland, both partly relieving the need for, and complicating the building of, roads into the interior.

The small-scale and diffused settlement patterns reflected the colonial economy, which was primarily extractive and based on fisheries, forests, and agriculture. Since the raw materials involved were dispersed over large areas, few economies of scale could be achieved through concentration. Lumber was milled and grain was ground at numerous locations where water power could be harnessed.

Industry was that of crafts and was extensively home-based. The fishing and whaling fleets were financed, built, fitted out, managed, and sailed from small ports. Profits and capital accrued locally. During the colonial period, the American style of business was, as the economic historian John G. B. Hutchins has noted, "adaptive rather than aggressive, competitive rather than monopolistic, speculative rather than planned, and personal rather than institutional."[1]

In 1700 the aggregate population of the three leading cities—Boston, New York, and Philadelphia—was approximately 15,500.[2] Ninety years later, that total had multiplied six times to 95,000. However, the growth only mirrored the overall population increase in the country at large to 3.9 million. Nevertheless, there were only twenty-four communities of more than 2,500, and collectively these towns had 201,000 persons, still less than 5 percent of the total population.[3] After 1820, a dramatic transformation began to occur, reaching, during the years 1840–60, the highest rate of urban growth experienced in American history.[4] By 1900, Boston, New York, and Philadelphia had become home to 5,291,791 citizens, a fifty-five-fold increase from 1790.

While seaports may have lacked water power, immediately available timber, and sites for larger-scale agriculture, they did have experienced mercantile leadership, a growing capital base, and access to recently immigrated trained workers. The ports also served as bases for developing trade networks that would continue to grow, through which products were funneled for transshipping. More so in the North than in the South, where geographic factors and cultural traditions sustained dispersed settlement, villages with locational advantages developed into towns, with local merchants specializing as wholesalers and extending trade networks to neighboring villages. Towns grew into regional centers as outlying villagers sold surplus products there and bought manufactured items that were produced or imported at the centers. In the 1830s and 1840s factories began to replace the small-shop production pattern of the colonial period, and increasing immigration and rural-to-urban internal migration eroded the former social, ethnic, and religious homogeneity of communities.

Cities evolved as their commercial, financial, cultural, and communication influences grew, allowing urban merchants to link trade from the interior hinterlands to that of the seas.[5] Banking became more sophisticated and centralized as more firms began to buy and sell in money exchanges rather than barter goods and services. The cities that captured and serviced the more extensive and profitable hinterlands grew faster, and, in turn, those hinterlands that were larger in physical size, population, and fertility supported the more rapid rise of cities.[6]

Transportation was a great facilitator of urbanization. In the early nineteenth century, new larger ships with deeper drafts began to bypass smaller ports to serve more navigable ones, further centralizing trade and development. Steam-driven engines increased the range and flexibility of shipping and travel. By the 1830s contract carriage became common among vessels chartered in freight markets, encouraging more concentrated management and ownership in the major coastal ports. Inland transportation networks developed beyond the initial rivers and roads to include canals and railroads that focused on transfer cities.

The fall lines of rivers offered outstanding locations for cities to capitalize on transportation advantages. Philadelphia, Wilmington, Baltimore, Washington, D.C., and Richmond, for example, lie along river fall lines at locations to which oceangoing vessels can navigate in order to transfer freight to the seaboard overland routes, including the road and rail lines that connect these cities along the higher ground above the Atlantic coastline. The emerging major ports had large, deep harbors and land available on which to build cities, qualities that the coastal towns, often situated in wetland surroundings, did not possess. Also to the newer port towns' advantage was the demonstrated vulnerability of coastal towns during the War of 1812, when superior British naval forces were able to approach them with relative impunity.

Major Cities

There were five important economic nodal forces on which the successful port towns capitalized to become important coastal cities: trade, transportation, production, finance, and business administration.[7] Efforts in these areas can be seen in the history of major cities, particularly Boston, New York City, Baltimore, and Charleston, which dominated urban growth along the Atlantic coast.

Of the seaports that became major cities, Boston had the distinct advantages of both having short lanes to the sea and being closest to Europe. It prospered early in trade and also developed a shipbuilding industry, enabling its vessels to replace those of the English and the Dutch as carriers of colonial commerce. Capitalizing on this success, the aggressive Boston merchants quickly came to dominate colonial trade in the seventeenth century.[8] However, while the Boston hinterlands were the first of the colonial regions to populate and thereby benefit their growing port, they were also constricted by the Appalachians, which lie close to the sea in New England. With its capital and entrepreneurial talent, Boston then turned not to manufacturing (it lacked sufficient water power) but to the financing and administration of regional industries, for example, the development of the nineteenth-century textile mills in Lowell, Lawrence, and Fall River, Massachusetts. In the process, Boston leveled hills and filled portions of its bay to gain more land for urban growth.[9]

Although New York City, then a trading post called New Amsterdam, initially languished under the control of the Dutch West India Company, its unrivaled location enabled it eventually to become the primary Atlantic port.[10] It had a large, protected, and deep natural harbor whose temperate climate favored navigation throughout the year. To the south, the Narrows opened to the Atlantic and the world; to the east, the East River gave passage to Long Island Sound and

New England; and to the north and the west, the Hudson and Mohawk River valleys provided good access to the continental interior. With the completion of the Erie Canal in 1825 and subsequent railroad linkages, New York City's hinterlands were extended into the Midwest. In and around Manhattan, ample flatland accommodated the building that commerce, shipping, and myriad trades and businesses promoted. By the early nineteenth century, New York City had replaced Philadelphia as the nation's financial and commercial center.[11] By 1860, more than 800,000 people crowded Manhattan and an additional 265,000 lived in Brooklyn, making the latter the third largest city in the country.

Baltimore also boasted an excellent harbor and was closer than the northern ports to the West Indies. Even more important, Baltimore became the major outlet for trade to and from the Susquehanna River region. As food demands grew in American cities and in Europe, wheat from Pennsylvania and western Maryland was shipped downriver to Baltimore rather than carried overland to Philadelphia. Unlike tobacco, wheat requires extensive central processing and proper storage. Being on the fall line, Baltimore had the water power for mills, and it also had land for storage and port facilities for shipping. Metal and textile mills soon joined the flour mills in and around Baltimore. Merchants then focused on the need for a railroad, and in 1827 the Baltimore and Ohio Railroad was incorporated, making Baltimore a particularly important terminal and a site for heavy industry.[12]

Lying on a peninsula formed by the convergence of the Cooper and Ashley Rivers, Charleston offered one of the few good sites for a port along the South Carolina coast. Charleston's early growth stemmed from the deerskin trade, which required warehouse facilities and capital and yielded significant profits to establish the town as a credit center. From this base, through extensive transactions with the back-country plantations, Charleston's merchants pursued trade in rice, slaves, and lumber. Like wheat, rice, which was introduced as early as 1690 in South Carolina, also requires central storage and processing facilities. Through the slave trade, merchants provided the means to work plantations and gained profits that further strengthened the city's role as a financial center. The opening of the Santee Canal in 1800, which greatly expanded the city's tributary system, and the growth of back-country towns allowed Charleston to rival the major commercial cities of the North.[13]

As these and other towns grew into cities, some eventually becoming metropolitan centers with sprawling suburbs, their social and physical qualities inevitably changed. In the preindustrial town, life was characterized by a high degree of communal order and stability, with the wealthy and the poor often residing close together—although not necessarily being neighborly. Activities of daily life were neither specialized nor radically different in character, allowing many to live and work in the same building. Communication was usually personal, as people frequently met directly to converse and trade with one another. As industrialization proceeded, activities became more specialized and aggregated, while land uses eventually codified into the zoning districts of the twentieth century. Social segregation increased as workers, immigrants, and the poor crowded into older sections of cities and members of the economic and social elite commuted by streetcars and then by automobiles from the urban centers to their suburban residences. Historic centers had to accommodate new functions, and, in the process, they lost their old character and adopted entirely different and larger scales. Fundamental relationships between communities and their surrounding water and natural settings, relationships that were the bases of the original settlements, were obscured, or completely lost, in these urban transformations.

The towns in this book avoided these cataclysmic changes. They were largely forgotten as this country, over a period of three hundred years, moved from being a land of marginal colonial status to a nation recognized as the dominant world power. These towns periodically participated in the national growth but then drifted into obscurity, preserving in that isolation their older coherence. Castine, Maine, is remotely located along the central coast of Maine, far from the major transportation lines and, with the exception of lumber, lacks the raw material sources that supported industrialization. Similar to Castine, Kennebunks' Port, Maine, had a limited hinterland as well as difficult soil conditions on which to build. Edgartown, Massachusetts, has been restricted in growth by its island location on Martha's Vineyard, as has Stonington, Connecticut, on its narrow, rocky peninsula. Ocean Grove, New Jersey, never intended to grow beyond its narrow boundaries for fear that expansion would weaken its social and religious integrity. New Castle, Delaware, while strategically positioned for defense during the colonial period, was poorly located for subsequent growth because of its low-lying land and its distance from the river's fall line and power source. Edenton, North Carolina, rests in a remote setting that is difficult to access either by land or by sea. Beaufort, South Carolina, is similarly arduous to reach by land and, moreover, is in a region that was largely unaffected by industrialization. In Florida, Saint Augustine's site on a sandy peninsula served early defensive purposes but hindered later growth and urbanization.

Qualities of Coastal Towns

Why do we appreciate historic coastal towns today? Why do many people find them attractive communities to visit and engaging places in which to live? Equally important, what can professionals learn from them to inform the design of new communities? There is, most immediately, the pleasure, the sheer delight of being in one of these towns. The light, often enhanced near the sea by reflections, the rise and fall of the wind, stronger around water and especially heavy in the South, the salty smells and tastes, and the constant sound of water meeting land all stimulate the senses. Here there are simple contrasts—high and low, warm and cold, protected and exposed, communal and private, maintained and neglected, tamed and wild—that are too often absent in our living environments.

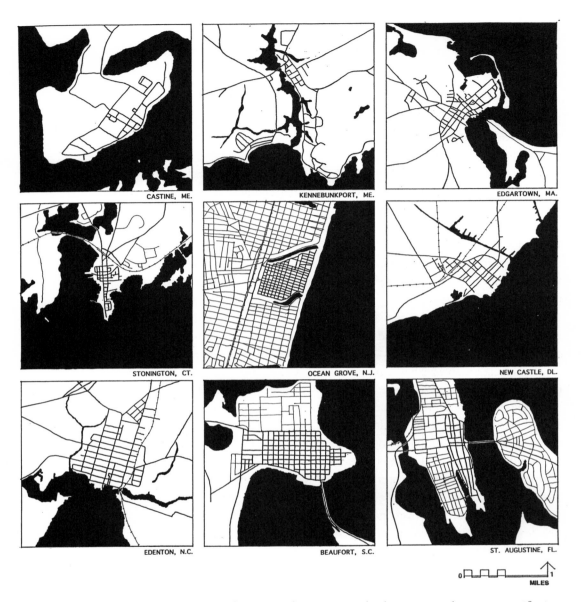

CASTINE, ME.   KENNEBUNKPORT, ME.   EDGARTOWN, MA.

STONINGTON, CT.   OCEAN GROVE, N.J.   NEW CASTLE, DL.

EDENTON, N.C.   BEAUFORT, S.C.   ST. AUGUSTINE, FL.

Fig. 1.1. Intricate configurations of water meeting land give unique identities to specific sites, while settlement patterns introduce a sense of community (drawings by author, from current U.S. Coast and Geodetic Survey maps).

More specifically, the historic coastal towns in this book share four distinguishing qualities: location, community, time, and scale. While the characteristics themselves are not unique to historic coastal towns, their individual and collective expressions are. In coastal towns these qualities gain distinct, intensified expression and reinforce one another in special ways. Though the values of location, community, time, and scale may be difficult to measure in absolute terms, these qualities have identifiable physical features that can be discussed and clarified through comparisons.

Location

Each of these towns could only have developed in its particular way on its respective site. Town form and town site are inseparable. Settlers knowingly responded to particular conditions, especially topography, climate, and landscape, in order to survive. They were intimately familiar with the sites, usually having lived in the area for years before establishing these towns. Viewing these towns today from an overlook, across a body of water, or from a typical public area on the waterfront itself, one can still understand the rationales for each town's location. Castine lies at the head of a bay and is the gateway to two rivers, allowing access both to the ocean and to inland resources. Kennebunks' Port is shielded upstream from the stormy Atlantic. Edgartown overlooks a protected bay near a major shipping channel. Stonington is situated at a point where Long Island Sound opens to the Atlantic. Ocean Grove, though on the mainland, is virtually surrounded by water. New Castle commands a bend in a major river estuary. Edenton rests at the end of a protected bay near inland rivers. Beaufort surveys a deepwater sound and captures cooling breezes off the water. Saint Augustine sits behind a barrier island. These towns belong where they are and derive character from their settings.

Settlers did not radically change the shape of the land. While sites varied from steep hills, such as at Castine, to flat land, such as at Edenton, Beaufort, and Saint Augustine, settlers accepted site conditions because they did not have the means to alter them. Instead they incorporated underlying landforms when siting roads and buildings. In Edgartown, for example, buildings tier up the town's slope, like seats in an amphitheater, to gain harbor views. In Stonington, a pattern of tight buildings loosens on the fringe to merge with meadows and marshes. In Beaufort, mansions alternate with groups of giant live oaks to accent the arc of the bay. Building incrementally in small clusters, settlers minimally disturbed the land, allowing town patterns to express the shapes of the underlying land.

Settlers viewed land symbolically as well as pragmatically. They preferred to place courthouses, churches, town halls, and schools on higher ground, and they built institutional buildings taller than surrounding houses, allowing steeples and towers to project above tree lines. Public buildings and churches still dominate uphill sites, especially in Kennebunks' Port, Edenton, New Castle, and Castine. Topography also conveyed social status. As towns grew and waterfronts became busier, the gentry relocated to higher ground, where, in relative seclusion, they could still survey their shipping investments in harbors below.

Giving a further sense of "location" to these communities, town forms and individual buildings responded to immediate climate conditions. Settlers planned towns to optimize orientation to the sun and prevailing winds. Castine and Edgartown slope southeastward to overlook harbors and to catch the warming sun.[14] Both Castine and Edgartown also have hills to the north that block cold winter winds. Town forms are "open" or "closed," depending on climate. In Beaufort, south-facing verandahs and the waterfront park capture cooling ocean breezes. Ocean Grove incorporates "flaring avenues" to funnel summer ocean breezes into the community, while Edenton has its Green and Saint Augustine its Plaza, both opening to the waterside to relieve torrid summer heat. In Kennebunks' Port, the village lies sheltered upriver and Dock Square is embedded within the town, protecting it from brutal winter winds.

Residents have adapted their individual houses more specifically to climate. In northern towns, barns and sheds interconnect with main houses to provide easier winter access, while in the South these structures are separated to maximize fresh air circulation around buildings and cross-ventilation through rooms. In the North, houses sit closer to public roads, which are diligently kept free of snow, while in the South houses lie further back from roads to gain privacy.[15] Year-round houses in the North are of simple shapes, with low ceilings to conserve heat, while in the South houses are of more complex shapes, with high ceilings to facilitate air movement. Northern porches shelter only front entrances, but southern porches stretch the length of a home to provide shade and serve as outdoor rooms. Southern houses are raised on masonry piers to induce cool breezes by convection and escape flooding in low-lying hurricane-prone areas. Steep building roofs in the North help shed snow loads, while shallow-sloped roofs in the South overhang to shade walls and windows.

The dictates of architectural styles have, at times, conflicted with climatic realities. For example, the Federal style, favoring shallow roofs and fence cornices, complicated snow buildup and removal in New England. Since World War II, however, mechanical heating and air conditioning systems have allowed buildings more climatic independence. As a result, owners have erected larger and more inward-oriented structures, which, in turn, have increased the scale of buildings and diminished the public life of these towns.[16]

Natural environments are integral to these towns and connect them to their locales. Unlike coastal towns of many other cultures, American towns do not wall off surroundings. Wild landscapes surround and even penetrate these towns. For example, salt marshes envelope Beaufort, uphill pine forests finger into Castine, and rivers and streams thread through Kennebunks' Port. Greenbelts in New Castle and Edenton bring wildlife into intimate contact with town activities. Few sea walls retain the shorelines bordering these towns.

Regional building materials crafted by local workers tie structures to sites and, collectively, further identify towns with their locales. Using rock and stone quarried on-site for walls and paths and wood from nearby forests for siding, shingles, and decorative details, buildings seem to be virtual outgrowths of the land itself. In Stonington, residents used local granite to construct both sea walls and polished pieces for sills and mantles. In towns with traditions of crafts-manship, artisans have inventively employed common materials. In Beaufort, "tabby" concrete, a mixture of local sand and crushed oyster shells, evokes maritime connections. Experienced carpenters in Edenton and Kennebunks' Port, some of whom had learned their skills in local shipbuilding, produced elegant scrollwork and corner, stair, and paneling details.

Community

These towns convey a sense of community that, while undoubtedly imposed upon some residents, produces interdependence among many others. To sur-vive, coastal residents had to cooperate: Together they have faced mutual threats of invasions, hurricanes, and floods—dangers over which they had no control. Residents have also had to work with one another to solve troubling internal conflicts arising over fishing rights, docking privileges, and, more recently, visi-tor regulations. Over generations, residents have developed a range of public spaces, from the large harbors to the more intimate streets, greens, malls, and cemeteries, where people could come together, exchange information, and rein-force belief in their shared destiny. Because these towns were often official ports of entry and seats of government, public buildings gained prominence and became everyday reminders of common needs. People from different social classes and with varying skills formed the community. They built houses to reflect their individual needs, tastes, and resources. Yet, they all respected a common building vocabulary that gave the town an overall identity. Even today, the economic and, to a lesser extent, the political and social activities in coastal towns remain visible.

These towns express a sense of community, a feeling that people regularly pursue common, purposeful tasks. Residents share similar beliefs and partici-pate with one another in associations that give form to the communities. Over many generations, residents have taken evident pride in their towns and imbued them with qualities that reflect their commitment.

Life in coastal towns fosters communal sensibilities. There are the dangers shared by all—such as the threats of hurricanes and floods—which require planning beforehand to avoid disasters and mutual assistance afterward to re-build. Even mild weather changes prompt conversations and civic awareness. As enterprises that carried great risks and could yield great rewards, fishing and trading ventures involved many citizens as investors, as active participants, or as dependent family members. Most local financially secure men—and a few women—owned shares in ships that originated from these towns. Consequently, people waited anxiously and gained news in public places, where seamen, hav-ing returned from exotic places, told their tales and where travelers and mer-chants came seeking hospitality. Understandably, residents shaped their towns to accommodate this active public life.

As people later began to summer in coastal towns, they enjoyed other types of public life—those activities centered on the pleasures of fresh air and sun. While boating, beach bathing, and golfing became more socially and spatially segregated than earlier popular activities, people still shared the public places of these towns for civic functions and everyday commercial needs. Today, tourism and shopping continue these traditions. In coastal towns, there is a heightened sense of public life because economic and social activities are visibly present. People enjoy seeing boats docking, fishermen unloading hauls, owners servicing boats, merchants displaying goods, and vacationers playing sports. Visitors and residents come together to see and to be seen, to overhear, to gauge shifts in public fashions, and to encounter the unexpected.

People with a range of skills and wealth constitute the community and, in turn, contribute to the spatial variety of these towns. Specific physical features of a town help to define public life and express this communal sense. With this in mind, residents have organized such coastal towns according to distinctive plans. Open spaces encircle these towns, public spaces encourage people to gather, public buildings symbolize common values, and walkable distances allow convenient associations.

During the towns' formative periods, activity was focused on the waterfronts. Ships and, later, trains typically arrived at ports and stations on or near the waterfronts.[17] In traditional maritime towns, warehouses, business operations, and institutions were congregated near port facilities. Especially in the early years of these towns, people walked to these centers. In towns such as New Castle, passageways exclusively for pedestrians are still open, while in other towns such as Stonington, residents are trying to regain them. The proliferation first of carriages and then of automobiles accelerated settlement dispersal. Recent commercial strips along arterial roads have rapidly blurred community edges in towns across the United States. If not defined by water or owned by public land trusts, open space boundaries are difficult to maintain in the face of contemporary development pressures. Fortunately, most of these towns have been able to maintain their surrounding open spaces and, in turn, their identities.

Each community has grown from a unique town plan that distinguishes it from other settlements. Residents identified with these plans, for such layouts established the patterns of everyday life—pleasurable walking distances, recognizable building rhythms, and memorable vistas. All these town plans are grid configurations, although they vary in plan geometry and block size.[18] In the South, central authorities imposed orderly and comprehensive plans on flat topographies. In New England, where topography is more varied and settlements sprang up before town design had been determined, plans were adjusted to site conditions. In Castine and Edgartown, for example, streets derive from public rights-of-way, which followed old property lines and were related to topographic features. Families with large property holdings subdivided land and added new roads as needed, but these too were fitted to the shape of the land. On the other hand, the plans of Edenton and Beaufort relate strongly to the

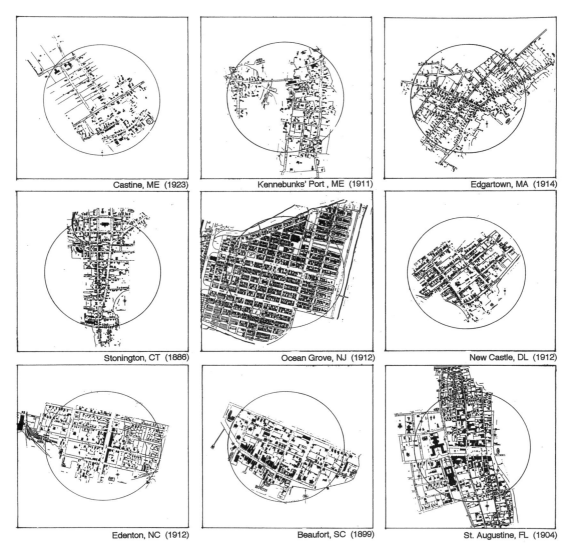

Fig. 1.2. Similarly scaled buildings fill these towns and lie predominantly within a circle half a mile in diameter (Sanborn maps, with buildings rendered black).

cardinal compass points and were platted before buildings appeared. In the North, street grids have been adjusted according to topography and the intensity of activity, becoming more compact where usage concentrates in the town center and loosening where activity disperses on the fringe. Street plans invariably orient to the edge of the major body of water. Town patterns often vary in block dimensions, use of streets, and building types as one moves inland from the waterfront, but they remain relatively similar parallel to the water's edge.

From expansive harbors to intimate streets, a variety of public spaces are still frequented daily by residents. These spaces, open and conveniently located, allow residents to experience and appreciate their communities. The most important space in terms of size, if no longer function, is typically the harbor. Many harbors have qualities that make them seem like large outdoor rooms, contained on three sides by the planes of trees or hillsides. Usually the distance across the harbor is less than half a mile, and it rarely exceeds three-quarters of a mile, allowing people to see one another from opposite sides of the shore.[19] While yachts and pleasure boats have replaced trading ships in these ports, waterfronts are still important activity centers in the majority of these towns.

In coastal towns that developed as resorts, such as Ocean Grove, the public has always enjoyed access to long stretches of the waterfront. In coastal towns that grew for trading purposes, such as Edgartown, waterfront access has been more limited. Streets often terminated at public wharves, but private interests controlled the remaining shoreline. As siltation and infilling enlarged waterfronts, adjacent property owners exercised riparian rights to gain valuable land. They built fishhouses, warehouses, and even factories on these sites and sometimes extended railroads to them. However, with the decline of maritime trade, waterfronts have become more publicly accessible although less active. In New Castle and Edenton, parks have replaced commercial waterfront areas, dramatically changing the character of these areas.

Each of these nine towns has a major public space. In some cases public spaces open directly to the water, as do Saint Augustine's Plaza and Ocean Grove's Ocean Pathway. In Castine and New Castle major public spaces are further inland to exploit the advantages of higher ground. Public buildings and churches are grouped around these spaces and rise above surrounding structures to dominate the town visually. Residences often casually mix with public buildings nearby. All major spaces have simple plan shapes, and their appearances are usually softened by landscape features. These spaces are also "permeable," allowing access from many directions.

Two types of major streets exist in coastal towns. One extends along the shoreline and is often called "Water Street," "Front Street," or "the Strand." The other type runs perpendicular to the waterfront through the middle of the town and is typically named "Market Street," "Main Street," or "Broad Street." The first type accommodated fishing, warehouse, and manufacturing activities while the latter provided sites for services, shopping, and institutions. Thus the focal points of coastal towns tended to be where these two roads intersected near the water's edge.

Stores and services developed along Main Street, usually favoring the two or three blocks closest to the water, while churches and public buildings were located further inland. Residents from adjoining neighborhoods, waterfront workers, and inland inhabitants could therefore most conveniently reach Main Street. For towns on narrow peninsula sites, the typical perpendicular relationship of these two primary streets was altered. For example, in Stonington and Saint Augustine the old commercial street parallels the waterfront one block inland, while churches and public buildings are on another street still further inland.

Main streets typically have defining spatial qualities and possess an identifiable sense of place. In the downtown business blocks, buildings are crowded together to maximize street frontages, forming street walls and spatial enclosures. The width of commercial streets, measured between faces of opposite buildings, ranges from eighteen feet in Saint Augustine to one hundred feet in Edenton. Narrower streets allow pedestrians to move easily from one side to the other, while wider streets provide more room for services such as town wells and activities such as temporary markets within the street space.

Public buildings are major town features. Custom houses, post offices, courthouses, town halls, fire stations, schools, and libraries are visually prominent and conveniently located. They terminate street vistas and dominate public spaces. Usually free-standing and constructed of granite or brick, making them more permanent and expensive than typical wood dwellings, these singular buildings exhibit a civic scale. Such public buildings also fit comfortably into the character of their immediate surroundings, keeping with the basic building rhythms, proportions, and setbacks along their respective streets. They are also approachable, having obvious street entrances. Since World War II, the space requirements of schools, firehouses, and county services have outgrown old buildings, forcing these facilities to relocate to town fringes. The old buildings, however, usually remain to house other functions.

Local capital and labor once sustained town economies, more so than they do today. Home-based industries, trade, and services provided employment and profit opportunities. People lived within a convenient walk, or at least a reasonable wagon or boat ride, from where they regularly worked and traded in town. Not until the latter half of the twentieth century, with the widespread use of automobiles and the construction of major highways, have many people regularly commuted long distances and regionally separated themselves from their places of employment.

House location and size reflected social rank. Those with power and wealth commanded the preferred sites. Sea captains, merchants, and planters—and, later, industrialists and "summer people"—chose sites with good drainage, quiet surroundings, attractive views, and refreshing breezes. The poor more often lived in lower-lying land susceptible to storms and climate extremes. Nevertheless, people of different social status lived physically close to each other. Compared to contemporary suburban living patterns, different classes lived in close proximity. If house size is used as an approximate index of wealth and social rank, insurance maps reveal patterns of different status groups living near one another. Several site-planning strategies facilitated these patterns. Typically, people of one social class grouped their homes along the same street. For example, the planter families in Beaufort resided on Bay Street, and the ship captains in Edgartown preferred Water Street. People living in more modest housing often resided around the corner, on a parallel street inland, down a side lane, or in midblock locations. Large residences also often housed extended families, in

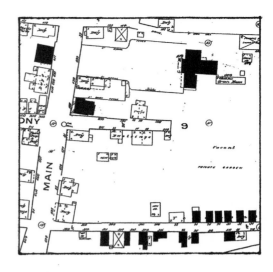

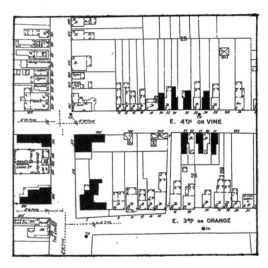

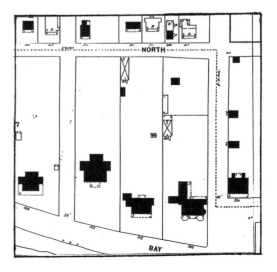

Fig. 1.3. Assuming house size as an indicator of social status, these plans illustrate site strategies to differentiate among groups while allowing residential proximity (Sanborn maps with selected buildings rendered black). Top: Stonington, Connecticut (1886). The houses of the gentry faced Main Street. The African Americans who worked as railroad and hotel porters lived nearby on a lane off that street, a location not nearly as prominent but still close to the town activities. Middle: New Castle, Delaware (1912). Lawyers and merchants favored large corner lots with access to light and views. Lower-income people lived nearby on smaller, narrower, mid-block lots in row houses with light and views only from the street and backyards. Bottom: Beaufort, South Carolina (1899). Mansions face south (toward the water) to enjoy views and benefit from the wind. Smaller, less desirable houses are inland.

cluding poor relations, elderly parents, and unmarried adults, as well as unrelated household help. Consequently, people of one social class were in close proximity to other types of people everyday.

While the towns' economies have changed, their physical patterns and relationships are still convenient and comprehensible. Their town plans connect home, work, public gathering places, and natural environments, thereby offering a range of experiences and allow residents, often of different status, to encounter each other informally. These patterns, not as evident in many contemporary environments, contribute to the quality of community in these towns.

Time

The quality of time is another readily apparent aspect of these towns, possibly more so than in any other type of community. Cultural, biologic, and geologic senses of time are tangibly evident. Human history permeates these towns in the collections of buildings, the changing attitudes toward the landscape, and the accumulated town patterns, which reflect the values of different periods. The oldest of these towns date from the very earliest European settlement of this continent, and they are living records of twelve generations or more. Animal migration patterns also relate to these locations—birds travel along the Atlantic flyway, fish swim through the nearby ocean currents, and each year the seasonal human vacationers come in search of the sun. Geologic time, the most ancient and usually most hidden dimension, is readily visible within the communities where water, wind, and sand have worn away the land's edges to reveal the past in the underlying strata. There are also the reliable rhythms of the tides and the more variable weather conditions of storms, which magnify the perceptions of seasons repeating and time passing. These evident indices of time, some that occur in repetitive patterns or cycles and others that transform as they age, are all essential attributes of coastal towns and, while not unique to them, are particularly expressive in them.

The towns examined in this book are among the oldest continuously inhabited settlements in North America. The towns record planning and settlement ideas brought to this continent by Europeans and which Americans, reacting to new-world concerns, changed. Understandably, each of these nine coastal towns reveals a different past. Ocean Grove is the accomplishment of primarily one generation, the fervent post–Civil War Methodists. Those who followed revered what founders established and sought to preserve it. Beaufort reflects most magnificently not one but several generations of antebellum planters, who, for more than a century, asserted their authority and importance. In Kennebunks' Port, Victorians built a community distinct from that of the earlier Federalists. In Stonington, New Castle, and Edenton, residents intermixed building types and structures from different periods.

Historical gaps or "lost" eras exist today. Some periods that, in retrospect, seem historically important are unrecorded in the environment. Fires, floods, and poverty have taken their toll, as has human neglect. For example, in New Castle today the seventeenth-century Dutch period and nineteenth-century industrial era are only faintly evident; the town chose instead to venerate the British colonial period. Saint Augustine was even more specific, electing to focus its preservation effort on 1763, the end of the first Spanish period of the town, consequently forsaking other periods.

We know more about the lives of the wealthy than those of the poor. The poor lived in marginal locations and insubstantial structures, susceptible to coastal storms and frequently demolished in order to put the land to more profitable uses. In the Kennebunks, few buildings remain of the fishermen and workers who had until recently lived and worked in the port. The wealthy, on the other hand, lived in grander, better-built houses in safer locations. While frequently used for other purposes over their long histories, many of these sturdy structures have survived to become dwellings again.

Regrettably, little evidence remains of the fishing activities that generated the original forms of many of these towns. Boathouses and fish shacks no longer line the harbors. Fish processing has shifted to offshore factory ships. Many small businesses, services, artisan shops, and industries that formerly flourished have closed. The 1889 insurance map of Stonington identifies at least one place of employment on virtually every street block. In Stonington today, residential use dominates almost exclusively.

Churches continue to be permanent town features. While a few are now residences, most still serve religious roles. Indeed, they remain as primary community contacts for families who have moved to outlying areas. Churches with adjacent burial grounds are especially time-laden environments. Particularly in southern towns, burial grounds shaded by ancient live oaks are extraordinary settings that dramatize the depth of time and the enduring nature of personalities. In their collective placement of grave markers, they also evoke the prevailing town building pattern.

Since World War II, suburbs have noticeably developed on the fringes of these towns. Built at lower densities with wider separations between buildings, accessed by curvilinear roads, dominated by homogenous land uses, and dependent on automobiles, these suburbs contrast with the traditional towns they surround. Roads that cross through these newer developments to reach the historic centers reveal changed values and lost opportunities. Passing through areas that were formerly wood lots, marshes, and farmlands, these town entrance roads are now often commercial strips lined with buildings and services for automobile travelers. Buildings face incoming traffic, seemingly unaware of the waterfronts from which the towns originated. Because of inadequate land-use controls along these roads, visitors can no longer appreciate the natural landscapes that were once part of the towns' overall environments. Visitors are only able to gain a small glimpse of Beaufort's marshlands or Edenton's swamps.

*Fig. 1.4. Church yards, such as this one in Beaufort, are particularly time-laden
environments. During the Civil War, these tomb slabs served as emergency operating tables
for those wounded in battle.*

Of all the towns discussed here, Castine has most carefully preserved its inland
approach road—a delightful unfolding introduction to the landscape, the town,
and its reflections of time.

Coastal towns have experienced different periods of activity. During the year,
times of relative quiet and rest followed those of productivity. People fished and

farmed when conditions prevailed, after which they rested and repaired to await the next seasonal flurry. Summer tourists visited on predictable schedules, and locals who had welcomed the vacationers were equally delighted to see them leave. With mechanical heating and air conditioning today, however, seasonal patterns are becoming more moderate. These towns now seek more diversified economies to reduce problems caused by seasonal employment cycles.[20] Yet the environmental sense of cyclical time still remains a strong characteristic.

These towns have endured periods of growth and decline. Most flourished in the Federalist period, prospered before the Civil War, then declined but enjoyed a brief resurgence in the late Victorian era as summer visitors discovered them. Their overall population continued to diminish through the Great Depression. Only since World War II have these towns experienced major population growth.

Significant expansion and contraction both occurred at the scale of individual buildings. Residents built new houses, usually one at a time, and incrementally expanded these houses by adding new wings, outbuildings, and more floors during prosperous years. In Stonington, owners raised a number of buildings on Water Street to insert new ground floors beneath the raised older floors. In less favorable times, they closed off building extensions and lived more compactly. Since World War II, expansion has occurred in outlying suburbs, beyond walking distance from the historic cores, aided by the widespread use of automobiles, the rapid population growth, and preservation laws that discouraged increased density in historic districts.

Throughout their histories, these towns had temporal anchors, seemingly immutable features that provided a sense of permanency as the towns changed. Water remains an obvious, profound, and constant presence. Cemeteries, churches, many public buildings, and houses of the gentry have been remarkably stable features even as workplaces and smaller houses have disappeared. Street patterns have been lasting. For the most part, public spaces continue to be open to all. Consequently, collective human memory relates to physical features of these towns that still exist today.

Evidence of time is pervasive not only in the built towns themselves but also in the natural environments of which they are a part. Natural environments virtually encircle many of these towns. The surrounding sea, ponds, rivers, marshes, forests, and woods exhibit cycles of growth and decay, migrations of animals, changes of seasons, and the ebb and flow of tides. In the sky above the meeting of major air masses—continental, maritime, polar, and tropical—can suddenly transform into turbulent storms. Where water and weather wear against the land, the underlying geology is often exposed, unlike in cities, where it is usually buried. Rock, gravel, sand, and mud overlay each other and record the ages.

Granite boulders in Castine welled up as molten masses from miles beneath the earth's surface millions of years ago. In Ocean Grove, the sand, ground

Fig. 1.5. In Beaufort, giant live oak trees shade a quiet lane.

fine by endless waves, continues to shift despite herculean stabilization efforts. Forces of change are unrelenting. Storm waves pound with enormous force, as much as twenty tons per square yard, hurling rocks and water against the exposed land to reshape shorelines. Erosion and deposition never cease. What the sea takes away from one place, it returns to another. In Kennebunks' Port, erosion and longshore drift transform granite headlands on one side of the river into sandy beaches on the other. In the areas bordering Beaufort, rich alluvial soil, washed down from the Piedmont and deposited as the rivers slowly meander through the Carolina Low Country, forms intricate marshes which remind us of the land's mutability. East of Saint Augustine, barrier islands continue to shift and confuse uninformed navigators.

The coast is not a line but a stretch of land influenced by oceanic forces. The coast ranges from locations only exposed briefly at low tide to those reached only by sea spray and tidal surges. Throughout this zone, there are many environments and opportunities for life, each with its own cycle of time. Factors such as exposure to storm waves, average temperatures, water salinity, light intensity, the size of rock particles, mud composition, and the presence of predators all influence habitats.

On sandy shores where animals and plants can cling to few surfaces, worms, mollusks, and crustaceans burrow beneath to survive. On rocky shores, invertebrates such as barnacles, mussels, snails, and starfish as well as seaweed find more dependable anchors. A wider range of life appears on muddy shores protected from the full force of waves. In fertile layers of soil, particularly marshes, plants such as sea lavender and cattails take root, and a wide range of birds, insects, and mammals visit. Sea turtles, whales, and seals drift in from the Gulf Stream, and weasels, wolves, and deer come from inland forests. The wild marshes along Bay Street in Beaufort, the woods and wetlands along the Kennebunk River, the marshes bordering Stonington, the greenbelt around New Castle, and the harbor islands of Castine are examples of environments that preserve varied habitats close to town and, consequently, enrich the sense of life and time there.

Human Scale

These towns have a delightful human scale. Confined, on one hand, by surrounding streams and marshes and drawn together, on the other hand, by the waterfront pursuits that established centers within them, these towns are comparatively dense and filled with human activity. As such, they relate to the pace, measure, and attention of people moving on foot. Based on what people can see and the ease with which they can walk convenient distances, the towns emphasize the common and everyday rather than the monumental and exceptional. Early residents easily went from home to work, to school, to the town hall, to church, and to stores, observing and participating in a range of environments and experiences along the way. They passed through streets framed by buildings related to one another, forming spaces that were engaging to explore. People on foot were, and are, the basic measures of these towns.

These environments are designed on a personal scale—particularly with individuals and small groups in mind. The buildings, streets, and spaces are comfortable and convenient, and most necessities of life are located within manageable walking distances. In an age that builds huge, forbidding structures,

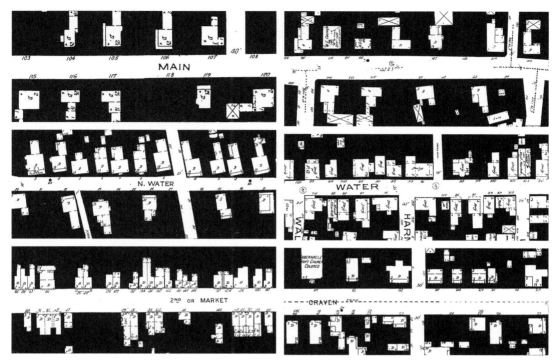

Fig. 1.6. These layouts illustrate the comparative character of residential streets in towns along the Atlantic coast (Sanborn maps, with ground rendered black). Top left: Main Street, Castine (1923). Large, free-standing, orderly sited houses respect common setbacks and house placement across the street. Generous side yards allow views downhill to the harbor (right) and access to the sun. Top right: Maine Street, Kennebunkport (1911). Separate buildings face the street. To the rear, additions and attached barns align with those of neighbors to create informal spaces. Fronts of houses terminate views up perpendicular streets. Middle left: North Water Street, Edgartown (1914). Ship captains' houses congregate on the uphill (top) side to gain views of the harbor opposite. Angled building placement emphasizes each house and facilitates views. Middle right: Water Street, Stonington (1886). Buildings crowd front property lines and each other. They define the street space and maximize backyards in this town with small blocks. Bottom left: Second Street, or Market Street, New Castle (1912). Favoring the north (top) side, which receives more sun, houses press to the street side on very narrow, long lots. Small houses group to form clusters similar in size to a large house. Bottom right: Craven Street, Beaufort (1899). Buildings orient to the street, while building porches preferably face south (bottom) to gain cooling breezes from the water.

amassing great numbers of people and machines and forcing people to travel great distances, the scale of these towns is reassuringly human. Routes are direct and public in character. Buildings and streets interrelate. Architectural details express what residents have defined through use. Fronts of buildings facing streets display bay windows, porches, and entrances that allow pedestrians and residents opportunities to communicate.

Streets in these towns have identifying characteristics, making them seem more like specific locations than anonymous routes. They possess different building rhythms, spatial enclosures, lengths, and vistas. Usually they are open-ended and permit people to pass through on their way to the waterfront or other destinations. Yet special buildings at a bend or intersection visually terminate the vistas. Streets are places to explore and a means for public connections, not private enclaves or high-speed arteries. The narrow street widths, tight spatial enclosures, and pedestrian details warn drivers that they are the intruders.

Pedestrian streets have quantifiable dimensions. For these towns, the typical block lengths vary from 175 feet in Ocean Grove to 460 feet in Edenton, with an overall average of 306 feet (see Appendix). Main commercial streets range considerably in width. Measured between building faces, they vary from 100 feet in Edenton to 18 feet in Saint Augustine (the latter is now a pedestrian lane). The average distance between buildings on opposite sides of a street is fifty-eight feet—considerably shorter than eighty feet, the approximate distance at which one can recognize a particular individual.[21] The spatial needs of human perception underlie the pedestrian scale.

Density indicates the proximity of buildings and, to a lesser extent, the intensity of activity. In these towns, gross residential densities range from 1.7 dwellings per acre in Castine to 10.9 in New Castle, with an overall average of 5.1.[22] Resident population in these towns may increase as much as tenfold during summer seasons. However, the average number of people per dwelling has decreased in recent years.[23] Lot size and proportion also affect one's sense of building density. As measured on the Sanborn insurance maps, lots vary in average width from twenty-nine feet in New Castle to ninety-two feet in Kennebunks' Port, with an overall average of sixty feet.[24] Lot frontage is partially a function of lot depth. In Kennebunks' Port and Edgartown, where lots are relatively shallow, they are correspondingly wide. In New Castle, where lots are narrow, they are unusually deep. In towns with narrow lots, one views buildings as ensembles, seeing common themes and connecting elements rather than isolated structures.

Southern towns, in particular, were platted into regular parcels of identical size, whereas the northern towns were more often organized into large parcels and then subdivided. Thus, in northern towns a complex pattern of lot sizes evolved with few identical lots. Lot areas and house sizes vary, and it is not unusual for large houses to be on small lots. In all these regions, the relatively tight lot widths contribute to the cumulative sense of town scale. Passing different properties, the visitor sees frequent and subtle shifts in details, claims of ownership, and levels of upkeep.

A pedestrian environment also implies limits. There are comfortable distances for daily errands and visits beyond which people prefer not to walk. According to insurance maps from 1886–1923, a circle of one-quarter-mile radius includes almost all of the dense areas in these towns, a one-third-mile radius includes virtually all dense areas, and a one-half-mile radius effectively covers the entire town pattern. The topography of coastal towns, their irregular shorelines, and the focus of activity near the water distort these idealized circular catchment areas. Nevertheless, the patterns of development primarily occurred within a one-quarter-mile radius, a distance one can walk in approximately five minutes.[25] Except for waterfront transformations, building patterns within the one-quarter-mile radius have remained substantially the same. Beyond this ring, town plans change first to thinner densities and then to looser road patterns dominated by automobiles.

Residents enjoy access to and familiarity with a variety of uses and environments. Within a five-minute walk of many and a fifteen-minute walk of most town establishments, residents can conveniently experience numerous activities and visit a wide variety of places: stores, schools, churches, cemeteries, playing fields, friends' houses, and even the open countryside. In so doing, they meet a range of people—rich and poor, old and young, residents and visitors. In that sense, such activities are economic, social, and political experiences, although, undoubtedly, people have never thought of them as such because they are aspects of daily life.

Conclusion

Are the qualities of historic coastal towns still relevant? Admittedly, communities are built differently today. They are planned at larger scales, constructed more quickly, and frequently designed for unknown clients. Developers buy land and supplies in huge quantities and select from previously unimaginable varieties of materials and technologies. They must work with complicated government land-use regulations and environmental controls that, many argue, thwart creativity. Unlike historic towns, new communities must accommodate automobiles and service trucks while also taking into account human sensibilities. People appreciate the enduring qualities that root them in time and place. By working in more thoughtful and purposeful ways at the local level and seizing special opportunities when they occur, present-day community builders may be able to achieve the qualities many people value and, indeed, travel great distances to experience in historic coastal towns.

North Atlantic Coastal Towns

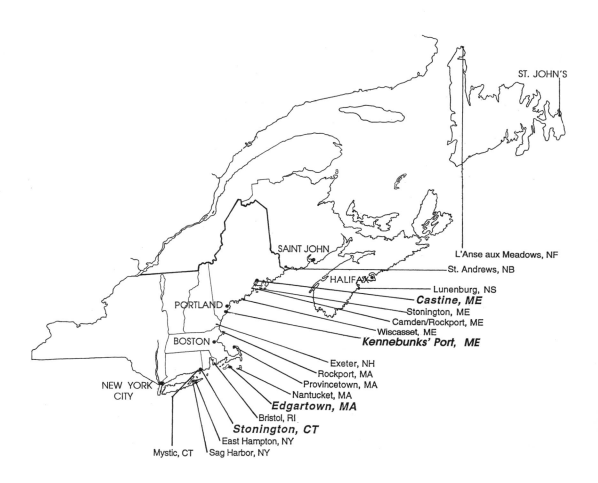

ST. JOHN'S

SAINT JOHN

HALIFAX

L'Anse aux Meadows, NF

St. Andrews, NB

Lunenburg, NS

Castine, ME

Stonington, ME

Camden/Rockport, ME

Wiscasset, ME

Kennebunks' Port, ME

PORTLAND

BOSTON

Exeter, NH

Rockport, MA

Provincetown, MA

Nantucket, MA

Edgartown, MA

Bristol, RI

Stonington, CT

NEW YORK
CITY

East Hampton, NY

Mystic, CT   Sag Harbor, NY

*Map 2.1. Map of North Atlantic coastal towns discussed in Part I.
Towns in larger type are the subjects of individual chapters.*

CHAPTER TWO

Overview

The North Atlantic coast extends from Newfoundland, the easternmost land mass of North America, to New York City, the southern edge of the area covered by glaciers during last great ice age. While geologically unified by its history of glacial activity, the region is politically divided into the Canadian Atlantic Provinces and the New England states. Its varied topography and character range from the rocky fjords of Newfoundland to the granite ledges of Maine and the broad beaches of Long Island. Its tides rise as much as fifty feet (the highest recorded tides in the world) in the Bay of Fundy to less than two feet off Long Island.

During the ice age 22,000 years ago, glaciers over a mile thick covered the North Atlantic region. Not until the last of them had retreated far into Canada (approximately 12,000 years ago) did this coast emerge in its present outline. As the ice sheet melted, it left terminal moraines (debris from the outwash) in the south and carved headlands and flooded valleys in the north. Granite and volcanic rocks have resisted erosion and remain, dramatically marking the high points of the coast and accenting its many small indentations.

The ancient mountains, having been covered and then released from the crushing glaciers, form the spectacular scenery we see today. Part of the Appalachians, they stretch across New England as the Green and White Mountains, and, as they arc northeastward and closer to the coast, they shape the Atlantic Provinces of Canada. After the ice sheets retreated, the land rose only partially. Although the land mass remained compressed from the weight of the glaciers, considerable amounts of water were still frozen in northern ice; soon after the glacial period, then, the coastal edge was approximately 200 feet below its present elevation and extended considerably further into now inundated areas.

As American Indians ventured into these lands ten thousand years ago, they undoubtedly lived along the coast, and, over the ages, their descendants retreated as the sea level rose. Thus, most likely sites of ancient precolonial civilization along the coast are now submerged and remain conjectural. Only in the last several centuries have most settlements become of such permanence that they will not be able to retreat and accommodate the ongoing rise in sea level.

In the ocean, higher areas of the continental shelf were drowned by the melting ice and became the great fishing grounds that have sustained the region's coastal towns over recent centuries. Much of the coastal North Atlantic shore faces the Gulf of Maine, which stretches from Cape Cod in Massachusetts to the Bay of Fundy in Nova Scotia. This sizable gulf, which geologists believe to be about 16,000 years old, is still relatively young compared to the Atlantic Ocean itself, which is about 150 million years old. Even today, with a higher overall water level in the oceans, the gulf has benefited from its position as a sea within a sea and has been extraordinarily fecund.

Marine temperatures work inversely to land temperatures in terms of supporting most marine and shoreline life. Cold water contains more of the dissolved gases such as oxygen and carbon dioxide that are essential for sustaining life. More important, particularly for the Gulf of Maine, are the convective currents that stir deepwater nutrients closer to the surface. In the Gulf of Maine, the cold currents from Labrador curl around Nova Scotia and into the Bay of Fundy before washing south along the coasts of Maine, New Hampshire, and Massachusetts. At Cape Cod, this cold water meets the warm, deflected Gulf Stream, not only defining the climate there with the resulting moody fogs but also contributing to the ocean turnover phenomenon, enriching the Gulf of Maine. In the spring, the upwelling waters provide mineral nutrients for the microscopic plankton, which form a virtual sea pasture in which other marine life feed, making this one of the most productive fishing areas in the world. The food chain leads to shrimp, herring, and cod, providing a rich bounty for the many fishers from coastal towns and, more recently, the factory processing ships. Unfortunately, overfishing since World War II has depleted these resources to the point of near commercial extinction; now only drastic reductions in allowable catches, if not total moratoria on some species, can reconstitute the ecological balance.[1]

Tides are a distinctive feature of the Gulf of Maine. Due to the converging edges and the rising bottom of the gulf, the tidal effect caused by the moon's gravitational pull is amplified as tidal waters move into the Bay of Fundy. When the tides retreat, they leave in their wake extensive salt marshes and tidal flats that become feasting grounds for the wildlife in the coastal habitat and the birds that migrate along the North Atlantic coast. The many islands, of which Maine alone has approximately five thousand, alter the range and effect of tides, thereby creating unique habitats. As the ocean currents swirl around these islands, the action oxygenates the water as the nutrient-rich colder water rises from the sea floor. The islands also cause greater quantities of water to be funneled through narrow passages, allowing filter-feeding invertebrates to flourish.

Along most of the North Atlantic coast, especially to the north, farming has proved difficult and, for the most part, marginal. Fertile soil is found only in pockets where marine mud was deposited by glaciers or in downriver valleys where sediment has accumulated over the millennia. Most of the remaining areas are dominated by rocky terrain or salt marshes. The growing season is short, ranging from two months in Canada to five months in southern New England, rather than the nine months that are common along the South Atlantic coast. Although there are countless indentations along the coast that provide safe, natural harbors, the rivers are navigable from the sea for only relatively restricted distances inland before encountering obstacles. Partly for these reasons, the North Atlantic coast developed around nucleated settlements supported by some family farming and sustained by the fishing available in these sheltered but conveniently located towns. The scarcity of fertile land and the difficulty of transporting products any distance by river eliminated the possibility of farming a single extensive crop, as southern planters so profitably did with rice, cotton, and tobacco.

The Atlantic Provinces of Canada include the island of Newfoundland and the three Maritime Provinces of Prince Edward Island, Nova Scotia, and New Brunswick.[2] At least a thousand years ago, Europeans, led by the Vikings, ventured across the ocean and sailed along the arc of land formed by Iceland, Greenland, and Labrador to Newfoundland, their first foothold in North America. They gradually came in greater numbers and extended their probes, first into the present-day Maritimes and then further south, in search of fish (especially cod, found in such abundance off the North Atlantic coast).

The great age of European exploration in this region began with John Cabot, an Italian (Giovanni Caboto), who, financed by merchants from the English port of Bristol, landed on Cape Breton in 1497 and claimed all of Nova Scotia for England, giving Britain justification for asserting its rights over the French who later came to occupy the area. In 1605 Samuel de Champlain, with Pierre du Guzy, established a settlement in New Brunswick on what is now St. Croix Island, at the mouth of the river of the same name that separates New Brunswick from Maine. However, Champlain and Guzy soon abandoned this location and moved across the Bay of Fundy to Port Royal in what is now known as the Annapolis Valley of Nova Scotia. The French used these settlements as outposts from which they could trade with Indians for fur and gain timber for ships. The great age of exploration concluded when the Pilgrims landed in Plymouth, in 1620. By this time, the coast had been extensively traveled and mapped, facilitating the region's colonization.

As the Pilgrims and their descendants pushed north and west from their base in Massachusetts and fueled the already conflicting claims and vested interests between the English and French, there followed decades of bitter conflicts known as the French and Indian Wars. With the Treaty of Utrecht, in 1713, the English formally gained most of French Acadia, although the borders remained vague. In Europe, as well as in Atlantic Canada, the English and French continued their power struggles. In 1755, after demanding but not receiving full compliance to an oath of allegiance, the English expelled the French-speaking Acadians from Nova Scotia. Eventually many returned, not to farm, as they previously had, but to fish. They settled on marginal land and established the numerous small towns that still exist along the coasts of Nova Scotia and New Brunswick. (Many of the others migrated to present-day Louisiana.)

With British control of Atlantic Canada secured, immigrants from England, Ireland, Wales, and Scotland, as well as Germany, began to arrive in increasing numbers. During the American Revolution, many of those colonists who wished to remain loyal to the Crown sought refuge in Atlantic Canada. A number of these newcomers were business and professional leaders, and, after relocating, they reestablished themselves in important positions. Boundary disputes continued as the French and English argued whether the Kennebec River, north of Portland, the Penobscot River (at the mouth of which lies present-day Castine), or the Saint John River would separate British and French America. Eventually they settled on the Saint John River, which became the seventy-five-mile Canadian boundary (Canada became a nation in 1867 under the British North American Act of Confederation). Yet, through all these conflicts threads the great unifying theme of the coast, with its similar way of life lived in small towns, a life based on fishing and supplemented by farming. Today, this coastal theme leads travelers to visit these towns and view the extraordinary settings in which they exist.

Selection of Representative Towns

Because of the geography and the natural resources of the North Atlantic region, many coastal towns developed there, and a sizable number of these still exist. Indeed, while the extraordinary number of towns is a delight to explore, it complicates the selection of representative ones. I chose four to study in detail: Castine, Maine; Kennebunks' Port, Maine; Edgartown, Massachusetts; and Stonington, Connecticut. As a group, they all display salient qualities of the region. They also represent a range of sites: Castine rises on a steeply sloped hill, Kennebunks' Port straddles a river, Edgartown is an island town embracing a bay, and Stonington clings to a rocky peninsula that projects a mile into the sea. Each is noteworthy for cultural reasons as well. Castine lies along one of the historically disputed borders between the United States and Canada. It was first a refuge for English loyalists and, after the American Revolution, a departure point for resettlement into Canada. Kennebunks' Port and Edgartown, on Martha's Vineyard, were both important seafaring centers and, more recently, have been the focus of national attention as presidential retreats. Kennebunks' Port is the summer home of George Bush, and Bill Clinton has favored Martha's Vineyard. In the early nineteenth century, Stonington was a major transfer point for people traveling between Boston and New York City.

Currently, all these towns are affected by tourism; each one is dealing with it differently. All four have exceptionally fine traditions of architecture and are engaging places to investigate. While these particular towns well represent the traditions and issues of the region, other excellent towns illustrate equally important features but can only be noted. These additional towns are grouped according to their province or state and are listed in each region's overview in geographical order from north to south.

Newfoundland

Although the great island of Newfoundland has impoverished soils, it has been rich in the bounties of the sea—at least until the last two decades, after overfishing had so depleted certain species. The Beothuk Indians have fished here for thousands of years; five hundred years ago they were joined by Europeans, who settled in the many bays and coves that notch the boulder-strewn Newfoundland coast. At first these European settlers came to fish, then they made temporary claims on land where they dried fish and eventually established more permanent settlements that became bases for exploration and contact with the natives.

At the tip of the Great Northern Peninsula of Newfoundland, approximately fifteen miles across the strait from Labrador is *L'Anse aux Meadows*, a UNESCO World Heritage Site. The remains of a Norse encampment have been discovered here, in which between eighty and a hundred people lived for several years. Consisting of eight buildings made of timber and sod cut out of the peat beds, and including three large halls, the encampment dates from the decade before or after A.D. 1000.[3] Established on the outer coast and accessible only by water, it was probably used by the Norse as a base camp for explorations to the south.

A few miles south of this ancient encampment is the small fishing village of *St. Anthony* (pop. 3,164), with its buildings clustered around a natural harbor.[4] Throughout this area in the spring, one can see huge icebergs (some as high as a hundred feet) that, having separated from the Greenland ice cap, majestically float by on the currents. Further south but still on the northern coast is the village of *Trinity* (pop. 500). Predating the settlement of Saint Augustine by the Spanish, an outpost was established here by English merchants in 1558. During the 1700s, it vied with St. John's as the leading island community. Today's buildings date from the late 1800s and are a picturesque assemblage of cottages, gardens, and winding lanes.

St. John's (pop. 105,363) became the largest city and the provincial capital. One of North America's most ancient ports, it officially dates from 1497, when John Cabot claimed it for England. The historic center is filled with brightly painted buildings that rise steeply up the slope from a beautiful deepwater bay on the Avalon peninsula. The name *Avalon* is attributed to Sir George Calvert, who, as Lord Baltimore, in 1621 founded a colony south of St. John's at present-day *Ferryland* (pop. 719*). He abandoned this colony in 1629 to establish his new colony in what became Maryland. On the south coast are the attractive towns of *Grand Bank* (pop. 3,528), named after the rich fishing grounds that have sustained it since the 1650s, and *Burin* (pop. 2,940), which Captain James Cook used as his base of operations when he mapped these coasts in the 1760s.

Nova Scotia

The predominantly shallow, acidic, and rocky soil of Nova Scotia has sustained more forests than farms. Succeeding waves of immigrants have, for the most part, gravitated to the coasts and oriented to the sea. Though dominated by people of British ancestry, different ethnic groups have contributed to the heterogeneous flavor of the province, and most have manifestly expressed their cultural backgrounds in the towns they developed.

In the north, Cape Breton projects into the Gulf of St. Lawrence and connects only by a causeway to the mainland. Cape Breton, of all the areas in the Canadian Maritimes, has the most convoluted coast and possibly the most dramatic scenery, culminating in the majestic Cape Breton Highlands. At the western entrance to the Highland's National Park is the Acadian fishing village of *Chéticamp* (pop. 3,100), settled in 1785. On the Atlantic side of the park and across the harbor from the modern town of *Louisbourg* (pop. 1,261) is the Fortress of Louisbourg National Historic Park. Founded in 1713 by the French to counteract British hegemony in the region, the old fortified settlement here was destroyed by the British in 1760. In 1961, the Canadian government began reconstruction of one-quarter of the town, using 1744 as the restoration date, to commemorate the town's history and to stimulate the local economy. Nearby are the villages of *Petit-de-Grat* (pop. 454) and *Little Anse* (pop. 217).

The sparsely settled northern coast along the Northumberland Strait is a land of gently rolling hills and coastal beaches. In the eighteenth century, Scots settled here after having been evicted from their Highland homes in Britain. They first landed in *Pictou* (pop. 4,134), one of the largest present-day communities on the Northumberland coast, and then established other towns in the area.

The southeastern coast, facing the Atlantic, is rugged and has forests growing down to the water's edge. The coast is heavily indented and has granite headlands alternating with narrow bays, along which some small fishing villages are found. Along the eastern section of this coast is *Sherbrooke* (pop. 397), a village restored to the 1860–80 period, when it was a mining, lumbering, and shipbuilding center. South of Sherbrooke is *Peggy's Cove* (pop. 120), a quintessential coastal village set on a granite shelf overlooking a tiny harbor. *Mahone Bay* (pop. 1,096), an old town and contemporary sailing center, is known for its three churches, which distinguish its waterfront.

Lunenburg (pop. 2,781) was settled in 1753 by German-speaking Protestants whom the British specifically brought to Nova Scotia to offset the influence of the previously dominant French-speaking Acadians. The British laid out the town according to their colonial standards on a peninsula between two harbors, with a primary orientation to the southern Front Harbor. The Germans then set about building on this layout a town of unusual character, an idiosyncratic yet coherent town, which is now recognized as a World Heritage Site by UNESCO. The layout is based on a grid pattern set parallel to the harbor and comprises six divisions of eight blocks, with each block subdivided into fourteen lots of forty by sixty feet.[5] From the Front Harbor, the street grid slopes up a steep hill until it reaches more level ground. The area in between, which is in the heart of the old town, bounded by the lower, more commercial district and the upper, more residential district, includes the four blocks originally designated as the "parade grounds." Since the town's beginning, these blocks have provided sites for public buildings; today half of the original four-block area is still open to the public. King Street, which is centrally located and unusually wide (at eighty feet across) connects this area to the harbor below.

Because of the small lots, buildings in Lunenburg are set close to the street, and rows of buildings run parallel to one another and the street. Since the site slopes, higher buildings are placed to maximize views over those below, taking advantage of each site's condition. The typical house is one-and-a-half stories tall and features a central architectural element composed of a five-sided dormer window extending over a porch and main entrance. Known as the "Lunenburg Bump," this whimsical feature has become emblematic of the town's domestic architecture, adorning, in a variety of interpretations, most of the houses. The buildings are also often brightly painted, expressing ownership as well as a sense of scale. Lunenburg today continues to be a major fishing center, although tourism plays an increasing role in its economy.

With the American Revolution, loyalists from the British colonies relocated to this section of the coast south of Halifax, then an English stronghold and today the provincial capital and major city of Nova Scotia. In 1783, nearly three thousand immigrants from New York City alone landed in *Shelburne* (pop. 3,436), and with more arrivals the population soon mushroomed to sixteen thousand before the newcomers dispersed to surrounding areas. Shelburne, a picturesque town situated at the end of a bay, is notable for Dock Street, on which a collection of restored warehouses and homes overlook the water.

On the northwestern shore facing the Bay of Fundy, great tides sweep through the salt marshes and tidal flats that gleam with red mud at low water. The coast is strewn with boulders, the remnant deposits of glaciers, which today make farming difficult. Some of the French Acadians who were expelled in 1755 returned to settle fishing communities along the western end of this seemingly marginal land. Numerous fishing villages today dot the shoreline, an area now known as the Acadian Coast.

Further to the northeast is the geological anomaly of the Annapolis Basin. Sheltered between mountains, this valley has fertile soils and a warm and humid climate that is particularly suited for growing fruit. *Annapolis Royal* (pop. 633), near the 1605 site of Samuel de Champlain's Port Royal, is a gracious old town with handsome houses and gardens set along broad, tree-lined streets. Dating from 1610, Annapolis Royal is one of the oldest settlements of European origin in Canada. In the same vicinity, at the head of a tidal river, is a town of Swiss origin, *Bear River* (pop. 774). In contrast to its venerable age, tiny population, and removed location, this town has embraced environmentally responsible planning with the building of a solar aquatic water treatment facility, where effluent is cleansed through biological processes using plants, snails, and solar energy.

Prince Edward Island

Formed in the Gulf of St. Lawrence as retreating glaciers converged, Prince Edward Island is a tripartite land mass with two wings reaching out from a central body. The north coast along the Gulf of St. Lawrence is an arc of barrier islands and beaches, in contrast to the south coast along the Northumberland Strait, which has jagged headlands protecting the narrow bays that house most of Prince Edward Island's harbors and towns. The smallest of the Canadian provinces, the island is a pastoral landscape spotted with colorful Victorian buildings. Its remote, formerly isolated location may no longer protect it; a new bridge, one of the longest in the world at eight miles—and disturbingly high, at 120 feet above the water for most of its length—now links the island to the mainland.

Charlottetown (pop. 15,396), the economic and governmental center of the island, enjoys a beautiful site on a point of land where two rivers empty into a bay. It is a compact city featuring brightly painted Victorian houses, tree-shaded streets and squares, and a restored waterfront area. To the west, *Victoria* (pop. 200) was laid out in 1855 in a grid pattern overlooking a sheltered natural harbor. No longer a prosperous shipping center, today it is a quiet, picturesque village. East of Charlottetown, *Georgetown* (pop. 716) dates from 1765 and also prospered during the nineteenth century as a shipbuilding and trading center, only to recede in importance during the twentieth century. However, Georgetown still benefits from its enviable location at the mouth of two rivers, overlooking an excellent deepwater harbor.

New Brunswick

New Brunswick has a northern and a southern coastal region, separated by the land connection to Nova Scotia. The northern stretch reaches from the Northumberland Strait, along the Gulf of St. Lawrence, to the Baie des Chaleurs ("Bay of Warmth") across which is Québec's Gaspé Peninsula. The southern coast is actually chillier, cooled by the Labrador Current, while the northern coast, affected by the Gulf Stream, is warmer. Noteworthy in the northern region is the historic coastal town of *Caraquet* (pop. 4,556), on the Baie Des Chaleurs. Founded in 1758 as a French settlement, today it is a picturesque fishing and cultural center.

The southern coastal region lies along the Bay of Fundy. At approximately the middle of its length is *Saint John* (pop. 74,969), the largest city and the capital of the province, situated at the mouth of the Saint John River. To the north of Saint John is the attractive fishing village of *St. Martin* (pop. 386*) which, after its founding in 1783, became one of the major nineteenth-century shipbuilding centers in the Atlantic Provinces. South of Saint John is *Sackville* (pop. 5,393*), settled in the seventeenth century by immigrants from coastal regions of western France, who applied their European knowledge of diking waterways and re-claiming land to the marshy areas of their new locale. Furthest south and imme-diately across from Maine along the boundary between Canada and the United States is the town of St. Andrews.

St. Andrews-by-the-Sea (pop. 1,652) lies on a peninsula extending from the northern shore of the St. Croix River into Passamaquoddy Bay. Although the peninsula was inhabited in the mid–eighteenth century, the settlement of St. Andrews stems directly from the American Revolution. Loyalists from New York City, Boston, and Portland first sought refuge in Castine, believing that the Penobscot River was to define the international boundary and they would thus be in British America. When the boundary instead shifted to the St. Croix River, approximately a thousand loyalists again relocated. For their new town, they chose a site that gently sloped to the south, not unlike Castine. Using a grid pattern, they set six streets running parallel to the waterfront and designated a main street to run perpendicular to the waterfront at a width of eighty feet instead of the standard sixty-feet.[6] Locations for a market square, a church, and public buildings were also assigned. The loyalists shipped a few disassembled buildings from Castine but otherwise built new ones. St. Andrews remained a loyalist stronghold and is still a provincial Georgian masterpiece, although, because of its remote location, it never prospered commercially.

In 1888 a group of Canadian and American businessmen, most of whom had connections to railroad and shipping interests, began promoting St. Andrews as a summer resort colony. They bought property in and around the town and built the elegant Algonquin Hotel. They succeeded in publicizing the region's beauty and benign summer climate. From 1900 to 1920, St. Andrews became one of the Northeast's most fashionable resorts. Numerous Shingle style houses date from this period and, along with the Georgian legacy, remain preserved on the penin-sula. Also during the late nineteenth century, on nearby Campobello Island, James Roosevelt, vice president of the Delaware and Hudson Railway and father of Franklin Delano Roosevelt, bought ten acres from a development company and built a fifteen-room house to which the future president would return to spend many recuperative summers.

Maine

The northern section of New England extends from the Canadian Maritimes south to Portland, Maine. Along this coast, old mountain ridges stretch southward into the sea to reappear as pine-covered islands on the horizon. These fingers of land break the force of the surging waves and provided many protected, though isolated, coves for settlement. In these villages and towns, generations have depended on fishing and lumbering for survival, as well as on farming when and where possible. To the north, the coast is more sparsely settled and the houses more modest and simple in shape to withstand the long, harsh winters. To the south, the coast begins to flatten into the coastal plain and beaches are more common. Here buildings are more varied, particularly in those areas vacationers have favored in recent years.

Founded in 1762 by settlers from Andover, Massachusetts, *Blue Hill* (pop. 700) lies at the convergence of a stream and a number of roads descending from the surrounding hills. These meet at the point where Blue Hill Bay joins the rise of land known as Blue Hill, the feature that gives the town and the bay their names. During the nineteenth century, first the lumber industry, then shipbuilding, and finally granite quarrying provided the solid economic base that resulted in the construction of grand and gracious civic buildings such as the library and the many elegant Neoclassical style residences that grace the streets and reflect the prosperous past. They contribute a larger-than-expected scale and sense of civility to this seemingly remote village.

Stonington (pop. 700) is arguably one of the archetypal towns of the northern New England coast. In the late eighteenth century, saltwater farmers and fisherman settled around a cove on the tip of Deer Isle. A century later, a boom of sorts occurred when the Deer Isle quarries opened and began providing the lovely pink granite used for, among other buildings, Boston's Museum of Fine Arts, New York City's Rockefeller Center, and the District of Columbia's Washington Monument. All such granite was shipped directly from Stonington village. Today the quarries are no longer busy, and the town has returned primarily to fishing, for it has an excellent harbor and is close to the fishing grounds. Increasingly, however, its clapboard buildings are catching the fancy of visitors searching for a second home. Like many of the traditional fishing villages remaining in Maine, its economic future will likely be determined as much by vacationers as by the success of its fishing fleet.

Visually and even acoustically, Stonington focuses on the harbor. Buildings tier up the granite ledges like spectators in an amphitheater. The simple gable-roofed houses adjust to the site to gain unobstructed harbor views and collectively act as a prism to catch the moving sun. Streets follow lines of least resistance as they wrap around the harbor and climb the hillside. Although there is not a completely granite building in the town, granite is a fact of life here. It ties the buildings to their sites with foundation walls, steps, and countless details. It has encouraged compact town development and has forced utilities such as tanks and wires to be above grade. The town's granite site limits expansion because of the difficulty of routing utilities through rocky soil and the fresh water lost through runoff that otherwise would supply aquifers. Unlike in other New England towns, churches and public buildings are not visually prominent in Stonington. It is, after all, a working-class town with a tradition of stone cutters, boat builders, fishermen, carpenters, and mechanics, who sought more prosaic forms of expression.

Monhegan Island (pop. 70*), lying a lonely twelve miles off the coast from Port Clyde, is one of the most dramatic islands along the Atlantic coast. With 150-foot headlands facing the open Atlantic and a haven on its sheltered side, the island has long been noted by seamen, who used it first as a fishing outpost. In 1498 John Cabot recorded it in his journals as he sailed the coast. A few hardy generations of residents have lived here year-round since 1674. Nearly all settlers gravitated to the protected side, where two smaller islands allow anchorage. A village slowly grew here along the paths fishermen wore from the beaches to their fish flakes and sheds. These early residents preferred to build houses back from the water's edge, to afford minimal exposure to the harsh northeast winds. Only after the "rusticators" discovered the island in the 1870s did summer cottages and studios appear in more exposed locations close to the shore to take advantage of the views.

In a remarkable way, Monhegan has captured the American artistic imagination. George Bellows in 1911 noted that "the island is endless in its wonderful variety. It's possessed of enough beauty to supply a continent."[7] Bellows, Robert Henri, Rockwell Kent, Edward Hopper, and three generations of Wyeths—N. C., Andrew, and Jamie—among many other artists, have lived and painted here. In 1954 Theodore Edison, son of the inventor Thomas, was instrumental in establishing a nonprofit organization, purchasing land, and protecting the extraordinary natural beauty of the island. Today, in ironic contrast to the Edison legacy, residents avoid electricity and automobiles. Instead of driving, they can easily walk the island and enjoy its variety: the open, wind-swept cliffs, the dense Cathedral Woods, and Lighthouse Hill and the nearby cemetery—both of which overlook the island, the marshy meadow in the middle of the village, and the harbor, the focal point for people coming and going.

Camden (pop. 4,022) and *Rockport* (pop. 1,100), two adjoining and equally beautiful but different towns, were part of the same jurisdiction until 1891. They still share the same dramatic setting where the ranges of the Penobscot Mountains slide into the sea and, as Captain John Smith once described the site, "against whose feet the sea doth beat."[8] In Camden the main coastal road, U.S. 1, squeezes through the town between Mt. Battie and the harbor; this road is often congested, especially in the summer. The larger of the two towns, Camden has a fanlike street pattern that slopes gently to the harbor. The movie *Peyton Place* (1957) was filmed in Camden because it was such an ideal setting at the time.

U.S. 1 bypasses Rockport, allowing a secondary road to pass through the town and serve the buildings arrayed high on the hillside overlooking the spectacular and capacious harbor. Both towns prospered in the nineteenth century as seafaring communities. Rockport shipped ice and lime to cities further south; the lime kilns are still evident today on its waterfront. Both towns are now popular summer vacation centers, with Camden suffering the brunt of the tourist flows.

Wiscasset (pop. 1,233), founded in the 1670s, achieved considerable prosperity in the late eighteenth century, when it was the center of extensive trade with foreign ports; it became the hub of economic activity in the local region. Today a number of handsome public, commercial, and domestic buildings line its main street, U.S. 1, and the nearby residential streets. Route 1 heads north through the middle of town and down the hill to the low bridge, which spans the Sheepscot River, where the remains of two four-masted schooners that went aground half a century ago have come to rest.

South of Portland and reaching to Cape Ann in Massachusetts, broad beaches punctuated by rocky headlands arc along the coast. This comparatively flat coast with shallow shores is part of a plain that extends from approximately ten to twenty miles inland to the rocky margins of the old postglacial shore. Fewer rivers and streams cut through this region, and the broad beaches permit fewer sites for coastal towns. These beaches and the close proximity to metropolitan areas, however, have attracted summer visitors in recent years, particularly since Interstate 95 was extended up the coast, allowing easy access from Boston.

New Hampshire

Although the coast of New Hampshire is only eighteen miles long, it boasts beautiful sweeping beaches and, perhaps most magnificently, the estuary of the Piscataqua River. Unfortunately, the historic beach settlements of Hampton and North Hampton have been virtually ruined by commercial development stemming from U.S. 1. *Seabrook* (pop. 740), which fronts on a marshy inlet and was settled in the early 1600s, suffers not only from Route 1 traffic but also from being the site of a huge and highly controversial nuclear power plant. On the other hand, *Rye Village* (pop. 835) and *Newfields* (pop. 700), picturesque estuarine communities, are bypassed by coastal traffic and remain largely intact, with handsome eighteenth- and nineteenth-century houses and public buildings.[9] Two other notable communities that are bypassed are *New Castle* and *Exeter*, which represent two different types of historic coastal towns in the region that came to be dominated by Portsmouth.

Settled in the 1630s, *New Castle* (pop. 975), is a former fishing village and occasional fortification that developed on an island in the mouth of the Piscataqua River, immediately east of Portsmouth. With its strategic position, New Castle controlled passage into the harbor, and today ruins of military installations from the War of 1812 and the Civil War remain to remind the visitor that the village's past was not always as peaceful as its current appearance would indicate. Consistent in scale, materials, and modest appeal, the one-and-a-half-story "Cape Cod" dwellings, the wooden town hall, and a simple church crowd the northern rocky ledges of the island. Although New Castle is now connected to the mainland through bridges and causeways, it remains removed from the commercial bustle of Portsmouth, the tourist activity of the Strawbery Banke Museum Complex, and the navy yard across the river in Kittery, Maine. The town has become essentially a wealthy bedroom community for Portsmouth, while the southern, lower-lying areas of the island are filled with undistinguished suburban housing.

Initially called Strawbery Banke, *Portsmouth* (pop. 25,925) was settled in 1631 on a narrow peninsula two miles from the mouth of the Piscataqua River. Prospering during the Colonial period because of its deepwater, ice-free harbor, the major one between Boston, Massachusetts, and Portland, Maine, it rapidly developed into an important shipping and shipbuilding center. By 1800 it was one of the wealthiest cities in the country, one whose constricted site and affluence had produced a town of density and unusual elegance, notable for its many two- and three-story Georgian style buildings. Disastrous fires in the early nineteenth century initiated mandates requiring that all buildings over twelve feet be constructed of masonry. Subsequent buildings, particularly those along the waterfront and those framing Market Square, today the heart of Portsmouth's historic district, are of brick and give the town its solid appearance.

After the Civil War, Portsmouth's economy declined, never again to regain its former significance. This decline, however, saved the town's collection of historic buildings from demolition, at least until the federal Urban Renewal Program of the post–World War II period became active. Under this program, many buildings were demolished to make way for new development. In the North End and the Hill districts, which had been home to some four hundred early buildings, only fourteen buildings were saved (ten were moved to a site where four remained). The Strawbery Banke district also suffered, although not as severely. Within today's Strawbery Banke Museum, located on a ten-acre site where the town began, forty-two preserved buildings, featuring over three hundred years of cultural history, are now open to the public.[10]

The estuarine community of *Exeter* (pop. 12,481) has been blessed with outstanding resources over its long history. Settled in 1638 at the falls of the Squamscott River, it had extensive pine forests for shipbuilding, granite for quarrying, fertile soil for farming, and excellent water power for manufacturing. Although it could not compete in maritime shipping with Portsmouth, twelve miles east, it supplied the products that Portsmouth ships transported, and thus it prospered.[11] This wealth in turn endowed the town with elegant architecture, particularly that of the Federal houses along its main streets, and excellent cultural and educational facilities, most notably the Phillips Exeter Academy, founded in 1781, which still vitally contributes to the town. With the river cascading through the very heart of the town and its fine tradition of architecture, Exeter delightfully combines wilderness and civility as part of its town design.

Massachusetts

The Boston Basin

Sandy beaches, saltwater marshes, and occasional rocky or stony areas alternate along the short New Hampshire shore. To the south, Massachusetts' geography provided a more varied coastal setting for early towns and villages. North of the Cape Cod peninsula, the shoreline is marked by drumlins (the hilly deposits of ice-carried solids left by the retreating glaciers), by the granite outcropping known as Cape Ann, and by expanses of fine sandy beaches.

On the northern edge of the Bay State, at the mouth of the Merrimack River, *Newburyport* (pop. 16,317) flourished in the past and is, indeed, flourishing in the present, reclaimed after a period of decline. It is noteworthy because of its magnificent collection of historic homes and its recently restored and highly successful waterfront area. Opposite, on the barrier Plum Island, the cottages lining the pristine beach have been transformed by new families and real estate investors.

Immediately south of Newburyport lies *Ipswich* (pop. 4,132). No longer the major cultural center it was during the seventeen century, it still focuses on its green, laid out in the 1630s. From here, Cape Ann protrudes some ten miles into the Atlantic toward the rich northern fishing grounds. *Gloucester* (pop. 28,716) is on the southern side of the cape and is the largest community there. With its excellent sheltered harbor, it has become one of the great New England fishing centers.

Rockport (pop. 5,448), on the eastern side of Cape Ann facing the ocean, was settled in the 1690s by fishermen and farmers. The town grew around Sandy Cove without the benefits of a natural harbor; not until 1815 were sea walls constructed to protect against ocean storms. Commercial, institutional, and residential activities favored Sandy Cove (Rockport Center), while to the north Pigeon Cove became a thriving fishing base. Granite quarried nearby and shipped to cities along the East and Gulf Coasts supported further improvements in Pigeon Cove. During the 1920s fishermen's shacks were converted to studios as Rockport became a popular artists' colony. Today it is a busy summer community with activity focusing on Sandy Cove and the man-made harbor. With its breakwater, its beach in the center of town, its wharf developments, and its docks, Rockport offers a variety of ways to experience the water.

South of Cape Ann, the shoreline extends southwesterly to the Boston Harbor area. Especially noteworthy along this stretch of coastline is *Marblehead* (pop. 19,971), an old fishing village and later a manufacturing town, whose structures were built wherever an open building site presented itself among the rocky outcroppings. Today it has been adopted by those people seeking a civilized setting within a relatively easy commuting distance of Boston.

As one approaches Boston, suburban sprawl and urban blight have erased nearly all evidence of historic coastal towns. The area nearest Boston is therefore of less interest for the purposes of this book. South of the city, the shoreline bends in a southeasterly direction.

Cape Cod and the Islands

Melting glaciers originally deposited the soil, rock, gravel, and debris that created the area we know as Cape Cod, and ocean currents, wind, rain, sun, ice, and snow have been shaping it ever since. The familiar peninsula, shaped roughly like a flexed arm, juts out thirty miles eastward from the mainland, separating the colder waters and marine life brought down by the Labrador Current from those carried north by the Gulf Stream. It is therefore recognized as a major ecological demarcation line.

When the first European settlers arrived in this area in the seventeenth century, much of the cape was covered with fertile soil and a heavy growth of oak and pine. These new inhabitants cleared the forests for shipbuilding and agriculture, exposing the soil to the brutal, salt-laden winds, which carried it away. Today, the ubiquitous spare, weather-beaten Cape Cod houses seem derived from the scrubby, dried-out landscape that remains.

The numerous outstanding historic coastal towns that originally flourished on fishing are now sustained by vacationers and retirees. One of the last coastal regions to undergo the change to a vacation economy, the cape escaped the attention of tourists until the 1920s, before which vacationers claimed only Provincetown and Hyannis for their own. Then summer pleasure seekers discovered the warm waters and sandy beaches of the cape's southern shore. As time passed and the demand for places to summer or weekend within commuting distance of Boston increased, the northern bay side of the peninsula, until then left to the native Cape Codders, was also adopted by the new wave of visitors. In 1956, in response to the rapid development of this fragile arm of land, the federal government created the Cape Cod National Seashore. Its expanse of sand, dune, and sea will forever remain an eloquent reminder of how this area appeared before it was overwhelmed by buildings, asphalt, automobiles, and crowds.

On the northern edge of the Cape Cod peninsula, approximately midway between its beginning and the bend of the "elbow," lies the village of *Yarmouth Port* (pop. 4,271). The area was first settled in 1639, and throughout the colonial period it was not considered distinct from the town of Yarmouth. The village, built around a bay, experienced considerable commercial success in the nineteenth century, but, as in other towns of the cape, a sharp drop in the availability of ocean resources meant an equally severe economic recession in the latter part of that century. The population declined until resort life was introduced to the southern section of the town in the late 1900s and to Yarmouth Port itself in the early part of the twentieth century.[12]

Also located on the bay shore of the cape, midway between the "elbow" and the "fist" is *Wellfleet* (pop. 1,200). Like most cape towns, its shoreline is defined by the hillocks, dunes, and depressions that centuries of exposure to weather have wrought. The town was first settled in the late seventeenth century, when explorers discovered the plentiful fish, oysters, and whales available in the nearby waters. Development first occurred on the harbor islands and in the creek areas. During the late nineteenth century, the busy village centered around Duck Creek. Within a few decades tourism took hold, ensuring the town's survival and economic health.[13]

The quintessential linear coastal settlement, *Provincetown* (pop. 3,536) consisted of a single long street until 1873, after which only one more parallel route was added. The village now stretches more than two miles along the harbor. Originally buildings clustered at the wharves where fishermen brought in their hauls. Over time, gable-front houses and stores filled the intervening properties along Commercial Street, creating in their compactness an almost urban feel yet allowing through the slots between them views of the all-important harbor. It was here at the end of Cape Cod on 11 November 1620 that the Pilgrims first landed in the New World. Although the settlement grew slowly, by the mid–nineteenth century it had become an active fishing center and then in the early twentieth century, a major artists' colony. Painters and writers, particularly from New York City, came for the summer and extensively redeveloped buildings, converting old warehouses, sail lofts, and fishing shacks into playhouses, galleries, and studios.[14]

South of Cape Cod lie Martha's Vineyard, Nantucket, and the Elizabeth Islands. Like all islands of this shoreline, they were formed as the recent glacier receded northward. Each is a rough triangle with a base to the south and an apex to the north. Between the "sides" of these triangles, the glacier left ridges of debris that have fallen away on either side to sandy outwash plains and then to the surrounding ocean. On these islands, as along the coast, similar patterns of early settlement, nineteenth-century prosperity, and a long period of economic decline have resulted in villages preserved through time. All three islands have become well-loved vacation destinations, and all are subject to the same overwhelming forces that threaten historic coastal villages on the mainland.

Nantucket (pop. 3,069), a name which, to the island's original inhabitants (members of the Narragansett confederation of the mainland Algonquin tribe), meant "at the land far out to sea," is in fact only a short twenty-two miles from the mainland. This distance was, however, sufficient to guarantee the island an isolated and conservative existence for most of its history. Colonists from mainland Massachusetts and Martha's Vineyard arrived in 1661 at the small, three-and-a-half-mile-wide, twelve-mile-long island intending to farm and raise sheep in a settlement one and a half miles west of the present town. The twenty-seven original proprietors divided a small portion of the land among themselves but held most of the land in common. Around 1720, as prospects grew of harvesting the sea rather than the soil, they moved their settlement to the Great Harbor, where Nantucket town now lies sheltered. During this period Quakers arrived in large numbers, reinforcing the strong sense of community. By the end of the eighteenth century, they constituted half the population.

For a brief period during the 1830s and 1840s, the island town commanded the world market in whale oil, as its citizens ventured into the far Pacific and brought back oil to light the streets of European and American cities. The town grew correspondingly from a rural village to a cosmopolitan center. Everyone in the town was directly or indirectly engaged in the whaling industry. Ships from around the world plied its harbor and wealth flowed into the town.[15]

At the peak of Nantucket's prosperity, in 1846, a fire engulfed one-third of the town center. The town quickly rebuilt in the Greek Revival style, which was then popular and today still contributes to the town's remarkable elegance. It was at this time that lower Main Street was reshaped into one of the enduring great American public places. Here Main Street Square—a long rectangular commercial and civic space—slopes gently uphill. At the harbor end is the free-standing Pacific Club, also called the Rotch Warehouse; facing it and terminating the space on the uphill side is the Pacific Bank. Both these landmarks are austerely proud buildings and indicative of the town's far-flung trade history. On the remaining sides of this elongated rectangle, commercial buildings line the paved space. Downhill Main Street extends into Straight Wharf and the heart of the harbor and uphill, into a row of magnificent ship captains' houses, making the "square" an important gathering space within the town.

In the mid–nineteenth century, with the discovery of petroleum oil in western Pennsylvania and the advent of the Civil War, Nantucket's halcyon days came to an abrupt end. Its long depression lasted until the late nineteenth century, when the first city dwellers began visiting the remote island. Today tourists come to Nantucket in boatloads, particularly in the summer, when the population may increase up to seven times. Physically, however, it remains the unique town created during the mid–nineteenth century by seafaring Quakers of enormous wealth.

In recent years, a combination of private and public forces have coalesced to freeze the town and the island in time, emphasizing the era of its heyday, around 1846. In the 1960s, Walter Beinecke, Jr., a wealthy longtime summer resident, purchased 80 percent of the town's commercial waterfront real estate and significant areas of the town center. He restored many buildings, added others, and established a trust fund to maintain landmarks.[16] In 1966, the town was declared a National Historic Landmark District, and in 1970 the Historic District Commission was established to act in a design review capacity.

To protect the island, the Nantucket Conservation Foundation was established in 1963 with private donations; it was founded with the intent of acquiring 25 percent of the island's area. Further strengthening this effort was the formation, in 1983, of the Nantucket Land Bank, which, through a 2 percent transfer on all island real estate transactions, is able to purchase land to be left in a natural state for public recreation. Through these means Nantucket, which historically has been conservative and wealthy, is in a sense returning to the past—to the building character of 1846 and to the common-lands policy of the first colonial settlers.[17] More so than any other coastal community, Nantucket is prohibiting change, and, in so doing, it is guaranteeing the continued prosperity, desirability, and beauty of the island town. At the same time, by driving housing costs up, these policies are also prohibiting less-affluent citizens from participation in life on Nantucket.

Oak Bluffs, Martha's Vineyard (pop. 1,984), started as a planned resort in 1867, and *Wesleyan Grove*, founded as a Methodist camp meeting in 1835, together form a unique summer colony on the northern side of Martha's Vineyard.[18] Jeremiah Pease from Edgartown, six miles to the east, chose a secluded grove of oaks on a slope that looked inward away from the sea as a site for the camp meeting. Eventually, five hundred gable-front, two-story cottages, trimmed in scrollwork and bedecked with porches, filled the thirty-four-acre site of Wesleyan Grove. Three hundred of these cottages still cluster tightly together in small neighborhoods around a central park, where a great iron tabernacle 140 feet in diameter shelters the site of the original preacher's stand. Although larger in scale, Oak Bluffs continued the architectural and planning themes of Wesleyan Grove. However, it celebrated not internal views but ocean vistas. Its Victorian houses edge two sides of Ocean Park, a seven-acre, triangular site on a bluff, open on its long side to Nantucket Sound. This colony today still has a powerful sense of place; one can recognize in its scalar arrangement the family unit and the collective whole, themes also evident in Ocean Grove, New Jersey (see Chapter Eight).

Rhode Island

Narragansett Bay, the main geographical feature of this tiny state, extends inland more than twenty-eight miles. Offering more fertile soils, better-protected harbors, safer seafaring ways, and a more moderate climate than exposed Atlantic locations, the bay first attracted American Indian inhabitants, who settled in the area possibly as long as ten thousand years ago. The first European settlers, led by Roger Williams, came in 1636 from the Massachusetts Bay colony to seek greater religious freedoms. While first Newport and then Providence grew into the state's primary cities, other bay settlements remain relatively more obscure and intact as small coastal towns.

On the eastern side of the bay, *Bristol* (pop. 21,625) was settled in 1680 on land sloping upward from a well-protected harbor that proved excellent for colonial shipping and trade. Unusual for a New England town, it was laid out in a rigid grid pattern of eight blocks of one acre each. These and the elegant Greek Revival style buildings that today line its broad streets, of which Hope Street is particularly outstanding, lend a distinctive and stately scale to the community.[19]

Little Compton (pop. 3,339*) lies to the east of Newport across the Sakonnet River in an area where the land gently slopes, indeed seems to slide, into the water. By at least 1674, settlers had arrived here, many from the Plymouth Bay Colony. Benefiting from the area's deep fertile soil, they and their descendants prospered from farming as well as fishing. While these activities continue today, the properties are increasingly used for retirement living and second homes. Although not immediately on the water, Little Compton Common, the village center of the area, clusters around a triangular graveyard placed where the roads come together in the middle of the township. Here several old churches and more recent community buildings blend together to reinforce the public role this center continues to serve.

In 1639 refugees from the Massachusetts Bay Colony founded *Newport* (pop. 81,000) at the mouth of Narragansett Bay, where the island that would later give its name to the state cups at the bay's southern end to form one of the finest natural harbors along the Atlantic coast. From its beginning, the town thrived on shipbuilding and international commerce, attaining its greatest relative prosperity during the years 1740–1775.

Although Newport is a city today, its central area has qualities of a small town and is recognized by the federal government as a National Historic Landmark District. Thames Street parallels the harbor and serves as the commercial corridor of the area. The old shipping wharves that extend into the harbor are now filled with tourist services and stores. Spring Street, uphill and parallel to both Thames Street and the harbor, stretches from the Old Town Spring and point of Colonial settlement south along the hill. Connecting these two streets are numerous narrow side streets, which have a variety of architectural styles and mix of uses. The two- and three-story buildings of this quiet neighborhood are close to, or abut on, each other and the sidewalks and, because of the slope of the hill, are near yet separated from the busy commercial life of Thames Street.

Approximately one mile south of this district begins the area of the great post–Civil War mansions that extend along Bellevue and Ocean Avenues. Splendidly sited on the jagged coastline, individually surrounded by lush gardens, and opulently designed by the most fashionable architects of the day, they are the ultimate expressions of the Gilded Age (1870–98). More so than anywhere along the Atlantic coast, these two districts, the compact town of the Thames Street area and the collection of mansions on the point dramatically juxtapose the two great traditions of American settlement patterns.[20]

To the west of Newport, at the mouth of Narragansett Bay on Conanicut Island, is *Jamestown* (pop. 4,040). Established in 1678, the village grew around the landing of the ferry from Newport, and in the late nineteenth century it became fashionable as a resort community. Today, turn-of-the-century buildings, including an old hotel, remain in the center of town, and, on land sloping further up from the water, Shingle style houses overlook the bay and Newport. A bridge one-half mile north of the town has replaced the ferry service and fortunately allows vehicular traffic to bypass the community.

On the western side of the Bay, *East Greenwich* (pop. 10,211), founded in 1677, lies along the old Pequot Indian coastal trail, which became Route 1. Overlooking a cove, the town terraces up the slope on three levels. On the first level, the waterfront and harbor are now separated by the seaboard rail line from the second level, which is Main Street, the old coast road. Above these is the third level, Pierce Street, where major civic buildings and fine residences are located.[21]

Eight miles south of East Greenwich is the village of *Wickford* (pop. 2,750), platted in 1709 in an area Europeans had settled by 1639. The village lies on a road that connects the old Pequot Trail to a small cove on the bay. On the edge of the cove, this road became an intimate street defined by buildings set on the front property lines. It remains one of the best-preserved and most memorable early colonial streets in New England.

Connecticut

The sheltered and brackish waters of Long Island Sound are edged on the south by the sandy moraines of Long Island and on the north by the marshy coast of Connecticut. The marshes, some of which extend miles inland, are periodically broken by granite headlands, left after the glacial retreat, and small beaches. Creeks, inlets, bays, and mouths of rivers also intricately configure the shore, allowing tides to ebb and flow through the low-lying region and boats to find safe harbors. The colonists chose sites in the river lowlands and tidal marshes, often on narrow points of land that offered defense and adequate pasturage for their animals.

South of Stonington, Connecticut, and originally part of it, is Mystic (pop. 5,650). Lying on both sides of the Mystic River, the town was settled in 1654. Although the river valley is only five miles long, it profited from being a short haul to hardwood forests and offered excellent sites along its banks for shipbuilding. For two hundred years, until 1870—when iron and steel replaced wood in ships' hulls and steam rather than sail began to propel vessels—Mystic was unmatched for a community of its small size in the number of ships it produced.[22] Active in the whaling trade from 1830 to 1850, the town subsequently gained distinction for its clipper ships, which combined cargo space with exceptional speed.

The reconstructed Mystic Seaport, which dates from 1929, has helped preserve America's maritime heritage. A "living museum," it has over sixty buildings on thirty-seven acres of land and features exhibits of historic vessels, demonstra-

tions of shipbuilding crafts, and an outstanding maritime library and manu-
script collection. Interstate 95 passes approximately one mile north of the town
center, allowing the nearly 400,000 tourists who come each year direct access to
the nearby Mystic Seaport Museum, which dominates the east side of the Mystic
River.

Today the seafaring tradition is carried on, albeit on a more modest scale, by
the many sailing enthusiasts whose crafts crowd the banks of the river. The Old
Post Road, now U.S. Route 1, meanders through the center of town and across
the river on a draw bridge. A densely packed two-block shopping area is adjacent to the drawbridge on the west side of the river. Serenely sited on a steep hill
overlooking this busy main street is the Union Baptist Church, a graceful local
landmark.

Two miles southwest of Mystic, *Noank* (pop. 1,371) rests on a peninsula,
sheltered at this point from the open Atlantic by Fishers Island, which lies two
miles offshore. A church, a few stores, and simple, dignified, nineteenth-century
houses cluster on the top of a small hill. A road wraps around this high point and
connects to others that descend to contrasting destinations—the old harbor,
rocky points of land, and quiet marshy coves. Rarely is the sea out of sight.
Indeed, so humanly scaled is the topography of the site and the buildings
occupying it that children appear to use the entire village as their playground,
and adults commonly walk rather than use their cars for local errands.

While no major city developed at the mouth of the Connecticut River, a
cluster of early colonial towns was established there and remains today. To the
west is *Old Lyme*, (pop. 6,681) settled in the 1640s. It prospered as a shipbuilding and commercial center and today still has many old houses built for ship
captains by their carpenters. These buildings, along with the shady streets, the
elegant Congregational church, the quiet meadows, and the rugged shoreline
attracted American Impressionist painters (among them Childe Hassam, Maurice Prendergast, and John Twachtman) during the first part of the twentieth
century and made the town a fashionable summer artists' colony. It retains these
qualities today, although a highway overpass spans the north end of Lyme Street
and intrudes on the idyllic village character.

Across the mouth of the Connecticut River on its western side is *Old Saybrook*
(pop. 2,281). Briefly settled by the Dutch in 1623 and then claimed by the
English in 1635, it grew up around a fort built by the English on present-day
Saybrook Point to deter Dutch encroachment into the Connecticut River Valley.
It was an active commercial town, first in the days when people traveled primarily by water and then later, when they traveled from Boston to New York City
via the Old Post Road, which passed through the town. In the early Colonial
period it was an ecclesiastical and educational center. Here, in 1701, ten Puritan
ministers founded Yale College, then named Collegiate School. Classes and
commencements were held here until 1716, when the college moved to New
Haven. Today, the town and surrounding area quietly host summer colonists,

although strip development mars much of the natural beauty of the setting, and few of the early buildings remain.

Upstream, on the same side as Old Saybrook, *Essex* (pop. 2,473) lies on a narrow neck of land. Probably settled in 1675, this town was famous during the eighteenth century as a ship building center; at one time eight shipyards thrived here. At a remove of only five miles from the Route 1–Interstate 95 transportation corridor, this town has nevertheless remained far less affected by the heedless development that characterizes so many villages dating from the same period. Its quaint streets, lined with Colonial houses and carefully tended gardens, its docks and marinas, and the tree-framed views to the water still attract faithful summer and year-round residents.

Guilford (pop. 2,588) was established in 1639 and named after the town in Surrey, England. Near but not directly on the water, it prospered from farming, shipbuilding, and transporting goods to Boston and New York City, as well as fishing. A variety of buildings—four churches, a library, the Town Hall, historic houses, and stores—surround the Green, all unified, perhaps even overwhelmed, by the grandeur of this space, one of the largest in New England. The community has preserved a remarkable number of its eighteenth- and nineteenth-century buildings—approximately four hundred—which collectively define the physical character of the town.

Further west and closer to New York City is *Fairfield* (pop. 77,211), a Colonial town with urban amenities. U.S. 1, the main seaboard rail line, and Interstate 95 all pass through the area. Three historic districts on the National Register are in the town: Greenfield Hill, Fairfield, and Southport. Greenfield Hill is inland, north of the transportation corridor, and centers on its idyllic triangular Green and old Congregational church. Fairfield village developed along the Old Post Road, although today's commercial strip development is far more evident than the town's historic past. Southport focuses on its harbor and its architectural heritage. Approximately two hundred houses from the town's Colonial period still survive.

Maritime New York

Long Island marks the southern edge of the glacial cover during the last ice age. Deposits from these glaciers formed a ridge running the length of the island, leaving a ground moraine to the north and an outwash plain to the south. Consequently, the north shore has many high bluffs, while the south shore, from Montauk to Coney Island (a distance of approximately 125 miles), has a virtually unbroken stretch of wide, flat beaches. The Gulf Stream tempers these shores, turning the region into a pleasure ground for New Yorkers. Yet, in the fall and winter, hurricanes, nor'easters, and high water periodically lash the exposed coast, eroding and reshaping it and reminding property owners how precarious coastal development can be. The better ports—for example, Cold Spring Harbor,

Port Jefferson, and Sag Harbor—are on the northern, more sheltered side of Long Island, while the surviving south coast settlements—for example, the Hamptons—are inland and gain access to the ocean through bays and inlets or through the ports to the north.

Over the centuries, as *East Hampton* (pop. 1,402) became in succession a farming community, a whaling port, an artists' colony, and finally an exclusive resort community, it evolved slowly rather than radically transforming itself. During this time, East Hampton fortunately avoided devastating disasters—the fires, hurricanes, and even rampant suburbanization that have destroyed other historic communities. As a result, today it possesses remarkable architectural, temporal, and spatial continuity. The old village blends comfortably with the more modern resort community, and both of these communities intertwine with the beautiful and varied landscape of ponds, beaches, dunes, and woods. Yet it is not compact. Compared to other historic coastal towns, East Hampton is low in density, spread out, and, except in its small commercial district, favors driving, not walking.

Settled in 1648 by Puritans from Lynn, Massachusetts, not by the Dutch who claimed Manhattan, East Hampton still reflects in its town pattern and architecture its old New England ties. The heart of the village remains along Main Street, where settlement started. The early inhabitants first located their dwellings at the southern end on either side of a small stream that they enlarged into a pond. The village grew a mile and a half to the north, to encompass the location of today's commercial district at a major intersection. Main Street became an extended common, with the town's green and burying ground, along with the pond, stretching through the middle of town and domestic and civic buildings marking the sides.[23] Today, this sequence along Main Street, from the town pond in the south to the commercial center in the north, is one of the most graceful passages in any American community.

For the first two hundred years, East Hampton remained a quiet, economically self-sufficient community. Modest salt-box cottages lined the lanes, and windmills, built to harness the ocean wind to grind grain, dotted the landscape. A few of these windmills still exist. Whaling was profitable, as whalers first harvested whales beached on the nearby shores and then later pursued them from ships, usually out of Sag Harbor. Although a few British soldiers came here to rest and enjoy the water during the Colonial period, East Hampton remained isolated and disconnected until after the Civil War. Then in the 1870s visitors, primarily from New York City, began arriving by rail to Bridgehampton, six miles away, and by packet boat to Sag Harbor. Artists such as Winslow Homer, Childe Hassam, William Merritt Chase, and Thomas Moran were among those favoring the village, and through their paintings and writings they publicized the picturesque qualities of the community.[24]

East Hampton gradually became a genteel summer colony, Episcopalian and rich, although not as conspicuously so as Newport, Rhode Island, or even nearby Southampton. Summer residents favored the Shingle style, which had long been associated with the area and was then becoming nationally fashionable. In 1895 the railroad reached East Hampton, decisively linking the quaint community with New York City. Also in 1895 and possibly a related event, the Ladies' Village Improvement Society of East Hampton was established to "keep East Hampton beautiful." It has ever since been a powerful guardian of town character, taking up such causes from arguing for underground utilities to protecting historic structures and trees.[25]

During the first part of the twentieth century, East Hampton remained sedate and conservative although it was gaining in popularity as a summer retreat for New Yorkers. With the depression, it returned to its quiet and removed way of life, only to be rediscovered after World War II—again, first by artists, such as Willem de Kooning and Jackson Pollock, and then by others. Today it is a community frequented by the wealthy and socially prominent, a place to flee city life and be close to nature, while remaining near one's agents, clients, patients, or patrons. The community prides itself on its village qualities and its ties to a venerated past, even if many of the residents are as vitally engaged as any group in shaping contemporary culture.

In the village, parking lots are hidden behind buildings and large houses are discreetly screened by lush landscaping while maintenance trucks scurry back and forth. In summer, crowds are an ever-increasing problem as visitors overload local roads and dwindle water supplies. New developments are consuming the potato fields of the region and, through higher land costs, driving out the less affluent. Suffolk County, with its Farmlands Preservation Program, adopted in 1977, fortunately has the capacity to transfer development rights from agricultural areas to other, less fragile locations. Yet the beaches continue to erode, and changes to the delicate ecology may mandate even more forceful measures if East Hampton is to maintain its unique character.

The rise of *Southampton Village* (pop. 3,980) from a small, remote agricultural settlement to one of the most fashionable summer resorts and year-round communities in the East parallels that of nearby East Hampton. Like its neighboring town, Southhampton's center does not relate directly to the sea because of the danger of storms and coastal erosion. Instead Southampton has a well-organized commercial center and a magnificent collection of residences, perhaps most handsomely displayed on South Main Street, which runs south from the village center to the Atlantic Ocean. Beginning with the firm of McKim, Mead, and White at the turn of the twentieth century, the finest New York City area architects have built here and elaborated on the village's domestic traditions.[26]

Settled in the seventeenth century, the village of *Sag Harbor* (pop. 2,134) served first as a trading port for towns in the eastern region of Long Island and then, in the late eighteenth and early nineteenth centuries, became an important whaling center, surpassed only by Nantucket and New Bedford, Massachusetts, in the number of its ships. With the arrival of the railroad from New York City in 1870, it began its era as a resort town, which continues today. The town pattern demonstrates the port's importance. Roads from East Hampton and Southampton descend the low-lying hills to the harbor as branches converge at the base of a tree. Passing by old cemeteries and many fine residences set generously back, churches marking the high ground, the large Federal and Greek Revival style houses close to the street, and into Main Street with its rows of buildings— all legacies from the whaling days—one arrives at the waterfront and all too abruptly into the present. Fires in the nineteenth century destroyed the old buildings there, and the waterfront remains a world apart from the historical richness of the surrounding town.[27]

Several other coastal towns on Long Island have similar development patterns to Sag Harbor, although they may not be considered as historically important. *Greenport* (pop. 2,070) was settled in the eighteenth century by former residents of the New Haven colony. In an otherwise rural setting on the far eastern end of Long Island's North Fork, Greenport has a dense, picturesque collection of buildings on its waterfront. The buildings here and in the neighborhoods that spread out from the town remain relatively unchanged, and their dates of origin range from 1750 to the 1930s. North of Oyster Bay is *Orient* (pop. 1,000), which was established in 1661 but has the character of a nineteenth-century community. Its residences and public buildings possess a more uniform scale, indicative of an egalitarian past based on farming and fishing. Also nearby is *Southold* (pop. 5,192), settled in 1640. Further to the west is *Cold Spring Harbor* (pop. 4,789), which was settled by 1682. First prospering as a whaling port, Cold Spring Harbor became a fashionable resort after the Civil War, and, beginning in the early twentieth century, it developed into an affluent residential community just eighteen miles east of New York City. Particularly in its residences, it retains a nineteenth-century character in an area that has otherwise embraced the late twentieth century.[28] Immediately west of Cold Spring Harbor is *Oyster Bay* (pop. 2,109), settled in the seventeenth century. Nearby is the Sagamore Hill National Historic Site, commemorating the former farm and then retreat and home of Theodore Roosevelt, which served as the summer White House from 1902 to 1909.

Conclusion

In Canada and Maine, where coves created harbors and hills embraced the sea, and also in southern New England, where twisting rivers and sheltered bays offered havens, the topography of the North Atlantic coast defined pockets for settlement. The relatively unproductive land, on the one hand, and the fecundity of the offshore fishing grounds, on the other, encouraged settlers to harvest the sea. The colonists, then, clustered around their ports to be close to their ships.

Succeeding waves of immigrants seized the latent opportunities in these locations and built unique towns adapted to their sites. Cumulatively, these settlements created a rich legacy of coastal towns.

Many of these towns, especially those in southern New England, have had to adjust, as they have in the past, to changing conditions—most recently to a modern world serviced by convenient travel and instantaneous communication and pressured by metropolitan growth. The historic coastal towns along the North Atlantic (mainly those nearer the metropolitan centers) have found a new role, serving as places of respite for people from the metropolitan centers. The town environments, which had evolved for other purposes, are now valued for inherent physical qualities. The current problems, however, lie in maintaining a balance between traditional town character and contemporary needs which can sustain yet ensure the preservation of these towns.

Rendering by Peter Lorenzoni, after a drawing by the author.

CHAPTER THREE

Castine, Maine

Fig. 3.1. Street section of Castine, Maine.

Map 3.1. Old mountain ranges, raked by glaciers, descend dramatically into the ocean, with islands and long peninsulas trailing off into the sea. Castine, at the head of Penobscot Bay, tiers up one of these hills to overlook an island-protected harbor (U.S. Coast and Geodetic Survey, 1886).

The village of Castine, Maine, rests on a peninsula at the head of Penobscot Bay, where the Penobscot and Bagaduce Rivers converge. This one-mile-wide and two-mile-long knob of land rises over two hundred feet to deflect cold northerly winds from the village, which slopes southeasterly toward a protected and capacious harbor, one of the deepest natural ports on the eastern seaboard.[1] Historically, this was a strategic site—located between rich ocean fishing grounds and the great northern wilderness abundant with fur and lumber. During the Colonial period, when national boundaries were being defined, the British and French aggressively contested this region.

Later, in the nineteenth century, Castine became a major port, capturing the market on the crucial salt trade. Consequently, enormous wealth funneled into this small town, allowing proud merchants to erect elegant buildings and shape a village of rare quality.[2] In the late nineteenth century, summer visitors favored Castine for its comfortable seclusion and rustic charm, qualities that are still evident. Now a retirement and yachting center and the home of the Maine Maritime Academy, Castine offers a quiet and leisurely life in contrast with its stormy colonial origins and bustling maritime days. Today, removed from the flow of tourists who stream along the coastal road, the village preserves in relative isolation its nineteenth-century architectural character.[3]

On entering Castine today, the visitor soon senses the judicious and eloquent development of its unusual site. Approaching from the mainland, the entrance road rolls across hills, passes through marshes on the neck of connecting land, rises through the old upland pastures of the peninsula to the ridge overlooking the town, and then descends the slope into the center of town and the harbor.[4] Rimmed with islands and flecked with white boats, the harbor itself is a grand civic space and, understandably, the focus of the town. Fronting it are Water Street to the east, an older area with a mixture of uses, and Perkins Street to the west, a more recent and exclusively residential area.

Court and High Streets tier up the slope and offer even more panoramic views. Commanding the ridge are forests, land formerly used as pastures (now a golf course), and old Fort George, built in 1779 by the English, its earth ramparts still in place. It now hosts Little League baseball games and community theater productions. Main Street, with its handsome Federal and Greek Revival style clapboard buildings, ties the harbor and ridge together. The stores on the lower end of the street provide meeting places for people from surrounding neighborhoods. The Village Green, several blocks inland and uphill from the harbor, is a serene and intimate public space. Within a relatively small and

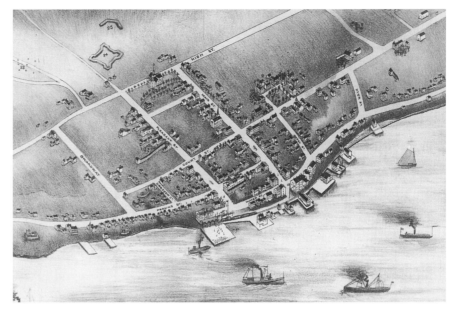

Fig. 3.2. While the railroad (shown along the water's edge) never reached Castine, this drawing correctly portrays a town with different centers of activity (Wilson Museum, 1889).

Fig. 3.3. In this view looking northwest, the surrounding sea contrasts with the intimate and orderly village. Within the village, the Maine Maritime Academy on the upper slopes and its training ship in the harbor contrast with the scale of the historic buildings (Aerial Photos International, Inc., 1976).

Fig. 3.4. Lower Main Street (ca. 1850–80). Although automobiles have replaced wagons, Main Street remains remarkably as it was in the last century (Doudiet 1978, 42).

Fig. 3.5. Public buildings, churches, and residences informally group around the exquisite Village Green (1990).

conveniently walkable area, Castine offers a variety of public environments engagingly related to its natural setting.

The village possesses a human scale, based on the module of the single, free-standing house, adapted to the hillside. While additions, barns, and sheds are often grouped together with houses to form complexes, these groups neverthe-less maintain an underlying modulated scale. Even late-nineteenth-century inns respected this characteristic. Buildings visually interrelate through the use of wood clapboard construction and white paint. They coexist with the landscape, with neither dominating. Often, century-old elm trees arc over houses and streets to provide summer shade while understory growth defines informal spaces and properties. Since buildings are free-standing, lawns and gardens weave through and slope between them. Only the Maine Maritime Academy, which otherwise has made contributions to community life, has violated the traditional scalar qualities of the village by erecting large blocks of brick dormitories and classrooms, which, sitting prominently on the upper slopes, markedly contrast with the scale of the village below.[5]

Stormy Years of Settlement

Soon after 1604, when Samuel de Champlain visited the area, Castine became the focus of continuing imperialistic contests between the French, the Plymouth-based English, the Dutch, and eventually the Americans. These tumultuous years are reflected in the more than fifteen forts built in the vicinity and the successive names given to the peninsula—Pentagoûët, Majabigwaduce, Bagaduce, Penobscot, and finally Castine.[6] In 1626 the Plymouth Colony of Massachusetts established a trading post here. For the next century the French would periodically seize and loot this settlement, only to have it later reclaimed by the English.[7]

Fort Pownall, built in 1759 on the west bank of the Penobscot River, secured the area for the English. In addition to housing troops, the fort attracted settlers willing to establish a permanent community. The British platted the peninsula in strips to give each owner access to water as well as to upland wood lots. These early property boundaries eventually set road alignments still used today. The settlers cleared the forests along the water's edge and built simple houses. They harvested a few crops, but the region's codfish proved more lucrative, found first in the bay and then beyond in the Grand Banks and the fishing grounds off the coast of Labrador. In addition to the profitable fishing, furs from Castine's hinterlands were fancied by ladies of the French court and proved to be a great source of wealth.

The British diligently settled the village to secure their claim to the growing regional trade. They constructed Fort George on the ridge overlooking the harbor, laid out upper Main Street to connect the fort and harbor, and cut a canal across the neck of land between the peninsula and mainland to link adjoining bodies of water and to discourage soldiers from deserting.[8] Throughout the Revolutionary War, the British controlled the town. Loyalists resettled here from regions to the south, especially after the British had burned Portland and evacuated Boston. The heart of the village now took shape around the harbor. Activity concentrated along the waterfront and up Center Street (now Green Street). The street pattern then, as now, had one set of roads running parallel to the harbor and another set perpendicular to the shoreline and aligned with established

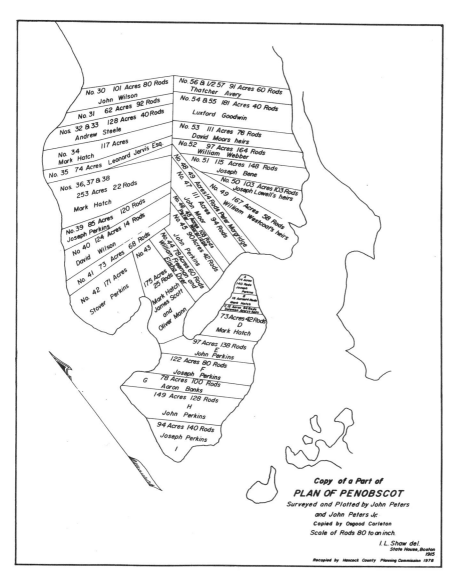

No. 30   101 Acres 80 Rods
John Wilson
No. 31   62 Acres 92 Rods
Nos. 32 & 33   128 Acres 40 Rods
Andrew Steele
No. 34   117 Acres
Mark Hatch
No. 35   74 Acres   Leonard Jervis Esq.
Nos. 36, 37 & 38
253 Acres 22 Rods
Mark Hatch
No. 39 85 Acres 120 Rods
Joseph Perkins
No 40 124 Acres 14 Rods
David Wilson
No. 41 73 Acres 68 Rods   No. 43
No. 42 171 Acres
Stover Perkins
175 Acres 25 Rods
Mark Hatch
James Scott
and
Oliver Mann
No. 44 78 Acres 60 Rods
William Freeman and
William Eliaha Dyer
No. 45 90 Acres 42 Rods
Joseph Perkins
No. 46 Peter Bridge 39 Rods
John Moor 111 Acres 94 Rods
No. 47 111 Acres 14 Rods Peter Marʼgriʼdge
No. 48 49 Acres 14 Rods
No. 49 167 Acres 58 Rods
William Westcoat's heirs
No. 50 103 Acres 103 Rods
Joseph Lowell's heirs
No. 51 115 Acres 148 Rods
Joseph Bene
No. 52 97 Acres 164 Rods
William Webber
No. 53 111 Acres 78 Rods
David Moors heirs
No. 54 & 55 181 Acres 40 Rods
Luxford Goodwin
No. 56 & 1/2 57 91 Acres 60 Rods
Thatcher Avery

A 14 Acres 140 Rods Joseph Perkins
B 16 Acres Mark Hatch
C 18 Acres 94 Rods Solomon Bene's heirs
D 73 Acres 42 Rods Mark Hatch
E 97 Acres 138 Rods John Perkins
F 122 Acres 80 Rods Joseph Perkins
G 78 Acres 100 Rods Aaron Banks
H 149 Acres 128 Rods John Perkins
I 94 Acres 140 Rods Joseph Perkins

Copy of a Part of
PLAN OF PENOBSCOT
Surveyed and Plotted by John Peters
and John Peters Jr.
Copied by Osgood Carleton
Scale of Rods 80 to an inch.
I. L. Shaw del.
State House, Boston
1915
Recopied by Hancock County Planning Commission 1978

*Map 3.2. Detail of a Plan of Penobscot (original ca. 1670). Early land grants stretch across
the peninsula. Subsequent roads followed these property boundaries. Recopied by Hancock
County Plan Commission, 1978, in* Castine Comprehensive Plan *1979, 18.*

property boundaries. In 1779 Castine was a village of about twenty small houses
on the lower slopes, with the primitive Fort George standing guard on the ridge.

The Salt Years

After the Revolutionary War, Americans briefly controlled the village until it
was seized once again by the British during the War of 1812. Americans finally
regained the town in 1815, and Castine began its period of great prosperity.

While fishing was modest until 1800, it grew rapidly afterward. Because of the village's entrepreneurial citizens and its proximity to rich fishing grounds, Castine became a major port, the place to visit before and after embarking on long fishing voyages. It was also important for the growing transatlantic trade, as ships transporting cotton between New Orleans and Liverpool regularly stopped here for supplies.

Castine's merchants reaped enormous fortunes when they captured the trade in salt, at that time the primary preservative for fish. These prescient entrepreneurs imported salt from Liverpool, England, and Cadiz, Spain, reselling it to ships coming back from the fishing grounds. From 1830 to 1840, Castine was the second-wealthiest town per capita in the country, after New Bedford, Massachusetts.[9] Enjoying a virtual New England monopoly on the commodity, the salt merchants forced trade to the area.[10]

Prosperity brought official recognition. Castine became a port of entry and gained the prestige of its own custom house. Shipbuilding flourished, with as many as twelve shipyards at the industry's height. These shipyards in turn supported other business and services. The J. W. Dresser's Line Company, which made "mackerel and cod lines known around the world," had a ropewalk building (a narrow shed in which separate strands of hemp were woven into rope) over 615 feet long and employed thirteen men, two women, and uncounted boys to "run" the rope. With its commercial success, Castine became the region's legal, financial, and market center. The town's population grew accordingly, reaching 1,357 residents before the Civil War.

With the growth of trade, the waterfront became a predominantly working-class district. Salt warehouses along with shipyards clustered on Water Street. The north waterfront (Oakum Bay), the oldest part of town, also housed taverns and brothels intermixed with a few old dwellings.[11] Noah Brooks, newspaper correspondent and close friend of Abraham Lincoln, remembered his youth here: "At odd intervals on the crumbling marge of this ragged bank were dotted the weather-beaten shelters of the oakum-pickers and fisher folk. . . . Under the bank were copper-shops, blacksmith-shops, and the like, and along its upper edge was a row of shabby cottages, the homes of fishermen (and) longshoremen."[12]

To distance themselves from this environment, the gentry moved further uphill, where they built dwellings on Center Street (now Green Street). John and Joseph Perkins, who owned much of the land in the central part of the village, sold property for development and donated land at the head of Center Street for the Village Common, or Green, which became the new focus for the gentry.[13] In 1790 a large congregational meeting house was constructed on the edge of the Common, and soon after, on the other side, a courthouse and jail (now a library) were built at the head of Center Street. Eventually, two schools and several houses completed this modest but stately group of buildings around the sloping lawn of the Common.

Fig. 3.6. Detail from the painting Castine Harbor and Town, by Fitz Hugh Lane (ca. 1850–
60, the Putnam Foundation, Timken Museum of Art, San Diego).

By the 1820s, sea captains were returning from long voyages with new wealth and, often, more liberal views which conflicted with those of the conservative town leaders.[14] The conservative members left the Congregational Church on the Common because of its liberal tendencies and in 1828–29 built the Trinitarian Church on Main Street, shifting the focus of activity again to a new prestigious residential area on upper Main Street (nicknamed "Quality Church on Quality Avenue"). Here, on higher elevations and in relative seclusion, the social elite (merchants, ship owners, professionals, and sea captains) built gracious Federal and Greek Revival style mansions.[15] The social status of residents soon paralleled the topography: the working classes remained low and close to the harbor and the elite placed themselves on the upper slopes. Yet village development occurred exclusively on the southeastern side of the peninsula, which faced the harbor. The backside, exposed to harsh winter winds, remained wooded.

The transferral of the county seat in 1848, from Castine to Ellsworth, more conveniently located on the mainland, signaled a decline in Castine's fortunes which became clearly evident by the end of the Civil War. Castine residents, whose fortunes depended on the sea, had lost many ships during the war. The federal government had also removed the profitable shipping and salt subsidies. More fundamentally, the nation was industrializing in the states further south and shifting to land transportation. First canals, and then railroads, replaced coastal shipping. Although better roads extended along the coast, they were inland from Castine, and the railroad spur that was proposed to serve Castine from Bangor never reached the town (Fig. 3.2). Castine, located on its remote peninsula and separated by mountains from the developing continental interior, became ever more isolated. However, summer visitors discovered Castine in the late 1880s and brought new life to the declining maritime village.

The Summer Visitors

Summer visitors came first from nearby Bangor. Soon wealthy Americans from the hot, crowded, industrializing cities of the Northeast discovered Maine's cool summer climate and rugged, untamed landscape. While the truly wealthy gathered in nearby Bar Harbor, a more modest but certainly prosperous group of families from Boston, Philadelphia, New York City, and Washington, D.C., favored Castine as their summer retreat.[16] Initially, these out-of-state visitors came by rail to Bucksport and then continued by stagecoach to Castine or sailed on the daily packet from Belfast.[17]

At first, many villagers who had already been boarding students from the Eastern State Normal School after it opened, in 1872, welcomed summer visitors into their homes after school had closed for the season. Gradually, these residents enlarged their houses to accommodate summer visitors more comfortably, and eventually inns and hotels were built. Even as the year-round population declined to about a thousand by 1890, the physical size of Castine expanded with the influx of summer sojourners, who soon began to build summer cottages west of the old village.

The western half of the peninsula had remained largely undeveloped until this period. Only a dusty cart track (Perkins Street) meandered from Pleasant Street, on the village's edge, to a lighthouse at the point. Once forested, this area was cleared in the early part of the twentieth century for pasturing and farming. The new summer population preferred the seclusion of this area and began to build large summer houses on Perkins Street overlooking the harbor. Here, on higher ground and larger lots, they could live a quieter, somewhat more Arcadian life.[18]

The popularity of this area prompted development of the southern point of the peninsula, called the "Sargent and Sylvester" lots. While ambitiously platted as early as 1872 in a regularized pattern of small village lots, the southern point developed less intensively, instead filling with large houses of different styles on generous sites. Unlike in the village center, where similar types of houses were oriented to the street, houses in this new area exploited local site opportunities; some houses were tucked into the woods for privacy, others sought optimum sun, and most reached for water views. In the late 1890s, summer residents built their first golf course (consisting of two holes) within old Fort George, and in the 1920s an eighteen-hole course was placed on the nearby upland pastures. Thus, those residents whose families had lived in Castine for several generations and the newer summer people tended to move in different orbits, the newer circling the older.

The summer vacation season began soon after Memorial Day, as visitors

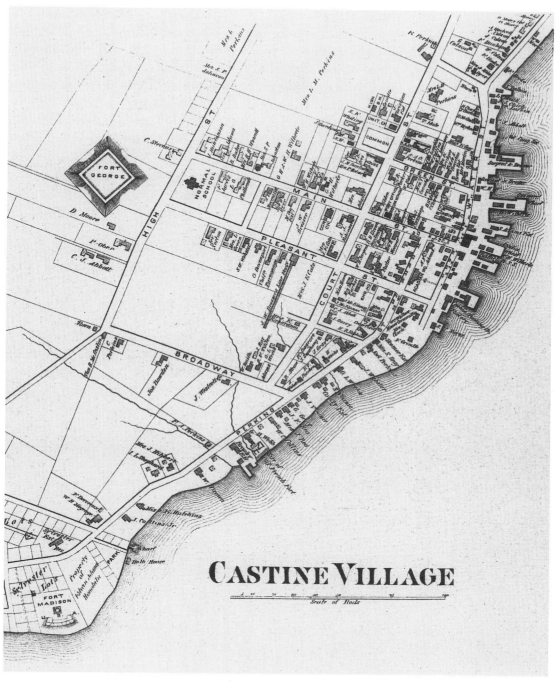

Map 3.3. Map of Castine, from the 1881 Hancock County Atlas. *The town extension to the south was never fully realized; houses on larger lots now fill this section (Wilson Museum, 1881).*

arrived with their steamer trunks. Women and children stayed till the end of the summer, while fathers tended to visit for shorter periods. It was a leisured, matriarchal society. Small parties hired boats for rides through the harbor and picnics on the islands. The younger set enjoyed hikes in the woods, buckboard rides on country lanes, and tennis games on private courts. Homes on the water had sailboats, yachts, and canoes readily at the disposal of the adventurous. Summer people had their own social club (now a private house) on Perkins Street at the foot of La Tour Street. They brought their domestic staffs from the city but usually hired local people as gardeners and caretakers.[19] Most summer residents belonged to the Episcopal church on Perkins Street, built around 1900, whose modest villagelike character belied its powerful social influence within the community. Across the street, summer visitors converted an old farmhouse into a Catholic church for their servants, and west of this, one year later, they established a museum. Informally, the summer people developed their own social and cultural facilities, removed from those within the village center.

Although the natives were relatively poor, the old village continued to be self-sufficient, and residents sustained themselves on fishing. Often the houses on larger village lots had gardens where residents grew food and small pastures where they kept livestock. One block up from the waterfront, a large house in the center of the village was expanded soon after 1865 and turned into the Acadian Hotel (demolished in 1943), which at the time became the most popular of the early hotels even though it overlooked a sardine factory. By 1894 a new hotel, the Pentagoet, was built nearby at Perkins and Main Streets. Summer people introduced the first automobiles into the village around 1910. With automobiles and better roads, the summer crowd began to favor the outlying areas even more, particularly the western side of the peninsula.[20]

The Twentieth Century

Land uses in early-twentieth-century Castine reflected the different living styles of vacationers and natives as well as the growing popularity of automobiles. For example, along the waterfront there were several inns in addition to the canning factories. There were also coal and lumber sheds, an ice house, automobile repair, machine, and paint shops, a telephone exchange (telephones arrived on the peninsula in 1893), and a movie theater (Castine had electricity by 1917), along with a variety of dwellings and stores. People traveled by boats as much as by automobiles, although the boats increasingly were motor powered.[21]

With the loss of wealth during the depression and the imposition of fuel rationing during World War II, fewer summer residents returned to Castine over those years, and those who did lived more modestly than before. Some year-round families whose ancestors had acquired wealth a century before continued to live comfortably, but other native residents were comparatively poorer than the generation before. While farming was still a way of life and provided food, taxes were low, and periodic odd jobs were available, Castinians increasingly had to look elsewhere for work. During World War II fishing was curtailed, further adding to economic hardships. At the beginning of the depression a paper manufacturing plant opened in Bucksport, twenty miles away, and continued through this period to be an important employer for workers from Castine. Others found work in nearby towns, in places such as the canning factories and the quarry in Stonington.

Families managed to survive over the course of the year by piecing together different jobs and opportunities in the region. Castine residents maintained farm animals in nearby fields and in the barns behind their houses, kept vegetable gardens, and supplied meat and milk to the declining number of summer visitors.

Fears of invasion during World War II prompted the federal government to install observation posts and alert systems along the coast. Otherwise, virtually no improvements were made to the town or the surrounding region, and property owners had neither the resources nor the optimism to invest in their buildings. After the long ordeal of the depression and then the war, the town was understandably unkempt. Houses needed repair, and public as well as private lands were not the tidy places we see today. Many of the active members of the old summer families had passed away or had lost interest in Castine, leaving heirs to sell once-treasured properties cheaply rather than restore them. The town and most of its residents were poor. For most of the 1940s, the town operating budget was approximately $30,000 per year. By 1991, this budget had risen to $1,474,360 while the population had increased from approximately 750 to 1,150 people.[22]

In the 1950s, retired middle-class people began discovering Castine. They bought houses and enjoyed the quiet town life during the warmer months. These outsiders remodeled old farmhouses and later built smaller houses for year-round living. With this increased interest in their village from outsiders, longtime residents became more concerned with Castine's appearance. Their first major effort at improvement was the restoration of the Green. The town soon began to rely more on tourism for income. It started advertising in state tourist literature, and throughout the 1960s tourists responded. New restaurants opened, and old hotels dating from before the war were revived. Residents discussed a comprehensive plan as early as 1957, but not until the threat of a mobile home park loomed in 1966 did they approve such a plan. The Maine Maritime Academy, housed in the former Eastern State Normal School, also expanded facilities within the town around this time, prompting concern over the need to provide additional police protection and utilities, as well as the loss of taxable properties.

During the 1970s, pressures for change and development grew significantly

*Fig. 3.7. New development in Castine. The Maine Maritime Academy's new buildings,
derived from urban prototypes, loom over the village (1991).*

as tourism increased, wealthier people moved in, and yachts and sailboats filled
the harbor. Residents feared change and sought additional means to preserve the
village character. The town passed subdivision regulations, stressed building
code enforcement, and, partly in response to the Clean Water Act of 1972, built
wastewater treatment facilities. Residents rejected a proposal to convert a Main
Street mansion into condominiums and a plan to make some streets one-way.
The Maine Maritime Academy, however, as a state institution, did not have to
abide by municipal ordinances and launched major construction programs that
produced buildings more appropriate for metropolitan centers than a quaint
village. Tourism and development continued into the late 1980s, when the real
estate recession offered a respite.

Possibly the most pervasive change during this post–World War II era was
that of the landscape of the village. While property owners carefully preserved
buildings, they made small but cumulative changes in the landscape that altered
the town character. Before the war, land within the town was more open. Yards
blended into pastures and one neighbor's land appeared seamlessly attached to
another's, as there were few physical demarcations to interrupt the sweeping
views. The town appeared more unified then, as indeed it was, since many families were related. Today residents, many of whom are new, increasingly mark off
the land they own with ornamental gardens and boundary plantings. There is a
greater sense of landownership, territoriality, and privacy than before, resulting
in a more suburban appearance. Where villagers once penned farm animals and
grew vegetables, retirees now cultivate flowers and enjoy secluded leisure.[23]

The Community Today

In 1990 Castine had a year-round population of 1,161, which increased by approximately 50 percent during the summer. Three primary groups of people—retirees and summer folk, Maine Maritime Academy personnel, and year-round natives—help shape community issues.

Retirees and summer vacationers constitute the largest group. While new to Castine, they have continued the traditions—the clubs, yachting pleasures, and church activities—that residents of past summers established. They have purchased many of the waterfront houses and, like the former generations of summer residents, prefer dramatic views of the water. They come from throughout the country and stay in the town for longer periods of the year than did the previous summer folk.[24] Visitors today are affluent, often having earned money in metropolitan areas of other states, and, since they also have raised their children in other places, they are less interested in the local educational system. With professional backgrounds and experience in addressing contemporary problems elsewhere, they usually feel more confident than the native Castinians in dealing with the complex problems facing the town—or at least those problems such as pollution and growth, which presently endanger Castine's physical character. As a group, retirees and summer folk have become the most insistent and vigilant guardians of the village.

The Maine Maritime Academy is the second major constituent group and illustrates the advantages and problems of having a relatively large institution in a small town. The academy has grown to accommodate an enrollment of over 620 students. With 150 on its staff, it is by far the largest village employer. The school no longer stresses merchant seamanship but rather concentrates on ocean studies and maritime management. To a limited extent, it opens its resources—library, recreation facilities, and meeting rooms—to the public. The academy makes annual payments to the town in lieu of taxes for the dozen or so houses it has acquired around the edges of its campus, but no taxes are paid to the town for the academy's primary properties. Because of the academy, however, residents enjoy a rich cultural life for a small town, a benefit retirees particularly appreciate. While students may at times cause nuisances, they add life and vitality to the village, volunteering for community projects and supporting local business. Academy staff members are also active on town committees.

Yet these benefits have not been without drawbacks, particularly in the ways the academy has affected the character and scale of the village. Whereas the earlier and smaller Eastern State Normal School had blended successfully with the community by using old residences or constructing similarly scaled buildings for classes and dormitories, the academy has erected buildings that violate village character. From this perspective, it has not been a considerate neighbor.

The year-round natives, or "locals," form the third village group. These people, some of whom trace their lineage in Castine back to the early Colonial

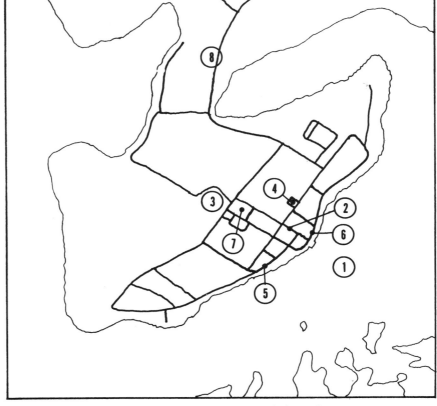

Map 3.4. Location Map of Castine, Maine (redrawn from current
U.S. Coast and Geodetic Survey maps).
1. Harbor; 2. Main Street; 3. Fort George; 4. Village Green; 5. Perkins Street;
6. Water Street; 7. Maine Maritime Academy; 8. Entrance Road.

period, are now finding it difficult to remain in the area.[25] Locals now have
limited employment opportunities in Castine and cannot compete with wealthy
retirees for housing. While viable fishing is slowly returning, thanks to reduced
pollution in coastal waters, retirees and summer residents object to the consequences of intensive fishing—the smells and noises it would bring, as well as
changing the image of the village into that of a processing center. Tourism and its
associated hotels, inns, sport fishing and yachting businesses, and boat repair
shops offer limited opportunities for anything more than seasonal employment
at minimum wages. Most of the teachers and staff who are employed at the
academy cannot even afford houses in Castine. The types of business open
throughout the year reflect more realistically the employment opportunities
available to native residents: real estate agencies, a few restaurants, one hardware
store, and one small market. Consequently, many younger Castinians have become transients, calling Castine home but seeking employment elsewhere for

long periods of the year. Because of its lack of affordable housing, Castine is losing its younger people, the ones who traditionally have staffed the village functions and services and who have family commitments to the area.

Conservation and Preservation

The overriding issue in the village today is the preservation of both its natural and historical environments. Organized conservation efforts started in the 1860s, when George Witherle, a member of a wealthy local family, bought Fort George and other properties along the ridge and backside of the hill. People willingly sold him their pastures and wood lots, knowing he would preserve the character of the land.[26] He opened "Witherle Woods" for public use, cutting trails through it for carriage rides and clearings for picnics. After his death, Witherle's daughter sold the land to private parties. However, the Hatch family bought large sections of the area and in 1985 donated that land to the Maine Coast Heritage Trust. This donation, and another in 1995 from the Foote family,

Fig. 3.8. The U.S. Post Office in Castine is the oldest continuously operating post office in the country. Reversing an earlier decision that would have moved functions to an outlying site, the U.S. Postal Service decided to retain operations here at this building, which also serves as a focus of village life (1991).

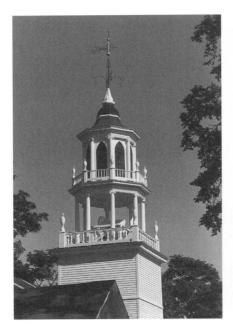

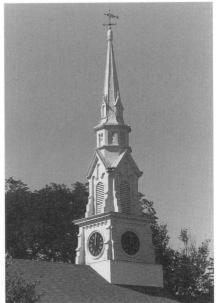

Fig. 3.9. Elegant belfries and spires announce the character of individual buildings and contribute to the village profile (1990).

have placed 130 acres of land on the peninsula in the land trust, ensuring that the majority of the ridge and backside of the peninsula's neck will remain undeveloped and open to the public. The Maine Coast Heritage Trust continues to accept land and easement donations in this area. It also seeks to preserve the natural character of fields and woods along the approach road onto the neck, as well as the islands and shorefront lands framing Castine harbor.

Most villagers hope change will occur off the peninsula and, even there, happen slowly. The decreasing availability of fresh water has been a recent deterrent to growth. For over a hundred years the town has relied on open-air ponds for fresh water. These ponds, however, have become increasingly susceptible to airborne pollutants. Responding to state concerns about safeguarding the water supply, the town is drilling wells for fresh water and will use the ponds only as backup sources. The town must also replace its old pipe network to ensure that plentiful water of good quality can reach all residents.[27]

While the town has been a historic district on the National Register of Historic Places since 1973, it operated without an architectural review board until 1995. Because village land values have risen, pressures to alter buildings and property have also increased. For example, some owners who have purchased expensive properties want to increase their rental income by subdividing units and introducing multifamily housing. Yet apartments would require additional parking. The architectural review board has resisted parking lots as violations of village character and prefers, as an alternative, to accommodate parking on the streets. Through zoning, the town has also prohibited commercial development in residential neighborhoods and along the entrance road, carefully specifying commercial locations to keep stores in the village center. Castine has the oldest continuously operating post office in the country.[28] Located in the center of town on Main Street in an elegant Federal style building, it has traditionally served as an informal social and cultural center as well as a mail distribution facility.

In the early 1990s the U.S. Postal Service proposed a larger facility on a site outside the village that would more easily accommodate parking and truck delivery. Town residents vehemently objected and launched a national campaign that ultimately involved the Postmaster General. The U.S. Postal Service reversed its decision and in 1996 began restoration of the historic building to utilize the interior space for contemporary needs and, more importantly, to retain the post office's role as a center of village life. As a result of this experience, the U.S. Postal Service is now reconsidering its policy for other small-town post offices throughout the country.

Castine, once the focus of imperial boundary disputes and international trade, is now home to retirees, second-home owners, and a sizable academic institution. Since its population is too small to support a range of jobs, stores, medical services, or educational opportunities, residents must seek them in the outlying regions. However, this does not discourage Castinians, who are proud of the village's history and setting and who recognize that they have benefited from Castine's peninsula location, far from metropolitan problems. With resolute land-use controls and vigilance, they are protecting that heritage. In the decades to come, even stronger efforts—including land banking and infrastructure improvements—will be required to protect this precious village and its remarkable setting.

Rendering by Peter Lorenzoni, after a drawing by the author.

CHAPTER FOUR

Kennebunks' Port, Maine

Fig. 4.1. Street section of Kennebunkport, Maine.

Fig. 4.2. With snow still covering open fields and lots, the Kennebunk River meanders to the ocean, creating a complex landscape of coves, ponds, and marshes. Kennebunkport slopes gently up from the river to the northeast, while the Lower Village of Kennebunk lies southwest of the river (Aerial Survey & Photo, Inc., 1988).

In Kennebunks' Port, water, land, and buildings occur in startlingly beautiful combinations.[1] From the wild islands off Cape Porpoise, the glacier-carved shoreline, and the crescent beaches of the coast to the forests, fields, and farms inland, the landscapes are varied and juxtaposed. Central to the settlement is the Kennebunk River, which meanders through town, rising and falling with the tides more than eight feet to fill coves, ponds, and marshes. Twice daily the tide surges in to fill the river basin, Mill Pond, and tributaries, and twice daily it abandons them, leaving mud flats and marshlands.[2] Water unifies this region and also defines usable areas—some sufficient only for isolated houses, others large enough for neighborhoods.

The old maritime village lies sheltered a mile upriver from the ocean. This once prosperous and bustling shipping port is now a busy tourist center and wealthy residential community. The historic district in Kennebunkport, filled with elegant merchants' and ship captains' houses, spreads over land gently sloping up from the river. The Port's commercial areas have few traces of the old shipbuilding days but teem with contemporary maritime activity, supporting yachting businesses, restaurants, and boutiques. With its intricate landscape and beautifully scaled houses, the Port invites exploration and appeals to individuals and small groups of people, not the summer crowds that have overwhelmed the town during recent years.

East of the Kennebunk River's mouth, an exposed granite coastline rises abruptly from the sea. Scoured by waves and strewn with boulders, this shore was largely ignored until the turn of the twentieth century, when summer visitors from Boston, New York City, and Philadelphia built elaborate Shingle style cottages that majestically face the open ocean. In contrast to the Port, where houses cluster together, Cape Arundel features mansions that stretch along the coast to exploit the drama of each particular site.

South of the river are Gooch's Beach and Kennebunk Beach, two sandy crescent bays. Inland, dunes alternate with salt marshes. Here, after the Civil War, summer visitors came to stay in the few scattered farm houses or, more simply, to pitch tents near the beach. Inns and hotels were built to accommodate the visitors, while those who sought lengthier stays began to build houses. Summer-house construction started as early as 1873 on Lord's Point, a rocky promontory, and continued during the following decades along the beach and inland. Today, second homes crowd the dunes and press into the marshes. While the beaches remain broad and expansive, the houses have become smaller and more numer-

Fig. 4.3. Water, land, and buildings occur in startlingly beautiful combinations and are ever changing with the tides in the Kennebunks' Port. Top left: *Kennebunk River and Town Park (1990)*. Top right: *Town Dock, behind Dock Square (1990)*. Middle left: *Tidal cove (1990)*. Middle right: *Mill Pond (1990)*. Bottom left: *Marina on Kennebunk River (1990)*. Bottom right: *Kennebunk Beach (1990)*.

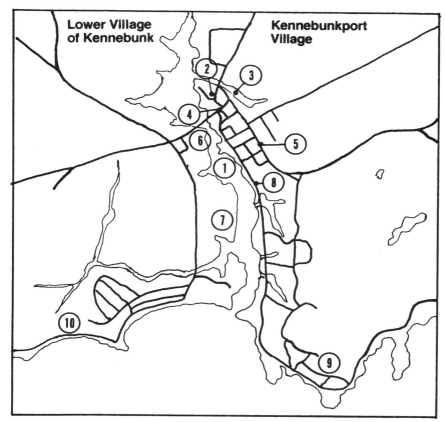

Map 4.1. Location Map of Kennebunks' Port (redrawn from current U.S. Coast and Geodetic Survey maps).
1. Kennebunk River; 2. Congregational Church; 3. Mill Pond; 4. Dock Square;
5. Maine Street; 6. Site of former train station; 7. Franciscan Monastery; 8. Ocean Ave.;
9. Cape Arundel; 10. Kennebunk Beach.

ous—they are built closer together and are not as carefully sited as before or as compared to the previous two communities, Kennebunkport and Cape Arundel.

Tentative Early Settlement

Before European settlement, the Indian population followed seasonal migration patterns to live near the coast during the summer and inland during the winter.[3] One of these tribes, the Sokokis, maintained a summer camp on Great Hill at the southern end of Kennebunk Beach. Indian descendants returned to the Port each summer until the 1920s, camping at Indian Canoe Landing near the mouth of the Kennebunk River, where they pitched tents, sold crafts, and rented canoes to the summer residents.[4]

Even before the Pilgrims landed in Plymouth, European fishermen cured fish on the islands off Cape Porpoise, three miles northeast of today's port. Gradually,

Map 4.2. This 1912 regional map of Southern Maine, from Wells Village (south) to Fortunes Rocks (north), shows the old coastal road threading through villages and, in turn, attracting development (U.S. Coast and Geodetic Survey, 1912).

they settled on Cape Porpoise. In 1620, colonists from the Bay Colony joined them. Enduring Indian attacks, these settlers tenuously established themselves in the Cape Porpoise area.[5] In the mid–seventeenth century, the King's Highway, a mere primitive path, meandered along the coast for overland traffic between Boston and Falmouth (later called Portland). As early as 1647, a ferry for this route crossed the Kennebunk River in the Port area.[6] Indians continued to menace the settlers and drove out many, but by 1720 the colonists had gained control and established themselves permanently.

From the coast, settlers moved upriver, building grist and saw mills. Farmers pushed further inland to supply these mills. Well into the 1700s, what few roads existed served to connect isolated farms to mills. When their first church in Cape Porpoise burned down in 1763, residents built a new one at Burbank Hill, four miles north of today's Port, at a central location to the then-settled area. They built roads to the new church and subsequent town hall, thereby creating a hub circulation pattern to this center that defines the district's road network today, even though this old center is no longer active. Thus, in the early years settlement was tentative and troubled, yet the inhabitants made locational decisions with far-reaching consequences.

The Age of Shipbuilding

After the American Revolution, shipping and shipbuilding became enormously profitable in the Kennebunks because of the protected river, ready access to inland timber supplies, and proximity to coastal shipping routes.[7] The Kennebunks prospered, growing most dramatically from the end of the revolution to the embargo of 1807. Early shipbuilding concentrated around "the Landing," a site two miles upriver from the Port. By midcentury, as the need for larger ships increased, ships came downstream to be fitted in the Port. Gradually villagers built more ships at the Port, and a settlement developed here on both sides of the river. On the east side, villagers enjoyed higher ground with better drainage and proximity to the older settlements at Burbank Hill and Cape Porpoise.

The commercial center evolved on the east side of the river around Dock Square. It was at the end of the bridge and served adjacent shipbuilding activities on either side. Nearby Union Square already served as the location of the old Post Office. Dock Square grew not from a plan but from the eagerness of competing merchants to locate in this desirable space. They infilled areas along the adjoining river to create additional land. One building in this square remains largely unchanged since its construction in 1775 and reflects in its sequence of uses the evolving economy of the square. Originally constructed as a warehouse for the Perkins West India Goods Company, it later accommodated a boardinghouse, the Post Office, a harness shop, a fish market, a grocery, an artist's studio, and now a book store. Dock Square is still an intimate space,

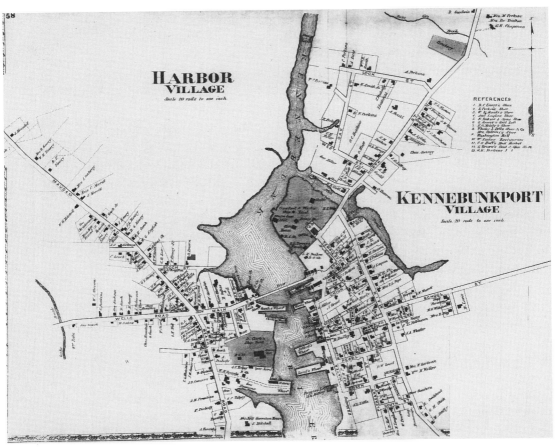

Map 4.3. *In this 1872 map of Kennebunks' Port, Kennebunkport Village is seen on the right and the Lower Village (Harbor Village) of Kennebunk appears on the left. Dock Square developed at the north end of the bridge (right side, noted with asterisk), midway between the ship yards on either side of the river (the Brick Store Museum, 1872).*

although it has been compromised by the automobiles and trucks that now funnel through it.

When it was officially named Kennebunkport, in 1821, the town had more than two thousand inhabitants. Only Portland surpassed it as the most important shipbuilding center in Maine. The wealth that flowed into the area chiefly benefited merchants and ship captains, who built elegant mansions on land sloping up from the river east of Dock Square. They organized this area into a loose grid of ten blocks, where they constructed complexes that combined house, office, barns, and sheds. Owners arranged these buildings into a town fabric, placing them to align not only with the streets but also with neighboring structures, creating a rich spatial pattern. Rather than following a rigorous, preconceived layout, the neighborhood evolved through carefully accommodating structures to sites and adjacent buildings as streets reached from the wharves to the houses uphill.

Maine Street dates from the early eighteenth century, when it was part of the primitive regional road network. Water Street (now Ocean Avenue) went only partway south along the river for waterfront use and until the late nineteenth century did not extend to Cape Arundel, a mile east of the Port on the Atlantic.[8] The streets between these two, which form the heart of the historic district,

Map 4.4. *Free-standing structures comprise the town, even in Dock Square (top center, marked with an asterisk), where they sit tightly together. Buildings consistently front the street, yet, rather than rigorously align, they adjust to local aspects such as placement of neighboring buildings and positions at ends of streets (Sanborn map with buildings rendered black, 1911).*

established in 1976, date from approximately 1750. Members of the Walker Family (Gideon, Daniel, and Daniel's son-in-law, Nathaniel Lord) were instrumental during the eighteenth and early nineteenth centuries in organizing this district and building impressive houses, such as the Nathaniel Lord Mansion (1814), on Pleasant Street.[9]

Of the 147 buildings in the historic district, 140 are of wood construction, and many of these have elaborate details. The remaining seven, including the

Fig. 4.4. In Kennebunkport, elegant houses and churches line Maine Street, which runs along the crest of the slope (1990).

Fig. 4.5. View from near the mouth of the river, looking north to the Port (ca. 1880). Water Street, later renamed Ocean Avenue, connects the Port in the distance to the "cottages" on Cape Arundel, further to the east (right) (The Brick Store Museum).

Fig. 4.6. Plentiful wood, skilled carpenters, and the popular Greek Revival style architecture produced a variety of handsome architectural details, such as these corners (1990).

old custom house (now the library), are masonry buildings.[10] White is the dominant and unifying color. The buildings are predominantly Colonial and Neoclassical (Federal and Greek Revival) style, with stately proportions and symmetrical facades.

The South Congregational Church is on Temple Street.[11] The church sits on a rise of land directly at the end of the street, allowing pedestrians a full view of the church, its steeple, and its portico (added in 1912). Indeed, the church steeple is the only structure to protrude decisively above the village tree line. In the early twentieth century, the nearby Parker House Summer Hotel rivaled it in size. However, a modest post office building replaced the hotel and, along with a community center, completes the group of public buildings on this street. Elsewhere within the village, churches give visual, if no longer exclusively religious, focus to their respective areas, as some have been converted to residences or galleries. During the nineteenth century there were two schools, but a consolidated school beyond the old settlement replaced them in the 1940s.

Before the opening of the bridge connecting the two villages, the Lower Village of Kennebunk had developed in a manner similar to, but relatively independent of, Kennebunkport Village across the river. It had its own church, school, and businesses, and villagers fitted and later built ships here. The road from the village center to the beach was little more than a cart track used by farmers to collect seaweed for field fertilizer. When the bridge opened, people from both sides of the river were immediately able to share more activities. In both villages fishermen, farmers, and merchants lived close to one another.[12] Not until the late nineteenth century and the development of Cape Arundel would social classes distinctly separate. During the 1800s, Port society, although certainly worldly, was relatively homogenous, unified by common backgrounds and, even more, by an underlying dependence on the sea.

The Era of the Summer Visitors

Shipbuilding continued until the latter half of the nineteenth century. From 1880 to 1894, about 750 vessels were constructed in the general vicinity of the Port. By 1850, however (long before 1912, when the custom house closed and its responsibilities were transferred to Portland), the area began to decline as a significant trading port. On the periphery of national commerce and suffering from a depleted lumber supply, Kennebunks' Port was less able to compete with either the steamships or the railroads, which increasingly commanded coastal trade and favored Portland, to the north, and Portsmouth, New Hampshire, and Boston, Massachusetts, to the south.[13]

At the end of the Civil War, a few Kennebunk Beach farmers began to rent to summer boarders. By the 1870s, seven trains per day made the three-hour trip from Boston to the Kennebunk station, four miles inland. A new era for the Kennebunks had arrived—that of the summer visitor. With the advent of railroad travel, wealthy people from crowded, industrializing cities could now more easily visit the region. By 1883 a rail spur came to a Lower Village station on the site of an old shipbuilding yard that had been created from landfill. Soon nine trains arrived each day, filled with summer visitors, servants, and trunks. As the place of arrival and departure, the railroad station area assumed new importance and attracted additional business.[14]

People from Boston, New York City, and Philadelphia were now a noticeable presence in the Port. Samuel Adams Drake wrote in 1875: "It is a quiet old place, or rather was, before it became translated into a summer resort; but now silk jostles home-spun, and for three months in the year it is invaded by an army of

Fig. 4.7. Looking east across the river from the Lower Village to Kennebunkport, the rail station, built in 1883, is in the foreground and several ships can be seen at anchor in the river; in the distance is the Parker House Summer Hotel (since demolished) and to the left is the South Congregational Church, still the local landmark (Thomas E. Bradbury, ca. 1900).

pleasure-seekers, who ransack its secret places, and after taking their fill of the sea and shore, flee before the first frosts of autumn."[15]

The popularity of the Kennebunks as a summer retreat continued, and real estate development followed. As early as 1872, four businessmen from Boston joined with two local associates to incorporate the Boston and Kennebunkport Sea Shore Company. They purchased more than seven hundred acres of land, stretching five miles along the coast from Cape Porpoise south to Lord's Point.[16] Local farmers eagerly sold them rocky, unproductive land for the elaborate summer community they proposed for the area just east of the river's mouth. While the planned community never materialized, summer people built grand Shingle style cottages, and the area remains one of Maine's major summer resort colonies. Former President George Bush's maternal grandfather, George Herbert Walker, built his house here in 1903 on a prominent peninsula, and it served as George Bush's summer retreat during his presidency.

These cottages were different from the older ship captains' mansions in the village. The summer people built houses of unpainted wood and local stone. On the bluffs, they sited houses that were seemingly independent of one another and unlike those congregated in the Port village. Summer residents favored houses with complex volumetric forms composed of elaborate porches, balconies, and turrets. They tucked stables, servants' quarters, and later automobile

Top: *Fig. 4.8. From the rocky shores of Cape Arundel, in the distance one can see the George Bush estate (1990). Bottom: Fig. 4.9. Cape Arundel cottages (ca. 1910, the Brick Store Museum).*

garages into the woods. Along with their private houses and dependencies, summer people also built a boathouse, a church, a casino (dance hall), tennis courts, and a golfing club.

As was done in other resort developments of that era, promoters first built a large hotel—the Ocean Bluff Hotel (1874), with rooms for two hundred guests— to establish a proper image for the resort and provide interested buyers with accommodations where they could spend a leisurely summer before committing themselves to buying property and building.[17] The Ocean Bluff burned down in 1898, and in 1914 the Breakwater Court (today known as the Colony Hotel) was constructed on the same site, where it still sits splendidly on its hill overlooking the ocean.

The summer visitors enjoyed canoeing on the winding Kennebunk River, sunbathing in the waters of sheltered beaches, driving in carts and buckboards through the quaint countryside, and attending literary readings, musicals, theatricals, and endless social gatherings at hotels. A water carnival brought the social season to its climax as summer people gaily floated in illuminated boats and canoes down the river and through the Port.[18] Artists and writers discovered the area to be conducive to work and creatively stimulating. The 1920s found Margaret Deland and Booth Tarkington there, along with native Kenneth Roberts, writing for national audiences about local lore.

As summer people began to stay for longer periods, they became increasingly interested in the town's appearance and convenience. In 1899 a group consisting primarily of summer people started the Village Improvement Society, to promote good roads, clean streets, sidewalks, piped fresh water, docks, waterways, and tree protection. By 1901 they even had electric lights installed on Ocean Avenue.[19] Eventually, the society persuaded the town government to assume these responsibilities. Yet this concern about the town's care added to social friction. The year-round residents, while grateful for the employment opportunities created by summer crowds, resented paying higher taxes for the requested "embellishments." In 1916, because of these disputes, Kennebunkport split into two municipalities, North Kennebunkport (now Arundel) and Kennebunkport.[20]

After World War I, Kennebunks' Port began a period of decline that would continue through the Great Depression. The Port itself was more economically dependent on vacationers than Kennebunk, four miles inland at the falls of a river, where a mill had developed and through which U.S. Route 1 passed. Major hotels in the Port area lost patronage as fashions changed and wealthier tourists began to favor Europe, the focus of recent war attention.[21] While Kennebunkport had installed a hand-dug town water system by the 1920s, its municipal income and services began to decline during the 1930s and 40s. Fewer tourists came to the Port, and those who did increasingly arrived by automobile and sought less formal vacations. They stayed in tourist camps with housekeeping cabins and in tenting areas. This new visitor preferred to travel from place to place rather than reside in one location for extended periods.

The Port area had numerous tourist camps, often in beautiful settings on the community's fringe. Within the town, small boatyards, fishing shacks, and coal sheds still lined the waterfront, while gas pumps, repair shops, and luncheon counters became new, informal centers of activity. The resident population of Kennebunkport declined from 2,130 in 1900 to 1,284 in 1930, its lowest point in the past 150 years. With the depression, resort activity fell even more, and natives had to sustain themselves as best they could—primarily through fishing, agriculture, and employment in the mills and factories in Kennebunk and Biddeford. Many residents could not pay their taxes and, in compensation, had to plow roads and haul refuse for the town. Except for the most basic services, the town deferred all public investments during this decade.

Post–World War II: Tourism and the New Gentry

The quiet, obscure, and impoverished Port, but one where nationally known authors still summered or lived, emerged from World War II to become an enormously popular resort and the focus of international attention. Within two decades, Kennebunks' Port became an enclave of wealthy, generally older people, reviving the area's Victorian tradition as a retreat for successful businessmen. As more automobiles came into use and better highways were built, the Port and its unique environment became even more convenient to Boston and its expanding suburbs. The new arrivals and the natives, however, often had conflicting views, particularly over the use of land (although both groups, fearing loss of property rights, resisted land-use controls). While the economy of the Port changed more than its physical character, development nevertheless seriously threatened the area's cultural heritage and its natural resources. The two municipalities that faced each other across the river and shared a rich history were, regrettably, unable to solve many common problems.

In 1947, as the harbinger of change, the first section of the Maine Turnpike (later Interstate 95) opened in southern Maine. Passing ten miles inland from the coast, it connected the Kennebunks to Portland, to the north, and to Portsmouth, New Hampshire, and Boston, to the south. "Outsiders" soon began to rediscover Kennebunks' Port. During the 1950s they gradually began buying fishing shacks and summer houses and converting them to small businesses and year-round residences. At that time, no building restrictions existed on what and where one could build. With the onset of uncontrolled growth, Kennebunkport officially began to discuss the possibilities of zoning in 1955. Yet most residents still would not accept zoning, viewing it as an infringement on property rights.[22]

In 1960, with matching state and federal grants, Kennebunkport started preliminary work on a comprehensive plan. The town, however, focused on traffic management as the primary means of guiding change, proposing one-way streets and creating new parking lots, in some cases even on landfill in the river. The Chamber of Commerce dominated public discussions and government

*Fig. 4.10. Through traffic and poor traffic management erode the historic character of
Kennebunks' Port (1990).*

decisions during this period. By the late 1960s, the character of the Port had
changed noticeably, as suburban residential and strip commercial developments
rapidly grew along the main roads entering the Port.

After years of acrimonious debate, Kennebunkport finally adopted a comprehensive plan in 1965 and its first zoning ordinance in 1972. The ordinance
codified uses then in place rather than attempting to redirect growth. Selectmen
zoned the town "free enterprise," permitting what the term implies. As a result,
small stores catering to tourists were opened wherever owners desired—in base-

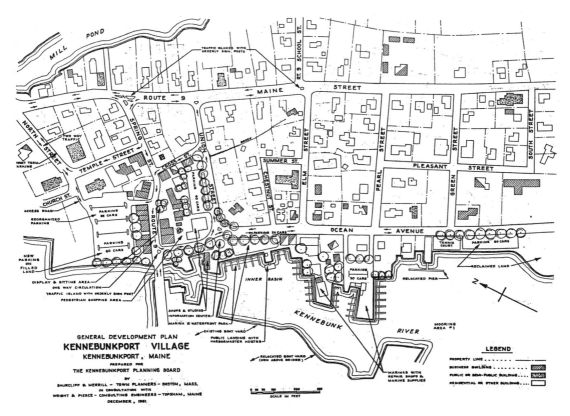

Map 4.5. Development plan for Kennebunkport Village emphasizes traffic flow and parking
(Shurcliff and Merrill, 1961).

ments, garages, and barns, as well as in converted old houses—and owners altered these buildings with patio doors, decks, and large display windows. Meanwhile, in 1972 the town finally installed sewers to handle waste disposal (before that, wastes were simply emptied into the river, even in crowded Dock Square). Recognizing the complexity of local problems, Kennebunkport voters adopted a town-manager form of government, but they still refused to support professional planning. Volunteer laymen comprised the planning board, then as now. They established policy and reviewed technical site plans. Throughout the 1970s, town officials proposed land-use ordinances only to have them rejected, either deemed by voters as too restrictive or found by federal and state agencies to not meet proper standards.

In the early 1970s a group of citizens, frustrated with the inability of the local government to address development problems and seeking lasting land-use controls not susceptible to the vagaries of zoning, formed the Kennebunkport Conservation Trust. Through land donations, easements, and purchases, this trust has since acquired strategic undeveloped land ranging from a small village park to islands off Cape Porpoise, and a "greenbreak" between the adjoining town of Biddeford. Town natives, not wealthy new arrivals, have been the primary donors, because they want the area to remain as they remember it.[23]

Tourism and commercial development increased in the 1980s as the economy prospered and George Bush ascended to the vice presidency. In the early 1980s, applications for condominiums, large single-lot housing, and subdivision construction soared. Developers continued to convert old residences for commercial purposes and erect new businesses in vacant yards. However, those who bought in the mid-1980s paid dearly for their investments. Faced with the recession of the late 1980s and burdened with high carrying costs, these investors were less willing to curb tourism. The tourist trade dominated the Port, evident in the restaurants, shops, and inns, most of which remained open nine months of the year. As cars and tour busses increased, the variety of goods and services diminished. Throughout this period, the town of Kennebunkport continued to stress traffic management, as more than twenty thousand cars and trucks each summer day squeezed across the narrow bridge and into the lanes of the Port (see Fig. 4.10).[24]

When development pressure was clearly rising in 1970, the town budgeted only $200 for planning (out of total tax receipts of $562,363). With 1,522 people, that amounted to thirteen cents of planning funds per resident. In 1990 Kennebunkport budgeted $4,000 for planning.[25] Its population had doubled, but its tax receipts had increased tenfold to $6,091,348. Kennebunkport still has no local official historic district even though its village and Cape Arundel have been historic districts on the National Register of Historic Places since 1976 and 1984, respectively. Consequently, no local board of architectural review exists to exercise control over historic buildings. Owners make whatever "decorative changes" they desire.[26] Fortunately, some residents, both old and new, have the wealth and expertise to preserve many old mansions as well as to support private conservation efforts.

Meanwhile, the town of Kennebunk has been more active in preserving the Lower Village across the river. By 1964, Kennebunk had prepared a comprehensive plan and funded its Preservation Commission, the first in the state. By 1990, Kennebunk was spending more than $58,000 on planning and employing a full-time professional planner.

Today the Port is a tourist center, and approximately ten thousand people visit the Kennebunks on an average summer day, more than twice the daily number of tourists during the mid-1970s. It continues to suffer major traffic problems in the summer, even as alternatives are sought in shuttle busses, fringe parking lots, and tourist trolleys. The Dock Square area has become a specialty retail center with restaurants and boutiques. Retail expansion in Dock Square has primarily been accommodated using older historic buildings. This expansion by itself has not radically changed the historic pattern of the area, but Kennebunkport's overwhelming parking requirements are producing detrimental side effects—the demolition of outbuildings, barns, and stables, and the paving of yards for parking spaces.[27] Subtly but pervasively, an important aspect of village character is vanishing. Fortunately, Kennebunkport does maintain a height restriction of two-and-a-half stories to preserve its handsome silhouette. Retail expansion has sought ground-floor space and has not pressured height restrictions, and most new retail construction has occurred in the Lower Village of Kennebunk. Here, the town of Kennebunk has purposely encouraged a neighborhood component for this commercial development by including convenience goods and service stores. Regrettably, the pattern of new development in the Lower Village has not supported pedestrian circulation because parking lots isolate store clusters into small islands of buildings.

Today, both towns are questioning the dispersed, automobile-dominated development that has evolved there since World War II. Kennebunk especially wants to return to the "village and countryside" pattern that favors compact settlement and complementary open space.[28] The town argues that such a pattern will better utilize land, be less damaging to the natural environment, and impose fewer costs on municipal services and utilities. Kennebunk also accepts congestion as inevitable during the summer peak season and recognizes that measures to alter this congestion now would simply be too costly and too damaging to the environment. Since the mid-1980s, Kennebunk has vigilantly protected its wetlands, particularly the extensive salt marshes in the Lower Village, a habitat that is relatively rare in Maine and offers exceptional opportunities for wildlife. Today, the grounds of a Franciscan monastery stretch for over half a mile along the lower edge of the river. Conservationists and concerned citizens hope that this property, formerly an estate with grounds landscaped by the Olmsted brothers, will remain undeveloped, a reminder of the river's edge during colonial times and a continuing preserve for wildlife.[29]

The Kennebunks possess a remarkably varied landscape. Over the past four hundred years, succeeding generations have focused on different aspects of this environment and, for the most part, have built sympathetically and often evocatively with the landscape. Residents appreciated the cumulative effects of water, land, and buildings. Today growth and congestion jeopardize these qualities. While the existing physical limitations of water supply and rocky subsoil may deter development, more concerted and coordinated planning will be needed to preserve this remarkable environment.

Rendering by Peter Lorenzoni, after a drawing by the author.

CHAPTER FIVE

Edgartown, Massachusetts

Fig. 5.1. Street section of Edgartown, Massachusetts.

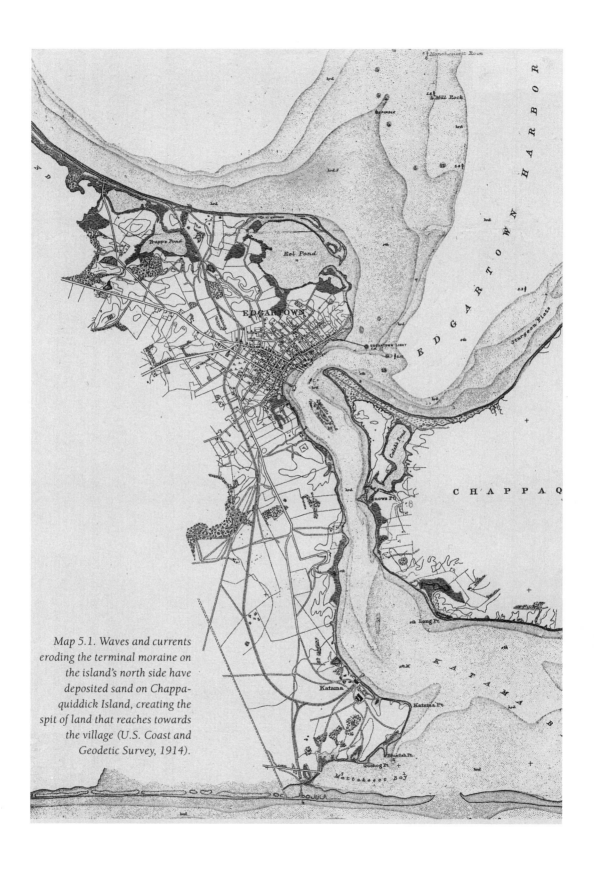

Map 5.1. Waves and currents eroding the terminal moraine on the island's north side have deposited sand on Chappaquiddick Island, creating the spit of land that reaches towards the village (U.S. Coast and Geodetic Survey, 1914).

Once known as Great Harbor, Edgartown Village overlooks an inlet on the southeast side of Martha's Vineyard. Shielded from storms by its land mass, which folds around the finger of Chappaquiddick Island, the village weaves a loose web of narrow and inviting streets lined with handsome buildings and overarching trees. The compact community gently slopes down to the expansive harbor and open, windswept Chappaquiddick beyond. This civic landscape blends a comfortable and convenient human-scale domain with a spacious natural setting. On the edges of the village are salt marshes, tidal ponds, sandy beaches, scrub oak thickets, and open meadows.

The historic village, some 150 acres, is part of the town of Edgartown, about thirty square miles in area and the oldest of six incorporated towns on Martha's Vineyard.[1] Warmed by the Gulf Stream, the island enjoys a benign New England climate and, in recent years, has become a national, indeed international, resort.[2] Martha's Vineyard offers a respite from city life for people seeking a change of pace and scene. Although it is a product of its insular location, five miles off the southeast coast of Massachusetts, Edgartown is no longer the isolated community that bred an eccentric, quaint way of life, nor is it the preserve of a relatively small number of privileged summer visitors. Instead, it is a community now accessible by ferry and air to people in the intensely urbanized northeast corridor who seek a pleasurable vacation destination and who, during the summer months, transform it into a crowded, sometimes highly congested resort.

The town began as a community of fishermen and farmers and rose to prominence during the nineteenth century's whaling days. Edgartown receded in importance after the Civil War, but it was rediscovered in the late Victorian period by a generation of summer people attracted to its beauty. Over the years, the village has evolved into an intimate pattern of businesses, homes, schools, workplaces, recreation facilities, and a cemetery, encouraging sociality and civic pride.

The harbor and Pease's Point Way are the boundaries of the historic village. Main Street runs directly from the harbor to the woodlands "up island," bisecting the town and serving as the primary commercial street and traditional meeting place. The old commercial district extends over the three lower blocks near the harbor. Buildings along lower Main Street are usually constructed of wood and remain free-standing, but they are built close together to appear almost as a continuous form. Further up Main Street, distances between buildings are greater. Civic buildings are most prominent, with the Old Whaling Church commanding the crest of the hill and the Dukes County Court House terminating the view down School Street.

Fig. 5.2. This 1958 photo of the Edgartown vicinity reveals the area prior to the latest era of development (U.S. National Oceanic and Atmospheric Administration).

On either side of Main Street are the old residential areas, each presenting a distinct character to the pedestrian. Some lanes are short and intimate, often ablaze with flowers in summer. Others are seemingly endless, with expansive views over the harbor. A range of architectural styles, building rhythms, and street setbacks enliven each street. Lanes end in distinctive vistas—a view of a civic building, an elegant residence, the cemetery, or the ever-present harbor.

Facing Page: *Map 5.3. The earliest map of the region (dated 1610) shows Martha's Vineyard as part of the mainland between the Elizabeth Islands and Cape Cod. The island noted as "Marthays Viniard" is the present-day Nomans Land, while today's Vineyard is north of that (Archives of Simancas, Spain, as reprinted in Banks 1966, vol. 1, 78).*

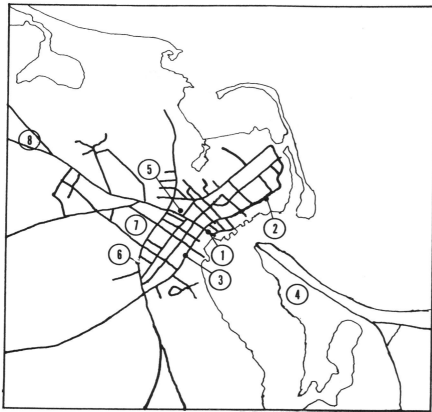

Map 5.2. Location map of Edgartown, Massachusetts (redrawn from current U.S. Coast and Geodetic Survey maps).
1. Main Street; 2. North Water Street; 3. South Water Street; 4. Chappaquiddick;
5. Old Whaling Church; 6. Pease's Point Way; 7. Cemetery;
8. Upper Main Street Commercial District.

Top: Fig. 5.3. An aerial photo looking north over the town. Marshes, beaches, meadows, farms, and cemetery, together with intimate streets and human-scaled buildings, create a civic landscape (Steve Gentle, 1985). Bottom: Fig. 5.4. View of Pent (South) Lane (1990).

Fig. 5.5. Details of Edgartown doorways express the individuality of owners as well as the collective character of the village (1990).

Other streets curve and entice the visitor to wander further. Many older residences serve commercial purposes, housing inns, stores, and even a newspaper office with printing presses, but they do so in ways respectful of the individual buildings and the community. On the edge of the village are a school and a cemetery, convenient to, yet separated from, the residential areas.

Commercial and residential buildings all employ a common vocabulary of scale, color, materials, and details. Yet within this vocabulary there is opportunity for individual expression. Entrances to houses, for example, display both common themes and personal identity. The physical qualities of the town evolved as it grew slowly; each generation respected what its forebears had built while adding features of its own. The town now wants to extend this vocabulary to a new commercial district developing on Upper Main Street beyond the historical village. More accessible to cars and trucks, this area now provides essential town services formerly located in the old village center, which is now dominated by tourists.

From Indian Paths to Property Lines

The Indians who inhabited Martha's Vineyard prior to European colonization were members of the Algonquin tribe. They lived in temporary settlements as they searched the island for food and sought agreeable seasonal locations, preferring the bountiful coastal inlets during the summer and the sheltering upland woods during the winter. Indians must certainly have frequented the Edgartown village area, since it offered both a freshwater spring and the protected bay. However, today we have little sense of how or where they camped in this area.

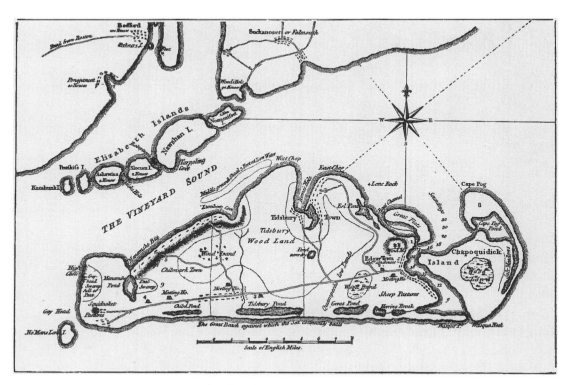

Map 5.4. This plan of Martha's Vineyard (1784), showing Edgartown, indicates island circulation routes still used today (from J. Hector St. John Crevecoeur's "Lettre D'Un Cultivateer [sic] Americain," as reprinted in Banks 1966, vol. 1, facing 396).

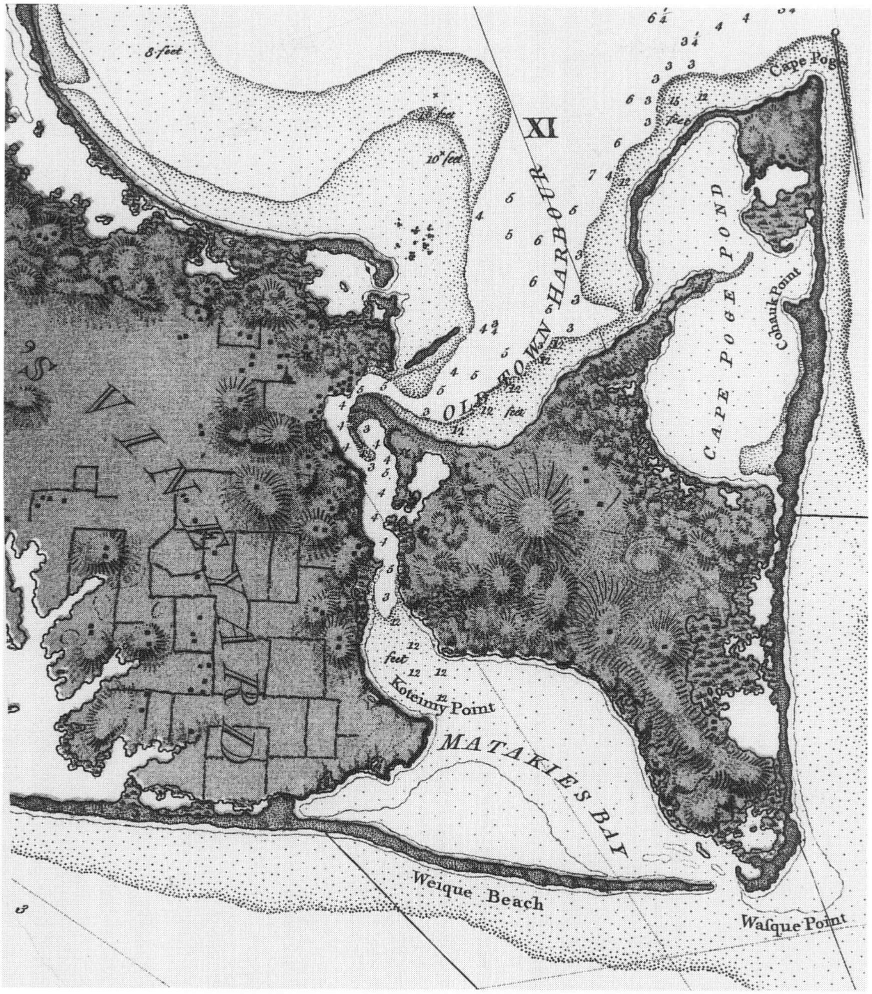

Map 5.5. *Detail of a map of Martha's Vineyard (1776), noting the Edgartown area, which was published for the British Royal Navy, part of the first detailed comprehensive survey of the east coast of North America (Des Barres [1780] 1966).*

We do know that an estimated three thousand Indians were living on Martha's Vineyard in 1642, when Europeans first settled. Within eighty years, this population was reduced to a quarter of its original size and relegated to undesirable sections of the island.[3]

The first Englishmen to visit were Bartholomew Gosnold and his crew, who in 1602 explored a remote section of Chappaquiddick. In 1642 Thomas Mayhew and his son led the island's official settlement, first calling it "Great Harbor" and then in 1671 renaming it "Edgar Towne."[4] The Mayhews cleared land on the western side of the harbor between the shoreline and Pease's Point Way. They divided land into twenty-five "home lots," which were allocated in long rectangular parcels ranging from eight to forty acres, with most about ten acres.

Each lot faced the harbor and extended inland, allowing these early settlers to fish, farm, and hunt to survive. The form of today's village reflects these early property decisions.[5]

Main Street dates from this initial subdivision, lying between the tenth and eleventh lots, near the midpoint of the allocated parcels. Other east-west streets—for example, Cooke, High, and Winter Streets—developed later, but these also stretched along boundary lines to access the harbor and out-lying fields. A meandering north-south path along the shoreline, probably of Indian origin, became today's Water Street. Further inland, Pease's Point Way, also probably originally an Indian path, twisted north-south around the inland side of the colonial home lots. Villagers introduced other streets, such as Summer, School, and Fuller Streets, in the nineteenth century as the town grew.[6]

By 1764 Edgartown had 924 residents. At least twelve houses, most of wood post-and-beam construction and enclosed with clapboards or shingles and painted white, remain from that period.[7] They typically had simple pitched roofs, which, collectively, became an important village characteristic.

Whaling Fortunes and Merchants' Mansions

If settlers during the colonial period established the backbone and basic street skeleton of the village, residents during the Federal period fleshed these out to create memorable places. During these years, enormous wealth from the whaling industry flowed into the village, allowing residents to grace its streets with handsome buildings. In 1789, immediately after the formation of the Union, the federal government recognized Edgartown's emerging importance, designating it a port of entry and establishing a custom house here. As the whaling industry expanded, Edgartown flourished, eventually supporting a major fleet of its own. In 1835, out of a population of fifteen hundred people, about three hundred—usually the young and able—were abroad hunting whales. The village also became a supply center for other whaling towns, as secondary industries such as cooperages and shipyards developed.[8] Edgartown's buildings reflected this new prosperity and confidence. Houses from the late Georgian and Federal period (1775–1835) are larger, more varied, more ambitious, and more decorated than earlier ones.

The period from 1835 to 1850 was Edgartown's golden age. The most magnificent building expression of this period, honoring the local whaling industry, is the Old Whaling Church on the crest of Main Street. Built in the Greek Revival style, the church features massive wooden columns and a distinctive tower rising ninety-two feet above the town. One hundred and twenty-five Greek Revival houses date from this period, many elegant examples of which can be found along Water Street.[9] Spare in massing and refined in proportion and details, they look proudly and serenely over the harbor from their bank on

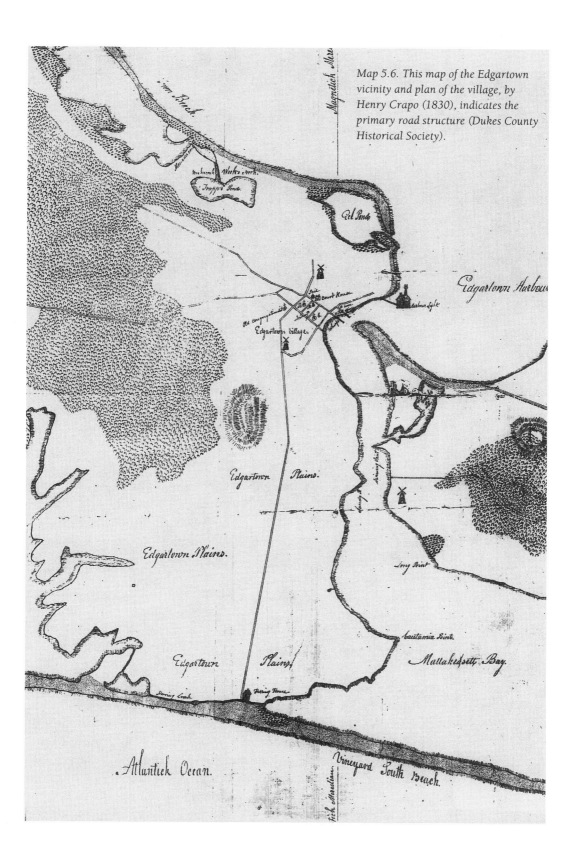

Map 5.6. This map of the Edgartown vicinity and plan of the village, by Henry Crapo (1830), indicates the primary road structure (Dukes County Historical Society).

Fig. 5.6. An aerial photo looking east toward Chappaquiddick Island. The Old Whaling Church dominates the foreground, while the compact village faces wind-swept Chappaquiddick Island, seen in the distance (Steve Gentle, ca. 1990).

Water Street. Yet this period, with its confluence of abundance and taste, would not last. Cheaper and more effective petroleum later replaced whale oil as the preferred energy source, curbing the profits of whaling expeditions. After the Civil War, Edgartown declined economically until it faced financial disaster. Between 1860 and 1870, its population dropped from 2,118 to 1,516. The seeds for its next major period, however, had been sown: summer visitors had discovered the island and would soon invade it in larger and larger numbers. The village's unique character would become its great attraction.

A Fashionable American Place

As early as 1835, Edgartown Methodists had begun to hold camp meetings in an oak grove outside the village. These meetings quickly grew to attract thousands of mainlanders, and they led to the eventual establishment of the town of Oak Bluffs. During these gatherings, visitors also became acquainted with Edgartown. In 1849 Daniel Webster saw the village and wrote letters, later widely reprinted, extolling its pleasures.[10] In 1858, yachtsmen sailing up the coast from New York City sought shelter from a storm in Edgartown and thus discovered the appeal of the village.[11] To guarantee they would visit again, they initiated annual yacht club returns to Edgartown. Wealthy whaling captains began to invest not in shipping but in island improvements. They helped to finance, among other ventures, a railroad, which in 1872 started to bring summer people to the village from the port at Vineyard Haven. The pace of village life quickened.

Not until the 1880s, however, did the growing resort activity begin to reshape the village. Development appeared first on Starbuck's Neck, the prow of land north of the village, beyond the rank of whaling captains' houses on North Water Street. Here summer people built grand cottages, more spacious and roomy than the Federalist houses, though built with materials sympathetic to those used in their construction. These Colonial Revival style cottage homes, sheltered by expansive gambrel roofs and surrounded by porches, allowed residents to spend summer evenings leisurely enjoying the panoramic ocean views. In 1891, summer residents built the Queen Anne style Harbor View Hotel, a large-scale version of one of their cottages, to serve as the social focus of their community as well as accommodations for visitors who came for lengthy stays.[12]

Off-islanders gradually purchased many of the roomy captains' houses in the village. Although they used them only for the summer, they nevertheless pre-

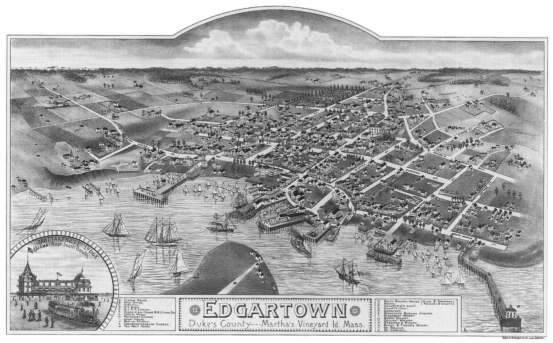

Fig. 5.7. *In this 1886 view of Edgartown, the grid of village streets is seen bending around the harbor with major entry roads into town terminating in wharves. There is no edge to the village, as the settlement pattern gradually shifts to that of farm buildings set close to roads. In the distance on the right, the rail line from Tisbury (Vineyard Haven) to south shore beaches swings by Edgartown (Library of Congress, Geography and Map Division).*

Map 5.7. *The basic village road pattern stems from initial colonial property divisions, with Water and Main Streets assuming the greatest importance. A common scale underlies all buildings (Sanborn Map with buildings rendered black, 1914).*

served the homes from deterioration. Year-rounders and summer people comfortably coexisted at first, socializing together in clubs and churches. Inevitably, though, it became clear that they viewed Edgartown differently. Because the summer people did not participate in the winter town meetings when villagers voted on budgets, they felt that their needs were ignored while they were unfairly taxed. The summer residents were, for the most part, a matriarchal and leisure-oriented society. While fathers remained in New York City and Philadelphia to oversee their business, the women and children enjoyed summer life in Edgartown. The islanders, on the other hand, viewed the newcomers as a moneyed class, there to seek pleasure while islanders worked to maintain an often meager standard of living. These tensions would continue, but as the generation of sea captains and their families passed on, summer people swelled in number and influence.

As Edgartown became a fashionable destination for America's social elite, the summer residents began to establish their own institutions. After first playing golf in cow pastures and then sharing a club with year-round islanders, in 1926 they formed the exclusive Edgartown Golf Club.[13] They also organized a yacht club, in which the pleasures of eating, drinking, and dancing were as attractive as those of the open sea. In 1927 this club bought the important but decaying village wharf and renovated it, giving it an ordinary warehouse exterior appearance that belied the elegantly finished interior. The wharf still occupies its commanding position at the foot of Main Street. Yachting, possibly because of its visibility and expense, abrasively dramatized the different lives led by summer people and islanders. In 1930, the New York Yacht Club arrived in Edgartown Harbor with more than one hundred sail and power boats in its fleet. One of these boats, the *Enterprise*, was worth $630,000. By contrast, the total operating budget for Edgartown that year was $95,570.[14] As summer people built other facilities—tennis, golf, and country clubs—they located them outside the village, decreasing social friction but also hindering public interaction.

No Longer an Island

Older residents still remember the difficult years on the island during the depression and World War II. Of those who did not leave to fight, many were unemployed and, being on an island, could not easily search surrounding areas for work.[15] At the same time, older residents look back at World War II as a cultural watershed for Martha's Vineyard and Edgartown.[16] People recall life before the war as simpler and more personable. Land, for example, was comparatively open. People could hike and hunt without encountering trespassing signs and fences.[17]

Since the war, there have been explosive changes. The Navy built an airport on the island before the war, relinquishing it to the county afterwards. This airport, possibly as much as anything, symbolized the island's new accessibility.[18] More people came, and they stayed for shorter periods of time. Land prices and taxes rose, inducing owners to subdivide and sell to developers. The countryside around Edgartown bears witness to these changes. New developments that were unsympathetic to the town's older architecture appeared on the Katama Plains south of the village, and the beginnings of a commercial strip emerged along Upper Main Street. Through the early 1980s, the town had no significant development controls, and the local water company granted utility connections to whoever requested them.

During the 1970s, the annual rate of residential construction in Edgartown was six times the rate of the 1960s. In 1974 this prompted the establishment of the Martha's Vineyard Commission, a regional planning agency, and in 1975 an islandwide building moratorium was instituted. Nevertheless, population growth and development continued. Between 1970 and 1980 Edgartown's year-round population increased by 49 percent, and between 1980 and 1988 it increased another 25 percent to 2,758 people, a growth rate exceeded by only four other towns or cities in the state.[19]

Retirees, as the group becoming the new year-round residents, are replacing young adults, who continue to leave Edgartown to seek education and employment on the mainland. In 1985 there were 18,114 seasonal residents and vacationers in Edgartown and 9,500 visitors.[20] Summer people now outnumber year-round residents ten to one. Nevertheless, seasonal residents pay 75 percent of total taxes for the island while using it less than 20 percent of the year, only about ten weeks each summer.[21]

During the season, tourists also visit the village for brief stays and intensely use community facilities. They do not support local institutions, unlike returning summer people who invest in the island and pay taxes for its upkeep. These new visitors are reshaping business activity in the village and, consequently, affecting the way that activity blends with village life. Gift shops, boutiques, and restaurants serving tourists have displaced neighborhood markets, shops, and the post office, which have since relocated to Upper Main Street. At the same time, the village street pattern exacerbates congestion, funneling auto traffic into narrow streets and lanes built for pedestrians and carriages, all of which confuses tourists driving on the island.

Since tourist shops are open only for summer months, the old business district is virtually lifeless for the remainder of the year. Older residents claim the village has lost not only convenient shopping areas but also the web of social relations these businesses sustained.[22] New shopping developments are growing on upper Main Street, a commercial district that lies beyond comfortable walking distance from the village but can more easily accommodate automobile access. In the meantime, people living in the old village neighborhoods endure

Fig. 5.8. In 1893, foot races on lower Main Street attract a small crowd, in a setting where trees and buildings complement each other and define a street space (Martha's Vineyard Historical Society).

Fig. 5.9. The old commercial setting of lower Main Street, with its domestic scaled buildings, now primarily serves tourists (1990). The major shopping area has shifted to Upper Main Street.

the seasonal influx of tourists, with whom they share little other than an appreciation of the village's quaint appearance.

In the Upper Main Street area, the town government wishes to have new development and, at the same time, retain village character. Design guidelines require that property owners screen parking behind buildings, adopt traditional setbacks, materials, colors, and details, share traffic entrances, and include mature landscaping to soften and shape the environment.[23] Hopefully, Upper Main Street will become another pedestrian environment; although shopping within building clusters will be easier than crossing the busy and wide thoroughfare to patronize other stores.

Throughout the 1980s, the role of planning in Edgartown has changed from development approval to preparing goal definitions and anticipatory actions. Edgartown also benefits from the Martha's Vineyard Commission, which addresses islandwide concerns. Meanwhile, Edgartown residents continue to debate the village's future role and character. To whom and to what activities should they give priority? Should they subordinate tourism and commerce to Edgartown's popularity as a retirement and second-home community? To what extent should they permit tourist automobiles into the complicated street pattern—or should they impose a summer ban on traffic except for service vehicles?

Local government hopes to achieve a more diversified economy by reviving traditional fishing and farming activities as well as encouraging new "location-free" telecommunication businesses, which could operate year-round and attract younger permanent residents.[24] Broadening the community socially will require affordable housing, a goal that will be difficult for Edgartown to achieve on its own. As part of this effort, the Martha's Vineyard Commission now requires that new developments assist in this policy.[25]

Environmental concerns also increasingly restrict development. Residents now realize they may lose irreplaceable resources that safeguard their health as well as provide aesthetic benefits if growth is not more carefully regulated. Water, in its various forms, lies at the heart of many of these concerns. The only convenient natural source of drinking water for Edgartown is its underlying aquifer. If this source becomes polluted, others would be exceedingly expensive to access. Edgartown's saltwater environment is equally precious—a remarkable combination of recreational, commercial, and natural resource areas comprising marshes, dunes, barrier beaches, grasslands, thickets, and tidal inlets. Fortunately federal, state, and local controls prohibit development in most of these habitats.

Open-space planning started with the first settlers, who set aside common land for grazing. More recently, in the 1920s, the state established an island forest, which now helps protect the aquifer. Large private estates have also preserved open space but have not been open to the public.[26] Since 1986, the Martha's Vineyard Land Bank Commission has focused on open-space preservation on the island and has since been held up as a model for similar efforts elsewhere. Voters in each of the island's six towns approved a bill from the state legislature subjecting the majority of real estate transfers to a two percent fee payable to the Land Bank.[27] Trustees use collected fees to acquire critical open space as well as scenic vistas and easements. Trustees maintain these lands in a natural state, allowing the public access to most for passive recreation, although they do not widely publicize property locations for recreational use.

Several trust lands are now used for farming, an activity considered virtually extinct on the island in the 1970s. A dairy farm, for example, operates on town-owned property bought through state and local conservation funds. Edgartown is also seeking to preserve a network of "ancient trails" to maintain a walking and riding network across the island. Altogether, Edgartown's major open spaces—drainage areas, farms and fields, wildlife habitats, and conservation and recreational lands—now encompass 10,600 acres, or 56 percent of its total land area. Currently, most of the island's conservation groups are focusing on land management rather than land acquisition. Competing demands exist for these lands, as tourists, conservationists, farmers, fishermen, and adjacent landowners all interpret "best use" differently. Management of the properties should ensure that land conservation does not become an exclusionary activity.[28] Through these efforts, along with the help of tax incentives, improved transportation management, restrictive ordinances, and public debate, the town hopes to direct development to areas that can serve people without degrading the surrounding environment.

Today, Edgartown and its setting constitute a civic landscape—an interwoven pattern of human-made and natural features. While it has become a cosmopolitan retreat, the town has retained treasured cultural and natural resources. Edgartowners today respect these legacies and seek sympathetic changes, even as they face growing crowds and crippling congestion in the summer months. As residents extend traditional patterns into new development beyond the old pedestrian village, they also realize there are limits to expansion that, if exceeded, will transform the town into a different entity. The community should continue its long tradition of cautious change.

Rendering by Peter Lorenzoni, after a drawing by the author.

CHAPTER SIX

Stonington, Connecticut

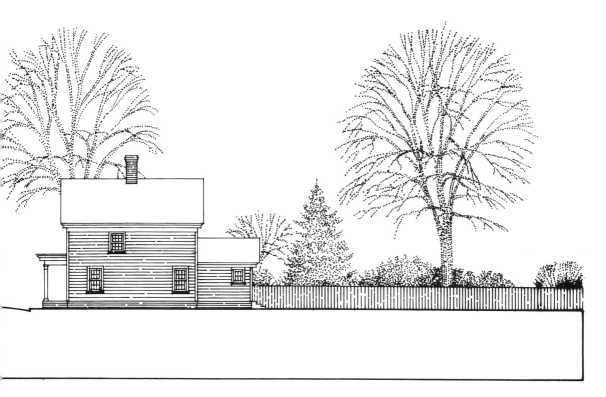

Fig. 6.1. Street section of Stonington, Connecticut.

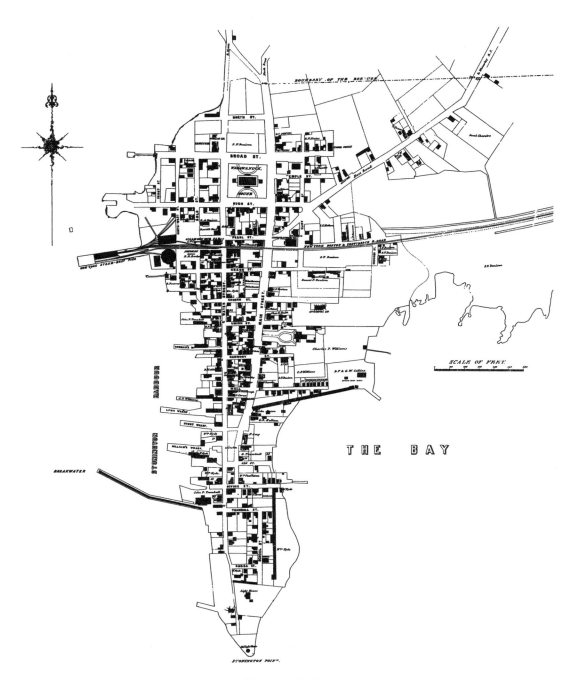

Map 6.1. Map of the Borough of Stonington (1851). The rail terminus transformed
Stonington into a bustling village. Rail passengers arrived from the northeast to board
steamboats at Stonington and travel down Long Island Sound to New York City
(Old Lighthouse Museum, Stonington, Conn.).

Stonington, Connecticut, is the result of tensions—geographical, cultural, and economic—that, over time, have created a community of uncommon character. The draw of the ocean, offering uncertain but at times immensely profitable ventures, competed against that of the land, offering the more tangible products of crops and trade. The town's ambiguous location, near the Rhode Island border, midway between Boston and New York City, and close to yet set off from the coastal road (now Alternate U.S. Route 1), encouraged the community to assert its own identity. The Portuguese and Italian immigrants who arrived in the nineteenth century challenged Yankee legacies to forge a compact community that allowed diverse people to live in close proximity. Through its long history, Stonington experienced economic cycles that put areas in the town to different uses and produced seemingly disparate building forms, from cottages to factories, that have survived to coexist comfortably and serve new purposes and constituencies. The town stands today as the resolution of these diverse forces, having acted upon one another in the fragile and beautiful landscape of the Connecticut coast.

Along this coast, the last glacial retreat left an intricate succession of sheltered bays, expansive marshes, and exposed rocky peninsulas. Stonington Village sits on a peninsula that juts southward into the Atlantic Ocean at Fishers Island Sound, between Little Narragansett Bay and Long Island Sound. The surrounding sea has profoundly influenced the community's history. Lying on the mainland at the eastern end of Long Island Sound, Stonington has enjoyed competitive access to the fishing grounds of the Grand Banks as well as the urban markets of Boston, Providence, and New York City. Stonington became a village with urban character, compact and heterogeneous. Today, the physical character of the village remains relatively untouched by the pressures of contemporary life that have swelled around it.

The village has a clear structure. Two streets, a primarily commercial western one, Water Street, and a predominantly residential eastern one, Main Street, stretch down the peninsula. Secondary streets connect these two, and the streets change character and scale as they extend further to the active harbor on the west and to the secluded marshes on the east. Dramatic contrasts exist between the village and the open sea, between one edge of the village and another, between Water and Main Streets, and between the public places located along them. Adding to these contrasts, numerous houses face a village street on one side and the open sea on the other.

Stonington Village, or Stonington Borough, covers some 170 acres, mostly on

Fig. 6.2. Along the glacier-carved Connecticut coast, Stonington Village sits on a rocky peninsula jutting southward into the ocean. The rail line, which once terminated here, forms the inland edge of the village (Aerographics, 1990).

the peninsula, and has a population of 1,111.[1] It is part of the town of Stonington, which encompasses about forty-three square miles and has a population of 17,360. Stonington Village survives today with its neighborhoods, commercial district, industrial buildings, waterfront, wildlife habitats, and even nearby farms still intact. However, the village is no longer the bustling port it once was. Rather, it has evolved into a quiet, sedate, and affluent residential community.

Vestiges of its past life remain. A commercial fishing fleet still leaves from here, and a few residents remember their parents speaking of old clipper ships crowding the port.[2] In recent years, however, residents and activities have changed. The Portuguese fishermen who once lived with their large families in small houses on the Point have since moved inland to the comforts of modern suburban houses, selling their old houses to new arrivals who value the historic character, unusual setting, and compact features of this village.[3] Members of the new Stonington gentry have become guardians of the village's past, preserving old houses and limiting new construction. In their zeal, they have even "over-improved" formerly unpretentious cottages. This once humble fishing village is now a coveted place in which to live.

Wadawanuck Becomes a Village: 1649–1819

One of the most densely concentrated populations of Indians in America lived along the Connecticut coast when Europeans began exploring the region in the sixteenth century.[4] Groups of fifty to one hundred and fifty Indians inhabited a series of sites along the coast, where they led a varied existence. Fishing for flounder in Long Island Sound and digging for clams and oysters in the streams probably provided the easiest means of sustenance, but the Indians here also hunted deer, bear, and turkeys in the forests for their meat and caught beavers and foxes for their furs. They also developed limited agriculture, clearing fields to sow corn. During the latter part of the sixteenth century, the feared Pequots (the tribe name translates as "destroyers of men") migrated from the Hudson River valley to conquer the more peaceable Connecticut tribes.[5] Europeans soon followed to displace the Pequots.[6]

After a series of probes into the Connecticut River valley, first by the Dutch in 1632 and then by the English later that year, William Chesebrough from the Plymouth Colony settled the Stonington area in 1649.[7] Several other families soon joined him. In Stonington, these colonists first inhabited the area around Wequetequock Cove, northeast of the peninsula, which they called Long Point and the Indians had named "Wadawanuck."[8] In the cove, the colonists found land for farming and gardening, timber for building material and fuel, and fresh water from springs. By settling in the cove, the colonists were able to have convenient access to the open sea yet avoid exposure to storms and the occasional marauders that drifted along the coast.[9] They cleared more land inland from the cove on which to cultivate corn, wheat, and beans. Cattle thrived on the coarse marsh grass, and the shipping of livestock around Cape Cod to New England became the first reliable source of income for this community. In addition to pasturing livestock on the peninsula, colonists also occasionally built boats to support their emerging coastal shipping ventures—first to the New England colonies and then, as the wave of Puritan immigration subsided there, to the middle and southern colonies. In 1662, town leaders built a dam and grist mill on a nearby stream, thus adding manufacturing profits to those of farming and shipping as the economic underpinnings of their community.

In the 1750s, colonists extended a road onto the peninsula and began settlement there in earnest. Stonington grew rapidly as traders recognized emerging opportunities in fishing and coastal commerce. Located inland along the streams, small mills and factories produced flour, sawn lumber, nails, woolen blankets, and tinware.[10] Traders shipped these, along with agricultural products from Stonington, first to nearby ports in New England and then further abroad to southern colonies. Shipping wood and food to New York City was relatively simple, while shipping to the West Indies proved to be dangerous but enormously lucrative.[11]

Stonington, then, developed a diverse and mutually supportive economy based on farming, fishing, shipping, and manufacturing. Main Street extended down the peninsula and connected to a latticework of primitive lanes. Water Street, now the main commercial street, was then only a rutted path along the marshy southern flank of the village.[12] In 1819 there were two churches, two schools, and two long sheds for running rope, as well as 120 dwellings. Approximately one-third of the buildings from that period remain today.[13]

The Village Industrializes: 1820–1865

Stonington flourished during the first half of the nineteenth century with the growth of the seal and whaling trades and the arrival of the railroad from Providence, Rhode Island. Village ships hunted seals and whales around the world on voyages that could last three years or more. In a good year, seamen unloaded 100,000 seal skins along with uncounted barrels of whale oil in Stonington. Profits from these ventures went into shipbuilding, manufacturing, real estate, and railroads.[14]

Because such voyages were dangerous, monotonous for long periods of time, and unremunerative for seamen, captains had increasing difficulty collecting crews in Stonington. Eventually captains began to stop in the Azores to enlist experienced Portuguese whalemen. Some of these Portuguese sailors returned to Stonington to settle in the tightly clustered streets on the southern end of the Point, an area then largely undeveloped because of its susceptibility to storms.

As a thriving port, Stonington was a logical destination for the railroad. To establish a coastal route from Boston to New York City, the New York and Stonington Railroad opened the first Connecticut terminus here in 1837, a seemingly bold venture at a time when there were only two thousand miles of track in the entire country. Passengers came from Boston and Providence to Stonington, where they transferred to steamboats bound for New York City, thereby avoiding the treacherous waters off Point Judith, Rhode Island, as well as the rutted mainland roads.[15] Until the 1880s, this journey was the fastest, most comfortable, and safest route from Boston to New York City; as many as twelve hundred passengers traveled it each day. For passengers in need of overnight accommodations, the railroad built the luxurious Wadawanuck House Hotel in Stonington. As a result, for the next fifty years, until the railroad bridges were

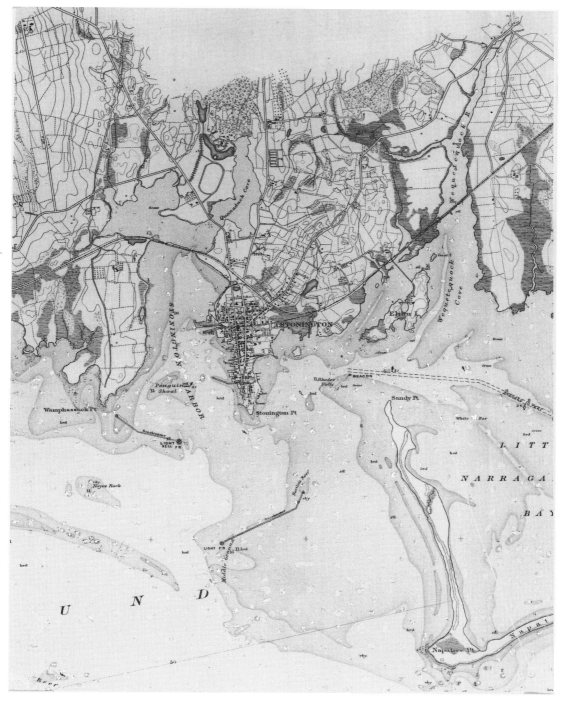

Map 6.2. Full of information, from water depth to property lines, this 1911 map of
Stonington Village and vicinity illustrates the complex topography of the Connecticut coast
(U.S. Coast and Geodetic Survey, 1911).

Fig. 6.3. View west on Denison Avenue, formerly Rail Road. Along this now peaceful greensward, trains cut through the village to reach the harbor on the peninsula's western side (1990).

completed along the coast, this small town enjoyed a remarkably busy and cosmopolitan life.

During this period, trains cut through the village to gain access to steamboat wharves on the western harbor side. Fearing fire from a smokestack's sparks, village leaders initially banned active locomotives within the village. Instead, teams of horses quietly, though inefficiently, pulled trains from the village outskirts to the wharves. Eventually the town fathers rescinded the ban and locomotives powered through. Freight and passenger service then expanded, and port facilities enlarged, adding more noise, smell, smoke, and congestion. One train could block five streets and effectively sever movement within the village.[16]

As the community prospered, shipping, railroads, and industrial activities came to occupy virtually the entire western side of the village. Ships needed rigging lofts and chandleries, and the railroads required a roundhouse, train sheds, repair shops, and water tanks. These additional industries and others soon located in Stonington, and German, Irish, and African immigrants joined the Portuguese, first to construct factories and then to settle here and work in them.

By the late nineteenth century, the town pattern evident in today's village had emerged. On the west side are shipping facilities and warehouses associated with the harbor. A commercial corridor along Water Street, the village's longest road, terminates at the southern point of the peninsula. A row of residential and institutional buildings lines Main Street, and to the east free-standing houses surrounded by gardens and marshes complete the village. A dozen smaller lanes cross Main and Water Streets, and public squares also tie the two long streets together and introduce a civic scale to the village. Moving down the peninsula the town pattern becomes more consistent in character, but moving across the peninsula one can see dramatic changes. This arrangement allowed people to live close to their workplaces and, at the same time, enjoy both active and secluded environments.

There are differences between "uptown" and "downtown" neighborhoods. Close to the southern tip downtown is the old Portuguese neighborhood, where houses are smaller and set close together on narrow streets. The northern, or uptown, neighborhoods have larger houses, usually free-standing and with larger yards. Within each neighborhood, different ethnic, religious, and social groups had their respective churches and social clubs. Villagers usually built

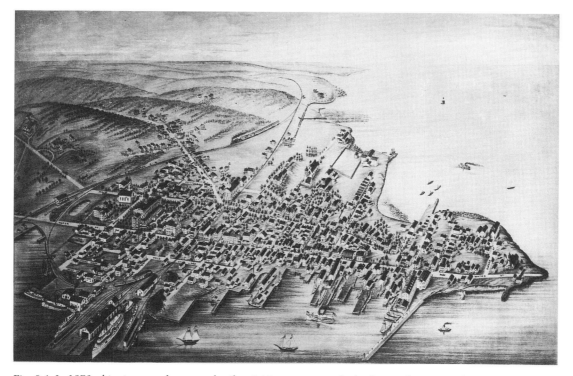

Fig. 6.4. In 1879, shipping, warehouse, and rail activities group near the harbor on the west side (foreground). Water Street runs the length of the peninsula. Beyond Water Street, Main Street connects with inland areas to the north (left) and terminates in the Town Square to the south (right) (Library of Congress, Geography and Map Division, 1879).

Fig. 6.5. On Water Street, looking south, clusters of houses alternate with stores. Some buildings were raised to insert ground-floor businesses (1990).

houses close to sidewalks to maximize space in their backyards for gardens, wells, and privies. According to an 1886 fire insurance map, virtually every block had residential as well as institutional or commercial uses. Buildings still typically occupy street corners except, most notably, around Wadawanuck Square, the primary public space.

Before the railroad's arrival severed it, Elm Street, which cuts diagonally through the street pattern, was the primary land entrance to the town from the east. Visitors now enter by a viaduct that passes over the tracks and descends into the town. A confusing route, especially the first time one travels it, this entrance protects the town by discouraging all but the most determined visitors. Arriving at the north end, visitors pass Wadawanuck Square, the park that connects Water and Main Streets, and, appropriately, the highest land within the village.

Wadawanuck Square is the first in a sequence of three public places one encounters as one travels south along the peninsula. Each place is different in scale, character, and purpose. Wadawanuck Square is an expansive civic space shaded by a mix of monumental trees. This was once the busy location of the grand old hotel and is now the quiet site of a smaller town library. Bordering the square are large houses, the town's post office, and a church. Eight blocks south, Cannon Square, a smaller and more intimate space, also connects Water and Main Streets and was once the old commercial heart of the town. A bank is still here, although the popular tavern and stagecoach stop are not, having discon-

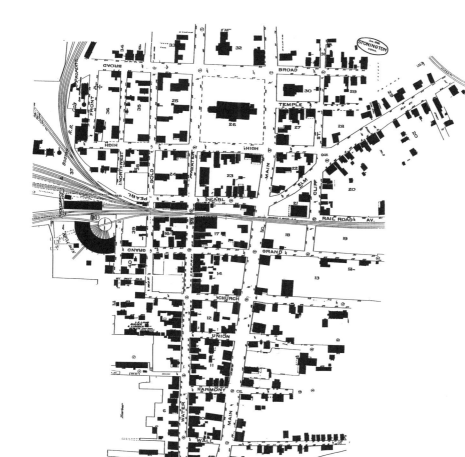

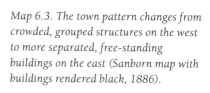

Map 6.3. The town pattern changes from crowded, grouped structures on the west to more separated, free-standing buildings on the east (Sanborn map with buildings rendered black, 1886).

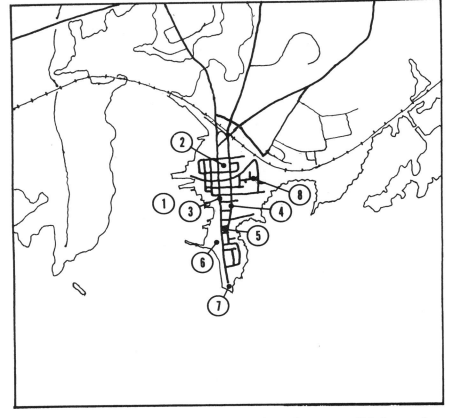

Map 6.4. Location map of Stonington Village (redrawn from current U.S. Coast and Geodetic Survey maps).
1. Harbor; 2. Wadawanuck Square; 3. Water Street; 4. Main Street; 5. Town Square;
6. Factory; 7. The Point; 8. Denison Avenue.

tinued their services in the late nineteenth century. Originally, an ocean inlet brought shipping close to the square's western edge, but that channel has been filled in to create sites for additional buildings and parking. Nevertheless, the space opens to the west and captures the late afternoon sun. At the end of Water Street, beyond the lighthouse and the other buildings of the village, the unpretentious but extraordinarily dramatic southern end of the peninsula called Stonington Point protrudes into the ocean. During the day, it is a place for leisure and recreation, but at night, when the sparkling lights of ships passing from the sound into the Atlantic are visible, it is a truly memorable sight.

Village houses range in style from simple Colonial fishermen's cottages to grand Victorian mansions. Most of the houses are made of wood, clad in shingles or clapboards. In the Colonial period, local shipwrights built houses of oak cut from nearby forests. Granite was plentiful, and villagers usually quarried it on or near building sites. Today, granite virtually roots the town to its site; villagers

Fig. 6.6. *From rough rubble sea walls to polished building details, locally quarried granite
ties the village to its site (1991).*

used it for foundations, seawalls, fence posts, paving blocks, and curbstones.
Important structures such as the lighthouse and the old custom house have
walls entirely of granite, and other buildings use polished granite for prominent
details.

Stonington has an enviable architectural tradition, distinguished by its quality and stylistic range. The Colonel Oliver Smith House (dating from 1761), at
25 Main Street, is an example of a modest fisherman's house (Fig. 6.7). Five bays
wide, it employs a central chimney and has virtually no decorative details. Near
the Smith house is the Peleg Hancox house (dating from 1820), at 33 Main Street
(Fig. 6.8). Built in the Greek Revival style, it has a temple front with ele-

Above: *Fig. 6.7. The Colonel Oliver
Smith House (1761), at 25 Main Street,
a modest fisherman's cottage with a
gambrel roof and central chimney, is
built close to the street and is typical of
Colonial period houses in the village
(1990).*

Right: *Fig. 6.8. At 33 Main Street, the
Peleg Hancox House (1820) with its
Greek Revival style temple front adds a
gracious accent to the village (1991).*

gant columns, pilasters, and friezes. Also nearby are two churches by notable
nineteenth-century architects. Richard Upjohn's Calvary Episcopal Church
(built in 1847) is the older of the two (Fig. 6.9). Constructed of granite in the
Gothic Revival style, its modest appearance gives the impression of an English
village church. Stanford White's Baptist Church (dating from 1889) is more
ambitious. This Shingle style building features a corner tower that became a
town landmark. Two commercial buildings are also especially noteworthy: the
Greek Revival Arcade, built in 1830 on Water Street (Fig. 6.10), which over the
years has accommodated a whaling office, a fish market, a bakery, and a jewelry
store, and now serves as apartments[17]; and the imposing harborside factory

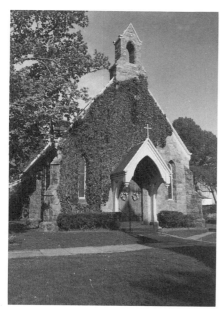

Left: *Fig. 6.9. One of the all-granite buildings in Stonington, the Calvary Episcopal Church, built in 1847, was designed by Richard Upjohn specifically to appear as a "village" church (1990).*

Below: *Fig. 6.10. Over the years, the Greek Revival Arcade (dating from 1830), on Water Street has accommodated a whaling office, a fish market, a bakery, a jewelry store, and now apartments (1990).*

that John F. Trumbull built in 1851, another granite structure. This building became the nucleus of a large factory complex and recently was the focus of community debate over adaptive reuse.

A Long Period of Slow Decline: 1865–1940

From 1865 to 1910, Stonington's economy shifted to industrial uses, as did the economies of many other Connecticut shoreline communities influenced by New York City's emergence as a national port. The Atwood Machine Company moved into the old Trumbull factory on Water Street to fabricate textile machinery.[18] This company, in turn, built housing for its managers and workers within the town. In 1904 the steamship line stopped operating, and in 1910 the railroad wharves permanently closed, ending the town's era as a junction for passengers traveling between New England and New York City. As waterfront activity declined, the town focused more on local affairs. In 1905 trolleys connected Stonington to nearby shore communities, although by 1910 there were still few cars and only dirt roads within the village itself. Nevertheless, Stonington was quiet and relatively self-sufficient. World War I brought a brief economic resurgence as shipbuilding revived.

Throughout this period, Stonington's old wealthy families remained active in village affairs, providing leadership and direction.[19] Some worked in New York City but regularly returned to Stonington, where they maintained family homes. As guardians of Stonington, they helped to establish the Village Improvement Society, which lobbied for street improvements. In 1924 they opposed the town selectmen who sought to remove stately trees on Water Street and widen and pave the roadways in concrete. The trees remained (at least until the disastrous hurricane of 1938), and the society continued its conservation efforts.[20] Wealthy families built large houses in the former pastures on the east side of the village, adopting the nostalgic Colonial Revival and Shingle styles popular nationally at the time.

The village, with its rocky shoreline, has never attracted large crowds of vacationers. Those seeking sandy beaches frequented nearby communities such as Watch Hill, Rhode Island. Those vacationers who preferred Stonington came for its village life. Mothers and children stayed for the whole summer; fathers commuted here on weekends from New York City. Most exited on Labor Day, leaving the village to its permanent residents. During this period, when Stonington was changing from a transportation and industrial center to a quiet residential community, it found a new revenue source in 1920 with the institutionalization of Prohibition. Because of Stonington's strategic location, it served as a refueling and supply point for rum-running operations. Of course, this minor renaissance lasted only as long as Prohibition itself. With the Eighteenth Amendment's repeal, in 1933, Stonington returned to its somnolence.

A Residential Village

During World War II, southeastern Connecticut prospered, thanks to its diverse industrial base, maritime resources, and skilled work force. In Stonington Village, manufacturing plants operated at full capacity and the fishing fleet expanded to meet the increased demand to feed new workers who flocked to these jobs and others along the coast. After the war, many defense workers remained to seek permanent work in peacetime industries and enjoy village life in Stonington. However, the economy again declined, and, except for the

Fig. 6.11. The harbor side reveals a succession of land uses; to the right is part of the factory complex started in 1851 by John Trumbull, to the left of it are recent condominiums, and in the foreground is a marina that has replaced commercial fishing wharves (1990).

major shipbuilding industry in nearby Groton, southeastern Connecticut did not maintain its prosperity long after the war.

As the old Stonington economy, based on fishing and manufacturing, declined, a new one emerged, turning the town into a prestigious residential community. The catalyst was the opening of Interstate 95 in the mid-1960s, three miles north of the village. With improved highway access, the post–World War II "baby boom" population spread out along the coast from the metropolitan centers and the older coastal suburbs such as Fairfield County, in western Connecticut. Stonington and other less discovered towns further east offered unique settings for this new generation. People now realized they could live in Stonington, enjoy the pleasures of village life, and commute to jobs in the region and even travel to events in New York City, Providence, Boston, and Hartford.[21] By the late 1970s, Stonington Village had become a desirable and expensive place to live. Stonington continues today to attract wealthy people, especially retirees. The average household size and total population have markedly dropped, while house prices have significantly escalated since the days when Portuguese fishermen's families lived here.

Residents today seek to preserve, not change, village character. Indeed, new buildings are rare because vacant land is scarce, and, to most residents, the village seems complete and should remain undisturbed. The best use is considered by most to be residential. Several condominium developments, though small, are prominent additions to the harbor side, where they have replaced an old boatyard and lobster pound. Regrettably, they differ in scale and site placement from traditional houses. The apartment condominiums that now fill an 1850's brick school building have been more successful for the preservation of town character.

The harbor and wharf area are disappointingly barren, as parking lots dominate. The commercial fishing wharf appears functional at best, and waste treatment facilities are also located here. A nearby public park is forlorn, particularly compared to its earlier years, when the park brimmed with activity during the shipping and railroad days. With modest landscaping, this area could instead emphasize the pedestrian qualities that otherwise make the village pleasurable. A plan proposed by a group of citizens to reopen old public rights-of-way encroached upon by private property owners would reenergize this area. Villagers have identified twenty-four routes, many of which once provided convenient pedestrian access to the waterfront.[22]

Current planning policies seek to preserve village character by maintaining the residential environment within the community while strengthening protective buffers around it. The sea surrounds the village on three sides. On the fourth, inland side, the rail line forms a barrier between the community and nearby developments. Beyond the rail line is an unofficial greenbelt, loosely consisting of streams, wetlands, and floodways that provide wildlife habitats, aquifers, and recreational opportunities. These environmental buffers further separate the village from inland development and reinforce residents' sense of community. With the protection offered by federal and state laws, local residents have carefully safeguarded these wetlands. However, in the late 1970's local environmentalists filed suit against developers of a residential project on nearby Quanaduck Cove, who, in turn, successfully countersued for loss of value, chilling community relations and lowering enthusiasm for subsequent confrontations.[23]

Commercial development has low priority, and villagers quietly but forcefully discourage tourism. There are now virtually no overnight accommodations within the village, a place that formerly had one of the grandest hotels in the country. The few existing restaurants cater to local residents as much as to outsiders. Tourists who visit nearby Mystic, Connecticut, and its Seaport Museum largely remain unaware of Stonington. Villagers appreciate this anonymity, for it preserves their community's peaceful life.

In recent years, the primary development threat to the village has been the old vacant factory complex on the harbor side. It remains classified as an industrial zone to forestall development. The future of this four-and-a-half-acre complex has been a focus of village debate. Should villagers encourage the reuse of the entire factory complex or only a part, particularly the old Trumbull building (1851), which played a major role in Stonington's industrial era? Should they support the demolition of sections to open visual and physical access to the water? If the complex houses commercial development, will it draw unwanted

Fig. 6.12. *Proposals for the vacant Trumbull factory complex have focused public debate on the future of Stonington Village (1991).*

traffic through narrow streets to its remote location? Most critical of all, if the site becomes housing, should a percentage be set aside for affordable dwellings to regain the traditional income diversity of the town and share the region's housing burden?[24]

While the village proper has been on the National Register of Historic Places since 1979 and has employed zoning ordinances since 1976, it has not introduced historic architectural controls, as most residents fear restrictions on individual property rights. Until now, few significant threats have arisen, partly because little vacant land remains in this compactly built community. Fragmented ownership and high residential values have also deterred developers from assembling property for commercial purposes.[25] In addition, Stonington's topography continues to protect the village from incursions—for example, its tight streets on the narrow peninsula discourage tour buses. Partly because of the restricted traffic, village retail trade has not thrived in recent years.

At the eastern end of Long Island Sound, Stonington is close to, yet sheltered from, the open ocean. While tidal currents are strong here, they also bring clean water. Yachtsmen prefer Stonington as a port because from here they have the choice of the open ocean or the calmer waters and scenic coastline of Long Island Sound. As in the past, commercial fishermen favor Stonington because it is the closest Connecticut port to ocean fishing grounds and enjoys highway connections to urban markets.[26] In its comprehensive plan, the town seeks to support the fishing industry, already subsidized, by improving docking facilities in the village. The town also recognizes that, as the region grows in population, more people will come to Stonington Village for boating and recreational opportunities. The comprehensive plan proposes to reintroduce a rail station on the edge of the village that, if realized, could encourage more recreational uses and promote development in the village's greenbelt.

Amid these shifting patterns, the physical character of Stonington Village has survived remarkably well. The visitor to Stonington today can experience a distinctive village in a unique setting. One can sense how a community, now less diverse than in the past, lives within a defined area and enjoys convenient access to a broad range of services, institutions, and pleasures. The surrounding sea, which from the beginning defined community life in Stonington, most recently has protected the town from unsettling change.

Mid-Atlantic Coastal Towns

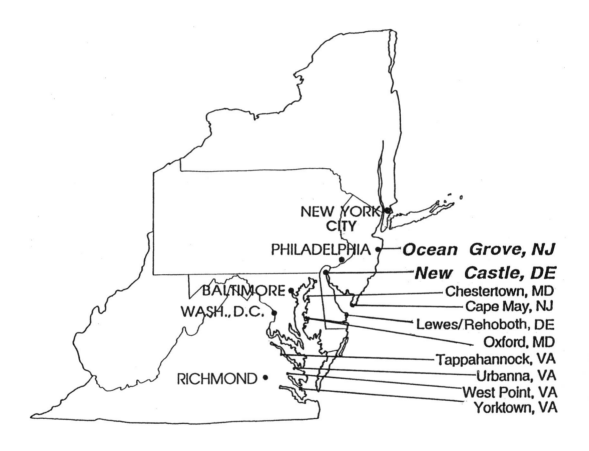

NEW YORK
CITY

PHILADELPHIA

Ocean Grove, NJ

New Castle, DE

BALTIMORE

Chestertown, MD

WASH., D.C.

Cape May, NJ

Lewes/Rehoboth, DE

Oxford, MD

Tappahannock, VA

Urbanna, VA

RICHMOND

West Point, VA

Yorktown, VA

Map 7.1. Map of Mid-Atlantic coastal towns discussed in Part II.
Towns in larger type are the subjects of individual chapters.

CHAPTER SEVEN

Overview

The topography of the coastal Mid-Atlantic region, which extends from New York and New Jersey through Virginia, gently slopes into the ocean as the coastal plain becomes the inundated continental shelf. Because the shelf is higher near the shoreline, the beaches are shallow for great distances, causing breaking waves approaching the shore to gain force and height. These powerful waves sweep up sand and heave it forward, building first submerged ridges and then, with continued deposits, thin barrier islands. Naturally unstable, these barrier islands continue to erode and reshape under the pressures of storms, currents, and tides. During storms, waves may even break over them, leaving sand deposits and altered contours in their wake. Where the islands are sufficiently separated from the mainland, they provide a sheltered route through the Intra-coastal Waterway for small craft wishing to avoid ocean passage.

These barrier islands, stretching along most of the Atlantic coast from Long Island to Florida, help protect the mainland. Behind them usually lie placid bays and estuaries. Where rivers and streams flow into these bays, sediment is deposited, helping to create marshes that nurture a rich biological life. Eventually, some of the islands even merge with the mainland, but this depends on the intervening distance and time. In any case, the lagoons are becoming filled with sediment and the islands are migrating, often at alarming rates.

Major river systems are also important features of the Mid-Atlantic coast. The Delaware River, whose estuary separates New Jersey and Delaware, allows ocean-going vessels to travel more than one hundred miles inland to Philadelphia. Of all the environments on the Atlantic coast, the Delaware River had the greatest potential for industrial and commercial development. Innumerable streams feed in on both banks, and the fall line a few miles inland permitted excellent mill sites. Further inland, rich, productive soil supported agriculture, while in the Wilmington-Philadelphia area, deposits of building stone, coal, copper, and iron ore provided raw materials for burgeoning industries.[1]

The early settlers in the Delaware River region favored sites that lay up tidal waterways, where the land was more stable and arable and fresh water more available. Though the area was settled first by the Dutch and Fenno-Swedes, it was the English colonists, especially the Quakers, who succeeded here. The settlers might have used the natural confining characteristics of barrier islands to contain animal herds, but they otherwise generally avoided building or living upon them, not wanting to assume more risks in their already precarious lives. Not until the industrialization of the nineteenth century did these shores and islands become popular, as dwellers in New York City and Philadelphia began to escape in great numbers to the New Jersey shore to avoid the hot summers in those increasingly crowded cities. Soon resorts developed on the island fringe facing the open ocean. What began as a few great resorts and scattered summer colonies, served first by steamships and then by the railroads, became after World War II a virtual carpeting of the New Jersey coast, as residents were soon able to drive to their second homes through the new parkways.

Lying further to the south is the Chesapeake Bay, one of the most important geographical features of the Mid-Atlantic coast. The lower Chesapeake was once the mouth of the Susquehanna River, and the Potomac, Rappahannock, and James rivers were mere tributaries before the melting glaciers caused the oceans to rise, flooding the bay some 175 miles inland. Although it is now one of the largest estuaries in the world, covering an area of more than three thousand square miles, the Chesapeake Bay is relatively shallow, with an average depth of only twenty-two feet. The shoreline is an extremely convoluted fringe of peninsulas and coves.

In the first decade of the seventeenth century, the Virginia Company of London, a commercial organization, initiated the colonization of Virginia, while an individual proprietor, George Calvert, the first Lord Baltimore (and later his son Cecilius, the second Lord Baltimore), led the exploration and development of Maryland. Both ventures sought structured colonization based on towns and villages similar to those in England—patterns that, not incidentally, would allow the developers to regulate and profit from trade. The many rivers, streams, and creeks that extend far inland on both the Maryland and Virginia sides, however, encouraged a dispersed settlement pattern that favored the local planters. As Thomas Jefferson observed in his *Notes on the State of Virginia* (1781): "We have no townships. Our country being much intersected with navigable waters and trade brought generally to our doors, instead of our being obliged to go in quest of it, has probably been one of the causes why we have not towns of any consequence." Even today the tidewater regions of Maryland and Virginia have few historic towns, particularly compared to the New England coast. Unlike the Delaware River basin, the Chesapeake region had few raw materials that would promote industrialization and thus encourage more centralized settlements.[2] The major cities of Baltimore, Washington, D.C., and Richmond nevertheless developed on the western side of the Chesapeake Bay, on the fall lines of their respective rivers.

In the Mid-Atlantic region, I selected Ocean Grove, New Jersey, and New Castle, Delaware—two towns that represent important regional contrasts: an ocean location versus an estuary location, social continuity versus ethnic succession, and the activities of a summer resort versus those of a commercial center.

Ocean Grove was part of the late-nineteenth-century wave of resorts that presaged the post–World War II vacation communities. Facing the Atlantic, the town flourished partly because of the compelling qualities of its coastal site and also because of the religious and social programs its plan facilitated. New Castle, on the Delaware River, was one of the first colonial settlements and became the home of different ethnic groups, and it later prospered in commerce and industry. Both towns have unique plans, beautiful public and private spaces, and proud architectural traditions. They have remained remarkably intact, given the astounding changes that have occurred around them.

New Jersey

The New Jersey coast extends in the arc of a bow approximately 130 miles along the Atlantic Ocean, from the north point of Sandy Hook, which overlooks Staten Island, to the southern tip of Cape May, at the entrance to the Delaware Bay. From this tip it bends inland as the estuary of the Delaware River. For most of its Atlantic edge, the coast is rimmed by low barriers of fine white sand, rising but a few feet above high tide level. Successive ridges and troughs, some filled with fresh water in the spring but dry in the summer, lie behind these, roughly parallel to the shoreline. Any older dunes not already lined with cottages may be covered with grasses, vines, and stunted oak and pine trees.

The Indians who lived in what is now New Jersey prior to European colonization belonged to the Lenni Lenape group of the Algonquin tribe. They had a network of trails threading through the region which linked their favored fishing places along the Delaware River to those near the ocean. Many of these trails became the roads of the later colonists. Giovanni da Verrazano, sailing for the French king François I, probably anchored off Sandy Hook in 1524, but it was the Dutch who, from their base on the tip of what became Manhattan, first explored northern New Jersey. They and subsequent settlers and inhabitants of that island established a sphere of influence over the New Jersey coast which New Yorkers have continued to this day. Meanwhile, the Swedes and Finns probed the Delaware River in 1636 to establish a base there, but it was the English who primarily shaped the character of colonial settlement in southern coastal New Jersey and the rest of the present-day state. In 1664 Charles II of England, basing his claim on John Cabot's discovery of the continent in 1497, asserted control over this entire region and seriously began pursuing English colonial ambitions.

Generally, it can be said that significant coastal resort development along the New Jersey coast did not begin until after the Civil War. There are the notable exceptions, however: Long Branch had a seaside boarding house as early as 1792 but its great bluffs and late-nineteenth-century hotels and ocean boulevards have since been washed away by storms; Atlantic City, before 1854 and the opening of the Camden and Atlantic Railroad, was known primarily as a dangerous sandy island strip five miles from the mainland where ships wrecked, but soon after rail service started it became the location of speculative resort development and eventually evolved into the great East Coast gambling Mecca; and Cape May, which was an easy sloop ride down the Delaware River from Philadelphia, was advertised as a summer "watering place" as early as 1800 and has endured and rebuilt from a series of devastating fires, today surviving as the great American Victorian resort. Following the railroad resorts and religious retreats of the nineteenth century, automobile-oriented resorts proliferated in the twentieth century. In 1891 New Jersey created the first state highway department in the nation, and by the 1940s, with the construction of the 143-mile Garden State Parkway which skirted the coast, motorists could access and—thanks to minimal zoning restrictions—build in previously inaccessible remote locations.[3]

Although I considered other towns in New Jersey, none captured as many of the regional qualities as did Ocean Grove. In northern New Jersey, *Keyport* (pop. 7,586) *Oceanport* (pop. 6,146), and *Red Bank* (pop. 10,636) prospered during the steamboat era as shore towns. *Spring Lake* (pop. 3,499), just south of Ocean Grove, developed in the late nineteenth century as a resort around a lake of that name. In southeastern New Jersey, a number of coastal towns emerged because of the rural glass, iron, and shipbuilding industries that developed nearby. These towns include *Port Republic* (pop. 992*), referred to by the British as a "nest of rebel pirates" during the American Revolution and the site of an early iron furnace, and *Tuckerton* (pop. 3,048), which was settled by 1699 and became an early port of entry for trading ships from England and the West Indies.[4]

Across the Delaware River from New Castle and three miles inland from its marshy river flats is *Salem* (pop. 6,883). Founded in 1675 by James Fenwick, it became the first English-speaking settlement in the Delaware River valley. Sadly, though the town still has gracious brick town houses lining its streets, today it is separated from the river by large industrial facilities. Sixteen miles south of Salem, on the Cohansey River, is *Greenwich* (pop. 911*), laid out in 1683, which, more than any New Jersey settlement, retains its colonial character. Residential, commercial, and public buildings and magnificent old maple and sycamore trees line its "Greate Street," yet it is still only a small village today. During the late nineteenth century, the fishing towns of *Port Norris* (pop. 1,701), *Dorchester* (pop. 600*), *Leesburg* (pop. 750*), and *Mauricetown* (pop. 550*), all on the Maurice River, were the center of the oyster industry in America. Today, Dorchester and Leesburg are still noted for shipbuilding, a legacy of their seventeenth-century Swedish settlers, and Mauricetown, for its distinguished architecture.

In the late seventeenth century, whalers from New Haven and Long Island settled on the sandy southern tip of New Jersey at the site of the present-day city of *Cape May* (pop. 4,853). Indians had long been camping here, and Henry Hudson viewed this land when he sailed up the Delaware River in 1609. The settlement grew slowly, profiting on fishing, lumbering, and a few tourists. After the War of 1812, the town gained international prominence as a spa. Situated where the Delaware River joins the Atlantic Ocean, it was ideally located for those coming by boat, the primary means of long-distance transportation at the time, from New York City, Philadelphia, Baltimore, and other cities to the south.[5]

Although it was eventually superseded by Atlantic City, which had better rail and highway connections to metropolitan centers, Cape May flourished throughout the early part of the twentieth century as the location of one of the great Victorian resorts. It now survives as one of the country's largest assemblages of Victorian buildings, boasting more than six hundred in all their bracketed, turreted, and multicolored extravagance.[6] While today there is an awkward juxtaposition of scales between, on the one hand, the large hotels and, on the other, the free-standing Victorian houses that otherwise fill the area, and while the street intersections do not feature important views, spaces, and buildings, the city of Cape May remains, in all its nostalgic flamboyance, a great American place.

Delaware

As he sailed around Cape Henlopen in 1609, Henry Hudson, the English navigator sailing for the Dutch East India Company, became the first known European to venture into the Delaware region, a name the explorers gave both to the river and to the Indians living along its shores and in the neighboring forests. The Scandinavians were the first colonists to settle the banks of the river. In 1638, with the sponsorship of the New Sweden Company and the support of the Swedish Government, Swedish and Dutch soldiers and sailors purchased land from the Indians and established the colony of New Sweden. Initially their settlements consisted of a series of forts and then a string of outposts that stretched from the south, near present-day New Castle, to the site of Philadelphia. Over the next fifty years, the Scandinavian colonists, particularly Swedes and Finns, spread up the tributary rivers and creeks. More Europeans arrived—French, Germans, Scottish, and Irish; the area was controlled by the Dutch in 1655 and then by the English in 1664. During this period of ethnic influx and change, the Scandinavian influence continued to dominate, particularly that of the Savo-Karelian Finns, who were especially adept at backwoods pioneering. From this foothold in the Delaware River valley, over the following centuries Fenno-Scandian culture spread west across Pennsylvania and south through Appalachia, introducing, among other innovations, log-cabin construction into American culture.[7]

Cape Henlopen today is a three-thousand-acre state park with six miles of public beaches fronting on the bay and ocean. In 1725, Philadelphia merchants built the first American lighthouse here to aid ships on their way to the growing inland port. That lighthouse and subsequent towers have been lost as the shore eroded and the cape shifted to the north, shoaling the harbor at Lewes. Cape Henlopen lies between the historic towns of Lewes and Rehoboth Beach, which, though only three miles apart, are markedly different.

Lewes (pop. 2,295) has had a succession of names—Sikonesse, Swanendael, and Deale—which, respectively, reflect the Indian, Dutch, and English inhabitants of the area. The Nanticoke Indians initially traded furs with the Dutch and in 1630 sold the land to them. A year later, the Dutch established a whaling station here on the inland side of a creek that roughly runs parallel to, and one-half mile in from, the shifting shoreline. Between 1664 and 1681, control of the area switched between the Dutch and the English, with English Quaker William Penn finally acquiring ownership. At this time the settlement gained the name *Lewes* after the town in Sussex, England, and, under Penn's guidance, a layout was established that ensured the common lands between the creek and the beach would, as in New Castle, further upriver, remain as open space.

Throughout the town's history, the strategic location of Lewes has made it susceptible to raids, beginning with those of pirates in the sixteenth century and continuing with the sacking of the town by privateers in the French and Indian Wars, its bombardment by the British in the War of 1812, and, finally, during World War II, its surveillance by the German U-boats that prowled the coastal shipping lanes. On the other hand, Lewes has been the key to safe passage on the Delaware River. For over three hundred years Lewes has been home to the river pilots who have guided ships up and down the river, taking ocean-going vessels as far as Philadelphia. These pilots have traditionally lived immediately west of the historic settlement in the Pilot Town neighborhood, where a row of houses overlooks the creek and the bay beyond.

The historic settlement itself is centered on the relatively small commercial area of Second Street. Although the earliest structure, the Ryves-Holt house, dates from 1665, most buildings in the historic area are from the late nineteenth and early twentieth centuries. In 1869 a branch of the Delaware Railroad arrived, and in 1896 the harbor was enlarged. Lewes Creek was later extended into the Lewes and Rehoboth Canal, in 1912, and became part of the Intracoastal Waterway. All these developments expanded and diversified the town's economy and prompted a surge in construction. Since World War II, tourism has replaced shipping as the economic mainstay, although the historic central area has remained intact.[8]

Rehoboth Beach (pop. 1,234) is south of Cape Henlopen and derives its name from Rehoboth Bay, which lies still further south and was named by English settlers in the seventeenth century. In 1670 James Mills acquired a land grant for the area, and for almost the next two centuries this land remained farms and pastures. Richard West purchased 3,960 feet of oceanfront in 1855 and had lots platted, and by 1869 a combination summer hotel and fall hunting lodge had been built. However it was a group of Methodists, first organized as the Rehoboth Association and subsequently as the Rehoboth Beach Camp-Meeting Association of the Methodist Episcopal Church, who determined the future character of the area.

Similar to Ocean Grove, New Jersey, which was founded in 1869, Rehoboth Beach became the summer destination for a group of Methodists who sought escape from the growing industrial cities. They purchased land in Rehoboth in 1872, acquiring 414 acres on which they planned a community with radial streets that focused on a central area for their tabernacle and allowed for communal gatherings and space for members' tents. As had their counterparts in Ocean Grove, they built a boardwalk along the dune overlooking the ocean to enjoy the public pleasures of the beach. Hotels followed and tents gave way to more permanent summer cottages. In 1878 the railroad made the area more accessible and thereby increased the number of summer visitors, including non-Methodists. Rehoboth proved less physically defined and controllable than Ocean Grove, however, and by 1881 the Methodists no longer organized camp meetings here, although members still came to vacation.

In the following decades the Rehoboth community continued to grow in population and in area as the town annexed land. Summer crowds also increased: in 1922 the resident population during the year was 690 but grew in the summer to 4,500. The opening of the Chesapeake Bay Bridge in 1952 reduced the travel time to Rehoboth Beach for people in the Washington, D.C., Baltimore, and Annapolis region. As the town continued to grow it became more crowded and commercialized, with seasonal shops catering to tourists and suburban houses and private clubs filling the surrounding marshes.

Today, a grid plan organizes the central part of the community, allowing vacationers immediate access in one direction to the beach, where streets dead-end at the wide oceanside boardwalk that the Methodists introduced. Running perpendicular to the boardwalk is a broad commercial street, Rehoboth Avenue, a riotous, concentrated cluster of tourist shops that presents a striking contrast to the boardwalk and the sedate residential areas buried in the groves of loblolly pine and holly—areas which, in their communal seclusion, also faintly recall the community's Methodist past.[9]

Maryland

European settlers first entered Maryland through the protected waters of the Chesapeake Bay. Having abandoned Newfoundland, judging it too inhospitable, the first Lord Baltimore, George Calvert, in 1632 gained proprietary control of the Chesapeake region for his next colony. In 1634 his son Leonard Calvert anchored off an island in the Potomac River and established the first settlement on today's Maryland mainland, the town of St. Mary's. The colonists then spread north along the shores of the Potomac River and settled around the many inlets that form the convoluted region of the upper Chesapeake Bay.

The Roman Catholic Calverts hoped to establish a manorial system similar to that of their Yorkshire, England, homeland, one based on nuclear families living in small organized villages, sustained by agriculture and supplemented by manufacturing.[10] However, the realities of the Chesapeake region dictated otherwise. A small group of Catholic gentry came to dominate a growing class of Protestant tenants (initially indentured servants who arrived as teenagers from the slums of London) and, after 1671, slaves imported from West Africa—all of whom were spread thinly throughout the watery region. In this emerging colony, marshy tongues of land determined property holdings more than geometric principles.

Maryland planters exported tobacco, their initial cash crop, from wharves on their property. Roads were primarily muddy paths that connected these landings to the nearby plantations, almost all of which were near the water. In 1683, in an effort to control trade, the Maryland Assembly passed the Act for the Advancement of Trade to establish custom houses, thereby leading to the creation of towns. A few outposts did become towns, but most did not. Unlike New England's terrain, the Chesapeake region's geographic reality conflicted with the growth of commercial towns—such that even today few towns of substantial size exist, particularly in southern Maryland.

As eroding soil from coastal tobacco fields silted the small waterways and the scale of export shipping increased, Baltimore became the dominant center for trade and commerce. By 1830, Baltimore was the second largest population center in the country. The subsequent urban and industrial development of the eastern seaboard at the fall lines of rivers and along the transportation lines that connected those cities largely bypassed tidewater Maryland. The few towns that did develop there have a distinct character bred of cultural crosscurrents and, until recently, shaped by the geographical isolation of the region.

Chestertown (pop. 4,005) is still a remarkably coherent and gracious town after three hundred years of existence and may be the quintessential Eastern Shore community. Lying on the low banks of the tranquil Chester River, the settlement started with the courthouse, which was located here in 1698, followed by the streets, which were laid out in 1707. The following year the town was designated as an official port of entry, a major distinction in an age when all important trade came by water. High Street runs perpendicular from the river, along a slight ridge through the center of town to the western countryside. Two streams define the outer edges of the town. As in New Castle, Delaware, grand Georgian and Federal style houses line Water Street, many of them built on filled river lots. Three blocks inland from the river where High Street intersects with Cross Street, the colonists located a church, a market house, and a cemetery, which, along with the courthouse, formed a civic area. Over the years this space became more refined as High Street was widened to enhance the frontage of these buildings and a row of commercial buildings was developed on the opposite side to complete a central area.

Located on the Old Post Road from Maine to Georgia, Chestertown grew slowly at first, reaching its greatest wealth and prominence around the time of the American Revolution, when it became a major tobacco and wheat shipping port of the Eastern Shore. Washington College, founded in 1782, dates from this period and, located on high ground to the northwest, is still an important asset of the town. During the nineteenth century, as Annapolis and Baltimore grew in importance, Chestertown receded into an isolation that protected it from change. Today, Chestertown possesses more pre-Revolutionary buildings than any other Maryland community, with the exception of Annapolis. It also benefits from the magnificent sycamore trees that were planted along many of its streets as part of a late-nineteenth-century effort to beautify the town.[11]

On the Chesapeake Bay side of Maryland near the Tred Avon River, *Easton* (pop. 9,372) developed around the Talbot County Courthouse, which has been sited here since 1710. The town began to prosper after it was named the administrative center for the Eastern Shore in 1788. This prosperity continued through the nineteenth century, when this region supplied produce and fish to northern cities. Today, Easton is surprisingly compact. In the heart of town, buildings (now filled with fashionable stores and law offices) typically line the sidewalks, while setbacks are judiciously used to feature important structures, most notably the courthouse, which still physically commands the town. Recent civic buildings behind the old courthouse demonstrate how new additions can complement, not compete with, the established character of an historic town.

St. Michaels (pop. 1,309) is more dispersed than Easton. Deriving its name from an Episcopal parish established here in 1672, St. Michaels was founded in 1778 and became a center for building oceangoing vessels, especially the sleek American privateers that frustrated the British during the War of 1812 and the shallow draft boats that could easily ply the many tributaries of the bay. Along a neck of land, craftsmen built these vessels and also constructed their modest houses, which were placed on small lots that today give the town a particularly fine scale. St. Michaels is now a popular recreational boating and retirement community.[12]

Oxford (pop. 699), on a thumb of land that juts out between the Choptank and Tred Avon Rivers, has one of the finest harbors on the Eastern Shore; indeed, in the eighteenth century it rivaled Annapolis and Chestertown as one of the most important ports in the region. Settled in 1669, Oxford was designated as a town by the Maryland General Assembly in 1684 and laid out as such in one hundred lots. In 1694 the assembly elevated it, along with Annapolis, to a port of entry. The town reached its peak as a shipping port in the years before the American Revolution, before the ports of Baltimore and Norfolk came to dominate trade. After the Civil War, Oxford emerged from almost a century of economic decline when the railroad arrived. For roughly fifty years thereafter, industry based on canning and packing Chesapeake oysters flourished, only to decline after World War II once the oyster beds had been depleted, again setting Oxford into a period of economic decline.

In recent years Oxford has experienced a new popularity and prosperity as a second-home community because of its town qualities, historic architecture, and proximity to Washington D.C., Annapolis, and Baltimore. Morris Street, the main entrance into town, runs the length of the small peninsula. Driving or walking along this street, one glimpses the Choptank River as one passes the town park (formerly the town market), which ends at the ferry, and another park known as the Strand. Sited on a peninsula, the town is defined by water, and each bay edge has a different scale of activity and mood. Within the town, functional areas and neighborhoods are grouped according to slight changes in elevations and water drainage paths.

On the south bank of the Choptank River, at a site where the river is nearly two miles wide and thus was not bridged until 1935, lies the town of *Cambridge* (pop. 11,703). Along with nearby Oxford, Cambridge was authorized as a town in 1684 by the Maryland General Assembly to encourage commerce and to enable the collection of taxes on tobacco, which dominated trade in this region up through the American Revolution. Cambridge developed along High Street, around the courthouse, initially built in 1686 (the present courthouse, built in 1852, was designed by Richard Upjohn and is on the National Register of Historic Places), and on either side of a creek that, over the years, has been lined with tobacco warehouses, shipyards, oyster-packing facilities, fruit and vegetable canneries, and, most recently, condominiums.[13]

Crisfield (pop. 2,924) is at the southernmost end of Maryland. Although the rail line that once carried fresh oysters to the hotels and clubs of New York City no longer runs down the main street to the pier (it is now a landscaped median), Crisfield remains a watermen's community, with warehouses, now storing crabs instead of oysters, choking the waterfront. Upper Crisfield was part of a tract of land registered in 1663. During the latter part of the nineteenth century, Lower Crisfield grew out into the marshes on foundations of discarded oyster shells, where fishing warehouses now line the water's edge.

St. Mary's City (pop. 0), the first capital of Maryland, lies on the St. Mary's River near the southern tip of the state on the western side of the Chesapeake Bay, six miles north of the Potomac River and approximately sixty miles southeast of Washington, D.C. In 1634 Leonard Calvert, son of the first Lord Baltimore, bought land from the Yoacomico Indians of the Piscataway Confederacy, who had a village in the area. He led a small group of colonists there, who formed a settlement that initially consisted of the Indian wigwams, a few new cottages, and a small fort. After his death, in 1647, Leonard Calvert's former house was purchased by the colony in 1662 and became the first official statehouse. By 1674, administrative activities had increased such that the colony began construction of a new statehouse specifically for the functions of the provincial assembly.

During the years 1665–70, the town was laid out in a new and more formal pattern, which arguably may have been the first use of Baroque town planning in America and may have presaged the plans of Annapolis, Maryland, and Williamsburg, Virginia.[14] Abjuring the conventional grid plan, St. Mary's planners, it was recently revealed through archaeological research, centered the town on a square approximately one hundred by three hundred feet, which probably served as a market place. From this space extended two triangular road patterns of equal size and shape. At the corners of one triangular pattern were the town square, the statehouse, and the water entrance to the town; the other triangular pattern comprised the square, a Jesuit chapel (Maryland was a Catholic colony at this time), and the land entrance to the town. Both the statehouse and the chapel were set about 1,400 feet from the square on visually prominent sites.

At the town's period of greatest activity, in the early 1690s, St. Mary's population probably did not exceed three hundred residents. In 1694, the Maryland Assembly voted to move the capital to Annapolis, which was more central to its growing colonial settlements. Most residents of St. Mary's City soon followed, and by 1708 the former capital had been largely abandoned and become farmland. For more than two hundred years the land was farmed and owned by one family, until 1980, when the state of Maryland purchased the property and opened an outdoor museum of history, archaeology, and natural history to commemorate early European settlement in the Chesapeake region. The site is now a National Historic Landmark, although there is no longer a city at St. Mary's City.

The site of *Leonardtown* (pop. 1,475) is at the head of Breton Bay, an estuary of the Potomac River, approximately fourteen miles northwest of St. Mary's City. In 1708 the Maryland General Assembly, after having received a gift of fifty acres here and having moved the capital to Annapolis, designated this location as the new county seat. Today visitors arrive along an approach road that terminates in a triangular public place dominated by a modern bank rather than the courthouse directly beyond it, which was built on the site of the original courthouse that overlooked Breton Bay.

Virginia

In 1607, colonists financed by investors in the Virginia Company of London, who sought both passage to the South Seas and gold from the New World, sailed up the Lower James River to establish a tidewater foothold at a site they called "James Towne." In the years that followed, settlement gradually moved up that river and on the banks of the long, parallel estuaries of the York, Rappahannock, and Potomac Rivers. London officials, annoyed at the dispersal of trade in the newly settled areas, sought unsuccessfully to centralize commerce in towns, first in Jamestown (despite its being poorly situated on a marshy site) and then in designated locations along other rivers and creeks. As early as 1622, the London Company directed "that the houses and buildings be so contrived together, as may make if not hansome Townes, yet compact and orderly villages; that this is the most proper, and successful maner of proceedings in new Plantacons."[15] The Virginia Company (and later the royal governor, after King James revoked the company's charter in 1624) had equally conflicting ambitions—to form "compact and orderly villages" and also colonize extensive territory. Town formation and territorial settlement proved difficult goals to reconcile.

London officials reluctantly relinquished the control of large tracts of land to individual investors, who, in effect, formed little colonies unto themselves, responsible for their own financing, trade, and internal organization. Along the James River, these subsidiary colonies were spaced, according to official policy, at least ten miles apart.[16] Land was also assigned on the basis of "head rights," with the largest grants going to those wealthy and powerful men who could assemble the most dependents to work for them.[17]

The growth of tobacco also deterred nucleated development, as dispersed farms growing tobacco along the rivers and creeks became the dominant settlement pattern. Introduced in 1612 as a crop from the West Indies by John Rolfe, within a decade tobacco became a widely cultivated crop and soon turned into the source of wealth the colonists had initially sought in gold.[18] This farming settlement pattern was reinforced in 1651, when Africans were brought to America, first as indentured servants and soon thereafter as slaves, to work the tobacco fields. As individual families gained control of these subsidiary colonies, their land holdings evolved into the great tidewater plantations. These plantations, with their complexes of clustered buildings, essentially became small self-sufficient villages, visually dominated by the mansions of the family patriarchs.

The English Crown, through its colonial government, continued to press for the development of towns through which all imports and exports were to pass, in order to allow the regulation of trade. In 1662 Virginia Governor William Berkeley promoted "An Act for Building a Towne," which stipulated the number and size of buildings for towns, and, in 1680, Virginia Governor Thomas Lord Culpeper initiated legislation for no less than twenty town sites. Additional acts in 1690 and 1706 further supported these efforts. The towns of Tappahannock, Urbanna, West Point, Yorktown, and Onancock are legacies of these acts. However, until the mid-eighteenth century the geography, economy, and cultural traditions of Virginia continued to thwart legislators' efforts and encourage instead a dispersed, plantation-based settlement pattern. The physical layouts of these towns, based on simple, unimaginative grid plans, are not remarkable. Their settings, however, nestled in marshy tidewater tongues of land, possess a quiet and even luxurious beauty.

The town of *Tappahannock* (pop. 1,550) lies on the Rappahannock River halfway between the river's fall line, at Fredericksburg, and its mouth, at the Chesapeake Bay. Constituted a town in 1680, it soon became an official port of entry because of its strategic location. Its ships traded around the world until the late nineteenth century, when the railroads were built and trade came to favor Norfolk and Portsmouth, Virginia. Today the river, creeks, and marshes define the extent of the old town, creating a small greenbelt around it except on its western side, where a commercial strip highway cuts across the site and erodes that edge of the town's historic character. In the town itself, the simple street grid is varied by two wider streets running perpendicular to the river. One of these serves the bridge traffic, and the other, the old commercial district. Between them lies a set of public facilities, including the courthouse, anchoring the inland end, and a public dock at the river's edge. The original 1728 courthouse building is adjacent to the current courthouse and now serves as a church. The buildings of St. Margaret's School line the riverbank and offer a stately view of the town from across the river. Beautiful trees and foliage, as well as the occasional delightful building, such as the wooden Gothic Revival Episcopal Church, also grace the town.

Urbanna (pop. 529), situated on land that slopes steeply to a small creek close to where the Rappahannock River meets the Chesapeake Bay, offers vessels shelter away from the fast-moving river current. The town was named after Queen Anne of England (*Urbanna* means "City of Anne") in 1705, and a plan prepared around that time shows three streets leading to the creek, tying the town to the water. A 1747 map shows a road wrapping around the waterfront, further strengthening this water connection. Tobacco was the dominant early crop, and Urbanna's merchants served the river plantations. Warehouses, a custom house, and a courthouse were built to encourage this trade. After the Revolutionary War and the waning of the tobacco trade, Urbanna declined until the late nineteenth century, when a seafood industry developed there to harvest the bay, bringing with it a new prosperity. Steamboats plied the waters linking the town to Norfolk and Baltimore, and it grew appreciably. This period of prosperity lasted until the 1950s, when the Chesapeake Bay became increasingly polluted and the oyster catch decreased significantly. Gradually, tourists and weekenders from Richmond and Washington, D.C., discovered the charms of the town: its mix of architecture from a range of periods, its irregular plan, and its secluded harbor, ideal for recreational boating. Unfortunately, the waterfront is no longer as accessible as it once was—a private marina now blocks the waterfront passages and suburban housing is filling up the fields, confusing the definition and sense of this beautifully sited and, compared to others in Virginia, surprisingly compact town.[19]

Formerly the site of an Indian village, *West Point* (pop. 2,938) was designated a new town under the 1680 legislation ("An Act for Cohabitation and Encouragement of Trade and Manufacture") and named for John West, from whom the land was purchased. West Point is strategically situated on a point of land where the Mattaponi and Pamunkey Rivers flow together to form the York River. The elongated point of land dictated a linear town, and today's plan follows the outline of a layout from about 1691. Ambitions for the town were never realized, and it remained a marginal settlement until the arrival of the railroad in the 1860s.[20]

Today, the town's architectural character derives from the buildings of the late eighteenth and early twentieth century. A network of three long streets and numerous cross streets run the length of the point. Along the beautiful tree-lined Main Street are residences, churches, and, in the midsection, the old commercial district. Anticlimactically, this street ends at the point in a minuscule park the width of the street itself. The perimeter streets are residential, with most buildings having been located on the firmer ground along the center spine of the point. At the bridge entrance to the town, a huge forest products factory, the town's major employer, casts an odor over the town.

Sited on a fifty-foot bluff on the south side of the York River near the mouth of the Chesapeake Bay, *Yorktown* (pop. 270) is in the Colonial National Historical Park and protected by surrounding federally-owned lands. The approach to the town through tidewater forests, more than the routes to any other coastal town, matches its historic setting. One of the twenty towns designated in the act of 1680, it soon became one of the most important towns of the Colonial period. During the Revolutionary War, British forces destroyed most of the buildings in Yorktown. However, it was here, on October 19, 1781, that Lord Cornwallis surrendered to General Washington, and today the town serves primarily as a museum to commemorate that victory. Main Street, on the bluff, parallels the river and is intersected by short cross streets to the waterfront. Unfortunately, in the original platting of the town in 1691, half the waterfront was excluded.[21] Today this area still stands in disorderly contrast to the village on the bluff. An even more startling contrast is the adjacent bridge across the York River to Gloucester Point, a grossly overscaled intrusion into this otherwise tranquil tidewater environment.

Smithfield (pop. 4,686) was initiated in 1752 by Arthur Smith as an effort in private land development. The town is located approximately one mile south of the James River at a bend in the Pagan River. A band of buildings on a ridge along Church Street follows the bend and marks the northern side of the town. Perpendicular to the bend in the river and extending southward is Main Street, along which is the old courthouse (built in 1750), now a visitors' center. The town is the home of the Smithfield Ham, shipped from here as early as 1779. The Victorian era was a particularly prosperous period for Smithfield because of the peanuts processed in its vicinity. Many of the houses on Church Street date from that period.[22]

Several other historic Virginia coastal towns are part of what is known as the Delmarva Peninsula (so called because it includes parts of Delaware, Maryland, and Virginia), that part of the Eastern shore that lies on the eastern side of the Chesapeake Bay. Until 1964, when the Chesapeake Bay Bridge–Tunnel was completed, transportation between the eastern and western parts of tidewater Virginia was by water.

Onancock (pop. 1,434) developed on a creek approximately five miles from the open bay. This was the site of an Indian village that dated from at least the 1620s, when European settlers first visited it. Established formally as a town in 1684, Onancock served as the county seat from then until 1786. It was a stop for steamboats journeying between Norfolk and Baltimore during the nineteenth century and on into the 1930s, when such steamboats finally were retired. From the harbor at the end of Market Street today, one can take the ferry to Tangier Island, twelve miles from the mainland and, until recently, one of the most remote communities on the eastern seaboard.[23] As Market Street enters the town from the east, it jogs to parallel a creek and, in so doing, creates interesting vistas that focus on buildings and a small park at the end of the commercial section. Along Market Street, churches project forward toward the street while residences, most notably the Kerr House (built in 1799), recede to accommodate gracious front lawns and luxuriant trees.

The present-day town of *Cape Charles* (pop. 1,398) dates from 1884, when the New York, Philadelphia, and Norfolk Railroad planned the town as the terminus of its rail line, the first down the Eastern shore. From this port, ferries transported freight and passengers across the bay to Norfolk. The main business street, Mason Avenue, edges the south side of the town and faces the rail yards and harbor. Substantial brick houses, often only six feet apart, give an air of solidity to this now depressed town, which has seen commerce shift from Mason Avenue to U.S. 13, the highway passing through the center of the peninsula and connecting with the Chesapeake Bay Bridge–Tunnel. The town is also notable for its open-space system: A public beach and boardwalk line the western edge of the peninsula along the bay. Forming an overall cruciform pattern within the town, four streets with grass medians run from the four sides of the town to a large central park. Unfortunately, the central park, originally intended to be an important feature of the town and a focus for neighborhood life, is today fenced off and inaccessible to the public.[24]

Conclusion

While the European colonists who crossed the ocean found in the Mid-Atlantic region an environment remarkably similar to that of their homelands, they had to forsake their intended nucleated settlement pattern for a more dispersed one in order to colonize the great territories before them. During the Civil War, the Mid-Atlantic region was between the North and South, and its inhabitants developed allegiances to both. On one hand, they sought to share in the commercial and industrial interests of the North, yet they wanted to maintain the agrarian traditions of the South. The region also became the gateway to the West, through which immigrants passed to settle the continent and to which the inland industries shipped the products that sustained the growing seaboard cities.

Many of the Mid-Atlantic coastal towns fell within the spheres of influence of larger cities, serving as commercial, judicial, or transport centers or becoming the resorts that offered city dwellers relief from crowded urban conditions. Topography, though an evocative part of these Mid-Atlantic towns, was less of a determining factor than it was for those in the North and in the South. The present-day forms of these Mid-Atlantic towns are therefore the consequences of geographic, cultural, and economic cross-currents, and, in accommodating these forces, the towns have produced a unique blend of buildings and settlement patterns distinguished by the domestic comforts of their residential areas and the modest civic grandeur of their public spaces.

Rendering by Peter Lorenzoni, after a drawing by the author.

Ocean Grove, New Jersey

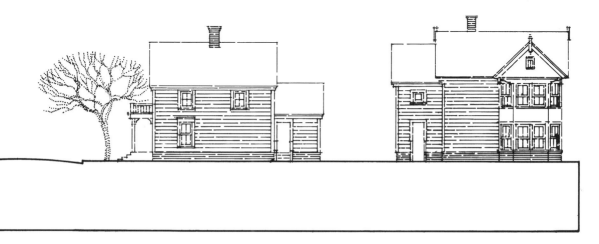

Fig. 8.1. Street section of Ocean Grove, New Jersey.

Map 8.1. Community and religious life focus on the Auditorium, seen here as the largest building, top center (Sanborn map with buildings rendered black, 1912).

Founded in 1869 as a Christian camp meeting ground and summer resort, Ocean Grove remains rooted in religious traditions.[1] For over a century, Methodist summer residents found fellowship and spiritual sanctuary in this once isolated area of sand dunes and pine thickets. Here, far from the hot, crowded, and "sinful" cities where they had to earn their living, Methodist campers worshipped and relaxed in a grove overlooking the sea. Here they passed the days with sermons, prayers, and concerts, not the gambling, drinking and racing common in secular resorts of the time.[2] In recent decades, however, problems of contemporary urban America, including those of how to care for the poor, have descended on this community and challenged its institutions and purposes.

Ocean Grove, one of the largest, most influential, and longest lasting of the nineteenth-century camp meeting communities, enjoyed phenomenal early success. Within ten years of its founding, the community had become a national resort frequented by presidents, senators, judges, and generals. Today, sixth-generation visitors still return to summer in tents tethered near the old grove of trees where Methodist leaders founded the community. Until 1979, the Ocean Grove Camp Meeting Association governed this enclave and controlled the town's government, police, and court system, enforcing their Protestant probity through the blue laws.[3]

The community's buildings and its plan reflect a concern for human fellowship. The most conspicuous building in Ocean Grove is not an ostentatious mansion but a place of religious assembly called the Auditorium, a voluminous tentlike structure in which thousands of people congregate. Streets are numerous and unusually short and intimate in character. Houses, while small and crowded together, have prominent front porches where residents can enjoy refreshing sea breezes and the company of neighbors.

Since 1979, courts have forced Ocean Grove to separate church and secular affairs, and the state has imposed deinstitutionalized patients and parolees on the community. Now older residents, who have traditionally enjoyed living close to one another because they share similar values, daily meet people who, often owing to a poor and disadvantaged background, display different social behavior than has been the norm for those of the Camp Meeting Association. As a result, Ocean Grove is experiencing what many private communities have assiduously tried to avoid—the realities of poverty and the need to adapt specifically designed facilities to different purposes. Ocean Grove residents have struggled

Fig. 8.2. Ocean Pathway leads from the shore to the Auditorium, visible in the distance. While crowded together, houses have prominent front porches and conform to staggered setbacks to allow inland residents views of the ocean (1990).

with these changes, seeking to address contemporary problems while still maintaining their sense of community.

The Camp Meeting Association

Camp meetings flourished in mid-nineteenth-century America as part of the religious backlash against the industrial revolution.[4] Reacting against an industrializing society that was becoming more urban and materialistic, many Americans flocked to remote countryside retreats for wholesome entertainment, fellowship, and spiritual uplift. As part of a growing middle class with new wealth and extra time, yet embarrassed by the notion of idle fun, these religious groups found that they could nevertheless use the expanding network of railroads and steamships to escape the confines of dirty, congested cities. Camp meetings provided perfect outlets. Here families could participate in old-time religion, celebrate patriotism, and enjoy a country, if not a resort, setting, all the while gaining the moral fortitude to win life's struggles.

By the 1860s, however, religious leaders began to feel that the social aspects of camp meetings had overshadowed their religious purposes. A group of Methodist ministers and laypersons led this reexamination and proposed an experiment in New Jersey. The group planned to form an association and buy the camp meeting property, then carefully direct the development and management of the meetings.[5] In 1867 the group commissioned Reverend William Osborn to locate a suitable site for summer camp meetings.[6] He searched the New Jersey coast and found a special site—one that is remote, largely uninhabited, on the ocean, and which featured the grove of pine trees that would give the community its name. Sand dunes matted with wavy grass rolled along the ocean. Behind the dunes, land was low-lying, even marshy, and tangled with wild scrub pine. The settlers would later level the front dunes to fill in the back areas. Even so, two different worlds existed—one near the ocean which was open and expansive, the other behind the dunes which was enclosed and limited. Subsequent development maintained these differences.

In the summer of 1869, twenty church members pitched tents and worshipped in the pine grove where Thompson Park now exists. In December of that year, thirteen ministers and thirteen laymen met in Trenton and established the Ocean Grove Camp Meeting Association of the Methodist Episcopal Church. To maintain civil order and protect the community from outsiders who might disrupt meetings in this remote location, the state of New Jersey granted a charter to the association in 1870, allowing it to manage its own municipal affairs. The association organized water, postal, fire, and police services. Reverend Osborn directed the arduous tasks of development, clearing overgrowth, leveling dunes, and grading paths and roads. By 1875, however, the association had assembled the 266 acres that constitute today's community.[7] In 1881, a father and son surveying team, Frederick and Isaac Kennedy, prepared a plan for the entire community that guided its growth.

During the early years, only dirt roads connected Ocean Grove to distant villages, but by 1875 the Farmingdale and New Egypt Rail Road reached nearby Asbury Park, and summer traffic boomed.[8] At first, ferries carried guests across

Fig. 8.3. This nineteenth-century illustration depicts Methodists at an evening meeting on the beach in Ocean Grove, where sermons were held for the many who came seeking old-time religion (Harper's Weekly, 31 August 1878, 692–93).

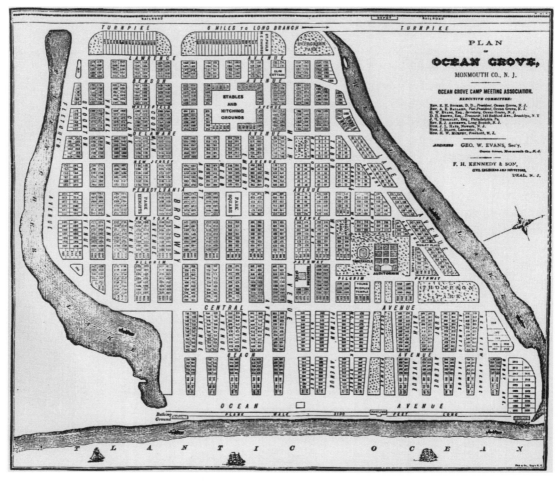

Map 8.2. *In the original plan of Ocean Grove, surveyed by Frederick H. Kennedy and his son Isaac in 1881, a thirty-foot lot length and width underlies the plan as the blocks increase in length from west to east. Along the flaring avenues, building setbacks enlarge to maximize ocean breezes and views from within the community (Ocean Grove Historical Society, 1881).*

the lake when they arrived at Asbury Park Station, but soon pedestrian bridges replaced the ferries. Substantial residences and boarding houses as well as more tents were erected to satisfy the growing popularity.

The early visitors needed food as well as accommodations. Area farmers willingly sold produce, others served meals, and some abandoned farming to open hotels. Since residents who built houses here were generally of modest means, they often added rental rooms for summer visitors.[9] This practice dispersed tourist accommodations and summer traffic throughout the community, allowing the town to maintain a consistent residential scale. Yet almost everybody went home by October, leaving the area to a few caretakers.

By the turn of the twentieth century, Ocean Grove had grown to more than a

Map 8.3. A regional plan of Ocean Grove. In the early twentieth century, settlements, separated by tidal ponds, clustered between the ocean and the coastal rail line (U.S. Coast and Geodetic Survey, 1901, reprint, 1912).

Fig. 8.4. In the early years, visitors arrived at the train station in nearby Asbury Park and then took the ferry across Wesley Lake to enter Ocean Grove (Harper's Weekly, 31 August 1878, 685).

thousand cottages and seventy-nine hotels, essentially becoming the compact community we see today. It forms a rhomboidal land area, approximately two-thirds of a mile in width and length. Its landward sides have distinct edges, and to the east is the open ocean. Unlike the development patterns along most of the New Jersey coast today, privately owned buildings in Ocean Grove do not separate public rights-of-way from the shore. Bathing, after all, was not only a popular recreation but also an occasion for fellowship.

A boardwalk stretching along the tops of the frontmost dunes formerly connected bath houses at either end of the beach. Today, benches for resting and viewing the promenade of people line the boardwalk. Adjacent to and inland from the boardwalk is Ocean Avenue, a street where motorists can watch as well

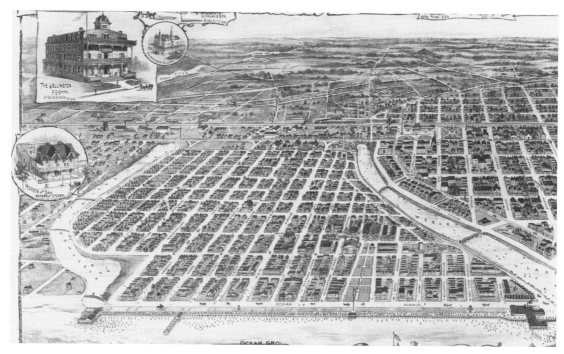

Fig. 8.5. By 1898, thirty years after its founding, Ocean Grove was substantially completed.
The Great Auditorium terminates Ocean Pathway near Thompson Park (right, near Wesley
Lake) where the camp meeting started (Library of Congress, Geography and Map Division,
1898).

Fig. 8.6. A grand boardwalk stretches along the shorefront of Ocean Grove (1990).

Top: *Fig. 8.7. Along the ocean at the tip of a flaring avenue, buildings crowd together, allowing two houses to be designed as an ensemble (1990).* Bottom: *Fig. 8.8. On streets perpendicular to the ocean, houses are set gradually further back to allow those behind to gain views and benefit from ocean breezes (1990).*

as become part of the passing parade. Together with the broad beach, the board-walk and Ocean Avenue form an immense space in which people are able to socialize in an open setting. Old wood-frame hotels congregate along the west side of Ocean Avenue, again allowing as many people as possible to appreciate waterside attractions. The first two blocks inland from the ocean are designed to be what the early planners termed *flaring avenues*. Here buildings conform to

Ocean Grove.

Top: *Fig. 8.9. Separating Ocean Grove from Asbury Park, Wesley Lake became a place for Victorian pleasures—boating, picnicking, and strolling* (Harper's Weekly, *31 August 1878, 692*). Bottom: *Fig. 8.10. Wesley Lake is now a quieter scene than it was in Victorian days (1990).*

*Map 8.4. Location Map of Ocean Grove, New Jersey (redrawn from current U.S. Coast
and Geodetic Survey maps).*
*1. Great Auditorium; 2. Asbury Park; 3. Wesley Lake; 4. Thompson Park;
5. Ocean Pathway; 6. Main Avenue; 7. Broadway; 8. Fletcher Lake.*

wedge-shaped setback lines, allowing more residents behind Ocean Avenue to
enjoy water views and breezes.

Along the community's north side is Wesley Lake, a finger-shaped coastal
pond that early planners separated from the ocean and developed for Victorian
pleasures. Visitors could stroll meandering walks, fly kites, or picnic on the
grassy embankments and islands within the pond, as well as go boating in the
calm waters. The dunes on the Ocean Grove side of Wesley Lake became a desirable location for single-family houses, since residents could enjoy the lake pros-
pect and still be close to the place of initial settlement and center of activities.

The western edge of Ocean Grove, along South Main Street, faces a more
hectic world. Here, the old coastal turnpike became the transportation, commercial, and industrial corridor of the region. Ocean Grove planners initially responded by adding small parks and later gates. They platted the remainder of
this edge for houses, but it soon became a service zone. Building-supply facilities

located here, and, with the arrival of automobiles, garages and service stations soon opened. Only three of the community's east-west streets connect to the bordering highway along this western edge, because founders wanted to control access to Ocean Grove. Furthermore, association officials always closed these three connecting streets on Sundays, prohibiting first carriages and then automobiles from entering and requiring residents to remove all transportation vehicles from within the enclave. Until 1979, residents did so, parking most cars in neighboring communities.[10] On Sundays everyone walked in a vehicle-free environment. Older residents still fondly remember this social ritual, even though it limited their choice of which church to attend.

Another freshwater pond, Fletcher Lake, marks the community's southern edge. This side is farthest from the Auditorium activities on the north and suffers from its low-lying topography. Consequently, it was the last to develop and today least exhibits the spirit animating other parts of Ocean Grove. The facilities there include only one service building, a children's playground, a shuffleboard, and tennis courts. The Ocean Grove Association filled the western half of the lake and now uses it as a parking lot.

Streets and Parks

The street pattern of Ocean Grove is its civic signature, clearly distinguishing it from surrounding developments. The pattern is small and directional: The grid on the west side is remarkably tight in the north-south direction, with the size of a block only 120 feet—approximately half the block size of those in adjacent communities.[11] In the east-west direction, the grid pattern expands towards the beach. Blocks incrementally increase in length from 150 feet farthest inland to 330 feet closest to the beach, and the number of lots per block increases from five to eleven. This grid and the resultant spatial expansion reflect the old landscape of dense thickets in back and open, rolling sand dunes in front. From a development standpoint, such a layout permits more house lots in the most desirable locations closest to the ocean.

The layout also orients people within what otherwise could have been an anonymous grid pattern. Inland one finds an intimate world of quiet streets, shaped by two-story buildings and shaded by overarching trees. Near the ocean, particularly along the flaring avenues, one enjoys the spatial orientation of the streets to the water and the cooling ocean breezes. Three- and four-story buildings, many of which are hotels and boarding houses, frame these streets. Landscaping is less important; while small front lawns are common, trees are restricted because they block views. The eighteen-foot right-of-way width, from curb to curb, of typical secondary streets contributes to the pedestrian ambiance.

Ocean Pathway is a grand mall that extends three blocks from the oceanfront to the Auditorium. With a length of fifteen hundred feet and a width of two hundred feet inland (widening to three hundred feet at the sea), it spatially ties the two great community social areas together—the Auditorium, with its intense, orchestrated, religious events, and the beach, with its leisurely, improvised pleasures. From the Auditorium, the illusion this space creates "pulls" the ocean back into the compact community through the reverse perspective of its flared shape. Ocean Pathway also provides a display area for the grand Victorian houses that edge this greensward. Meanwhile, smaller parks punctuate the community, providing places for people to gather within their neighborhoods.

Main Avenue is the primary vehicular entrance into the community. Two blocks of this street form the commercial core, separate from, yet convenient to, the Auditorium area as well as the beach front. Broadway, the other main entrance into the community, was more important when the south beach pavilion existed. Central Avenue and Pilgrim Pathway, running north-south, both provide access to the Auditorium precinct.

Architecture and Building Lots

Ocean Grove began in Thompson Park, just north of the Auditorium, the present center of the community. Initially, a simple preacher's platform encircled by seating stood in a grove of trees, and tents clustered in the surrounding woods. In 1894 the Auditorium replaced the open preacher's stand. This steel-

Fig. 8.11. The two scales of Ocean Grove—the communal and the individual—are dramatically juxtaposed here, where semipermanent tents cluster around the Auditorium (1990).

Fig. 8.12. *Three adjacent structures recapitulate the evolution of the Ocean Grove house type (from right to left): a tent, a simple wood cottage, and a two-story dwelling. All employ a gable form and front porch (1990).*

truss structure, with 161-foot spans across the interior, seats 9,600 people. It is an eight-sided pavilion with a bell-shaped roof and round cupola, contrasting in size and form with the rectangular cottages surrounding it. Of the former 600 tents, 114 still huddle around the Auditorium; the inner, or "first," circle of tents are held by those families who have been returning the greatest number of seasons.[12] The tents invariably have front porches, where small clusters of people gather to enjoy breezes and the companionship of friends. The diminutive tents and the grand Auditorium reflect a contrasting scale also found elsewhere in the community.

The "campground cottages" are endearing little houses that began to appear in the 1870s. They relate formally to the preceding tents and stylistically to the cottages at Wesleyan Grove in Oak Bluffs, Martha's Vineyard.[13] Ocean Grove's "wooden tents" are typically small, narrow, two-story buildings. On the front porch is usually a centered entrance with double-leafed doors similar to tent openings or church doors. On either side of the entry are narrow, arched windows. Larger wooden houses of differing styles quickly followed the tents—Italianate, Eastlake, Gothic, Queen Anne, and later Colonial Revival, Bungalow, and Foursquare styles.[14] However, virtually all of these display two important Ocean Grove themes—generous one- and two-story porches and gable house ends, often with fanciful wood details, facing the street.

A thirty-foot module organizes the community plan. Most house lots are thirty feet wide and sixty feet long, and houses are packed tightly together. Rear and side yards are narrow, often five feet or less. Understandably, fire has been a

Fig. 8.13. On gable-front houses, Victorian owners incorporated double and even triple level porches where they could enjoy refreshing sea breezes and the fellowship of neighbors.

recurrent danger, and three fire stations are strategically placed throughout the community. The Ocean Grove Camp Meeting Association owns all land within the community and grants ninety-nine-year renewable leases. New residents who buy old homes can renew ninety-nine-year lot leases at the nineteenth-century rate of $10.50 per year. For the Association, however, these low-priced renewable leases result in a lost source of income.

Illumination of the night, an important practice in Ocean Grove, not only contributed to religious mysticism but also allowed residents to use the community more intensively. Since the season was short, they crowded activities into event-filled days stretching from sunrise well into the night. During the early camp meetings, pine bough torches illuminated midnight preaching under the stars. Later, gas lamps lighted the boardwalk to encourage evening promenades. For a number of years, the Auditorium has also displayed a lighted cross on its top. Most magical of all are the canvas tents surrounding the Auditorium that, when lighted within, softly glow like giant lanterns.

After 1900, property developers built more hotels along the shore blocks and residents continued to make alterations to their houses. However, more profound changes were now occurring outside the community. Neighboring Asbury Park, founded soon after Ocean Grove, promoted an amusement park, a casino, and large hotels on its oceanfront, while, across the nearby countryside, developers built new automobile suburbs at much lower densities than pedestrian-oriented Ocean Grove. New highways improved access for those in automobiles and congestion increasingly became a problem, especially on summer weekends. Ocean Grove, however, with its extensive street network and dispersed pattern of accommodations, absorbed automobiles remarkably well. It also managed to remain a community for pedestrians, not become one dominated by automobiles.

Recent Years

In 1970, following riots in the Watts neighborhood of Los Angeles and Newark, New Jersey, violence on a smaller scale erupted in nearby Asbury Park. The state activated the National Guard to restore order.[15] From their enclave, Ocean Grove residents watched in dismay. The riot marked the beginning of economic decline in the area immediately adjacent, as middle-class black and white residents relocated. Vacationers, benefiting from the Garden State Parkway, began to favor more modern and remote resorts to the south. During this same period, New Jersey, like other states, began deinstitutionalizing its chronically ill mental patients. Rather than warehouse them in psychiatric hospitals, the state released these patients to the "least restrictive environments" of local communities. Asbury Park, which had empty boarding houses and hotels, became an early recipient of these former patients. Ocean Grove, physically and institutionally insulated, at first was not directly affected.

From 1980 to 1987, property prices increased in Ocean Grove. Speculation focused on old Ocean Grove hotels, which developers believed they could profitably resell as condominiums.[16] In 1988, however, the general real estate market dropped, and Ocean Grove's property prices became even more depressed after a local pollution scare caused by garbage and medical wastes washing up on the shore. Investors who had bought old hotels toward the end of the price escalation found they had large mortgages but few paying guests. At the same time, the New Jersey Department of Human Services was looking for ways to house its severely dysfunctional patients. Desperate Ocean Grove investors needing income accepted them. Within a brief period, parolees and formerly homeless people joined the mentally ill in the old hotels and boarding houses. Regrettably, the state did not provide sufficient local assistance to care for the sickest patients.[17]

While officially uncounted, the number of deinstitutionalized patients living in Ocean Grove has been estimated at near five hundred, which is about 10 percent of the total community's population. Crowded together and unsupervised, the deinstitutionalized are now an evident and noisy presence in this community, which prided itself on being quiet, family-oriented, and "Christian," in which buildings stand close together and people enjoyed public activity and street life because everyone shared similar values.[18] Now, intimate streets and narrow side yards instead promote social friction. Old vacationers, particularly women and children, who sustained the community for so many years, return less frequently. While younger families find Ocean Grove a potentially attractive year-round home, they are frightened at the thought of having deinstitutionalized patients as neighbors. Ocean Grove residents believe they have borne an unfair social responsibility. Strengthened by their strong sense of community and long tradition of local organizing, they are vigorously challenging the government programs that led to the influx of deinstitutionalized patients.

Less traumatic but even more profound has been the secularization of Ocean Grove's government. Ocean Grove is no longer an association-controlled community, but rather one of many districts competing for funds and services within the township of Neptune. In 1870, a year after the Ocean Grove Camp Meeting Association founded the community, the state of New Jersey granted the association municipal authority since no other political entity existed on the then undeveloped coast. Although it was not an elected leadership and unable to tax, the association provided some utilities, street maintenance, and police protection, paying for these with funds from ground rents, concession fees, and contributions. As the surrounding area developed and Neptune Township became the administrating jurisdiction, Ocean Grove residents paid taxes to the township but requested few services. By the 1970s, maintaining the police had become burdensome, and Ocean Grove relinquished these responsibilities to the township. In 1979 the New Jersey Supreme Court declared the association's form of government unconstitutional because it violated the separation of church and state.[19] Residents of Ocean Grove voted to secede from the township, but an overall election forced them to remain.[20] No longer permitted to govern themselves, Ocean Grove residents accepted township services, for which they already had been paying taxes.

The Camp Meeting Association still owns and leases the community's land, however. It owns and operates the Auditorium and its complex of facilities, in addition to the beachfront. With its relinquishment of civil administration, the association has had to redefine its mission and goals. It has broadened its activities and now organizes cultural events as well as religious programs. Increasingly, the association caters to the northern New Jersey shore and eastern Pennsylvania region, not just the old religious community. The Camp Meeting Association offers an active summer program, including concerts on Saturday in addition to its traditional Sunday services. Younger people, many of whom are unaffiliated with the Methodist Church, patronize these events. The beach, which was traditionally closed on the Sabbath, is now open on Sundays—although only after 12:30, when the Great Auditorium services end. Indeed, it is difficult to park convenient to the beach on summer weekends, forcing people now, as in the past, to use fringe areas and walk through the community.

Before 1979, the association had imposed land-use controls. Neptune Township then introduced zoning, codifying what had existed previously. At that time, the township also established a Board of Architectural Review. Realizing that the old high-density zoning had too easily permitted patients to move into the old hotels, the township has recently extended single-family zoning to restrict the spread of boarding houses and to encourage more families to relocate here.

In its transition from a homogenous, tightly controlled community to an open and more heterogeneous one, Ocean Grove offers insights for the growing number of "closed" communities that may face similar transformations in the future. Residential community associations—condominiums, cooperatives, and mandatory homeowners' associations—have grown enormously in recent years. Advocates argue that these associations allow self-determination and community control, greater land-use efficiency, more responsive services, stable property values, and more attractive neighborhoods. Critics question their lifestyle restrictions, types of governance, double taxation, and divided loyalties. They charge that when associations fail, the public sector must assume responsibilities and town residents pay for members' past privileges of exclusivity.[21]

Ocean Grove illuminates these issues. This community, originally developed for specific needs, has adapted to new, varied ones. While Ocean Grove's intimate physical environment aggravates relationships between radically different social groups, new buyers find the setting attractive and hope that once "unfair" government social programs are changed, the community will again be safe and supportive for family life. Township public services are now more professional, even if less personal. The township provides more resources—such as police, street maintenance, and elder care—than Ocean Grove could afford to fund on its own. The township also intercedes more forcefully than the association formerly could with other public agencies and utility companies.[22]

Ocean Grove's community facilities have meantime won new patrons. The Great Auditorium, built for large religious gatherings, now also hosts secular activities such as concerts by popular entertainers. The community beach and boardwalk are open to people from surrounding communities who do not have local beach access. Visitors pay a fee to the association, which still owns and maintains the beach. Ocean Grove volunteers also staff a civilian patrol which successfully coordinates with the Neptune Township police.[23] Ocean Grove has a prosperous business district, which outsiders patronize more and more, and which, in turn, contributes significant taxes to the township. In a region dominated by automobiles, Ocean Grove offers a pedestrian environment which residents and visitors enjoy exploring and find refreshing—if not as spiritually rewarding as in the past.

After a fractious period, Ocean Grove and Neptune Township are currently cooperating for mutual gain. Ocean Grove sustains its sense of community but does not provide municipal services. Neptune Township retains its tax base and offers economies of scale in services. With its wealth of modest yet personalized housing, a rich architectural tradition, equitably placed facilities, and small-town character, Ocean Grove still appeals to new home buyers as well as retirees. Isolated first geographically and then organizationally, after the recent challenges the community is now more of an integral part of its region in New Jersey. Determined to maintain their community, Ocean Grove residents have had to become actively involved in larger public issues.

Rendering by Peter Lorenzoni, after a drawing by the author.

CHAPTER NINE

New Castle, Delaware

Fig. 9.1. Street section of New Castle, Delaware.

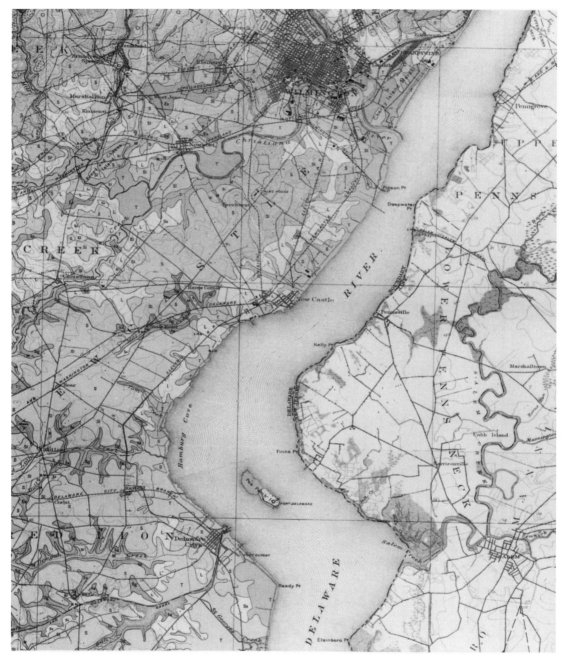

Map 9.1. This map shows New Castle, situated at a commanding bend in the river six miles south of Wilmington (U.S. Coast and Geodetic Survey, 1906).

Six miles south of Wilmington, on the flat, sandy banks of the Delaware River, rests the town of New Castle. Settlers favored the commanding river position encircled by wetlands for its defensive advantages.[1] Today marshes still isolate the community and preserve a town that combines a coherent and compact tradition of building with unexpectedly generous and gracious public spaces. The early citizens of New Castle hoped that their town would become a great Atlantic seaport and thus sought to create an environment worthy of their ambitions. While New Castle successfully served many roles—colonial assembly, state capital, court town, county seat, transportation hub, and market center— other more advantageously located cities surpassed it in these activities. New Castle is now part of the greater Wilmington area. Yet, with its compact small-town character and well-defined boundaries, it agreeably contrasts with the sprawling contemporary developments around it.

New Castle has three major environmental areas. The first is the town center, whose public spaces and tall, free-standing buildings on high ground dominate the surrounding community. This central precinct contrasts with the second area, the fabric of the town, structured by a grid of streets lined with houses, stores, and workplaces. Buildings here are orderly and unified, with common setbacks close to the sidewalks and similar heights of usually two or three stories. Within this order, buildings feature a variety of materials and engaging details. The third major environmental area, a greenbelt that dates from the early colonial period, encircles the town and comprises marshes, playing fields, and parks. Varying in width from one-half mile to over two miles, the greenbelt separates the town from surrounding development. The trustees of New Castle Common, a nonprofit organization that has fostered town improvements for the past two hundred years, owns most of this greenbelt. Delaware Street, the main approach route and commercial street, passes through each of these three environments to end at the town wharf on the river's edge.

From Colonial Fort to Federal Meeting Place

To control the Delaware River and capture Indian trade from the Swedes, Peter Stuyvesant, Governor of the Dutch West India Company, founded Fort Casimir in 1651 on a sandy hook of land at the foot of what is now Chestnut Street. By 1655 the Dutch had designated a green, or public area, on higher ground inland from today's Second Street. They bounded this area with streets, initiating the town's grid plan.[2] In 1656 the bankrupt Dutch West India Com-

Fig. 9.2. The town's major features are evident in this aerial photo: the greenbelt that surrounds the settlement, the park, formerly an industrial area (along the river bank in left foreground), Delaware Street, which passes through the town to a turnaround at the water's edge, and Front Street (The Strand), lined with row houses (Eric Crossan, 1997).

pany relinquished control to the burgomasters of Amsterdam, who renamed the town New Amstel and encouraged rapid settlement.[3] Immigrants built on the elongated lots, approximately 30 by 180 feet, which permitted many people access to river frontage while also providing some higher land for crops and storage.[4] To drain surrounding marshes, the Dutch built a dike, still evident north of town. Through these efforts, the Dutch, however tentatively, initiated measures that led to the three environmental areas of today's community.

The English seized the settlement in 1664. While immediately renaming it New Castle, they sympathetically continued the town plan started by the Dutch. They relocated the main fortifications uphill to the Green, affirming the public purpose of this site. They placed several public structures here: a blockhouse for defense, built in the 1670s, New Castle's first separate courthouse, built in the 1690s, and Immanuel Church, built in 1704, which, being the Church of State, could occupy public land.[5] The English also designated a market area on Second Street. Inland from the central area, they provided lots for a blacksmith, wood-cutter, wheelwright, brewer, and brick maker, generally relegating lower-status activities to areas along the marshy fringes.[6] By 1666, there were more than one hundred buildings in the town. However, citizens were still able to live where they worked—an arrangement they would not begin to alter until the end of the eighteenth century.[7]

During the seventeenth century, the river's edge lay between the present-day Strand, which was then underwater at high tide, and Second Street, also known as Market Street, which ran along the upper edge of the bank. Not until 1701, after it had been built up through years of river siltation, did colonists lay out the Strand.[8] Property owners on the inland side of the street controlled the land facing the river, parceled out in areas called "water lots." They first built wharves into the river, and later they filled that area to create more usable property, eventually extending this land as much as three hundred feet into the river. As the area prospered, merchants built larger houses along the Strand on this new land. While most wharves were private, a public wharf existed at the foot of Harmony Street as early as 1702, allowing general access to the river.[9]

New Castle emerged as a junction point in seaboard transportation. To avoid

Fig. 9.3. Since early colonial times, the town's Green has been dedicated to public use. Buildings dating from the seventeenth century align along the street to shape the space (1990).

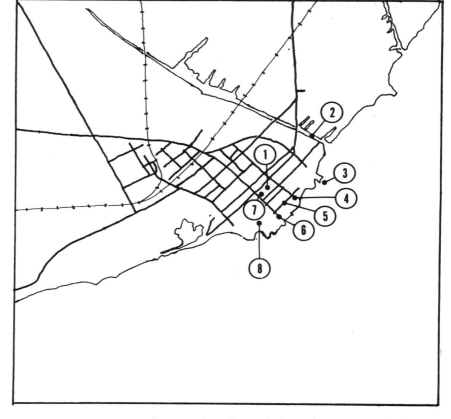

Map 9.2. Location Map of New Castle, Delaware (redrawn from current U.S. Coast and Geodetic Survey maps).
1. The Green; 2. Dike Canal; 3. Fort Casimir Site; 4. Harmony Street;
5. The Strand; 6. Delaware Street; 7. Court House Square; 8. Battery Park.

circuitous trips around Virginia's Eastern shore, travelers came by boat down the Delaware River from Philadelphia and transferred at New Castle for land journeys south to Baltimore, Annapolis, and, later, Washington, D.C. The town prospered as a place to meet people and embark upon journeys. Inns and residences as well as public spaces offered hospitality. New Castle citizens excelled at providing services rather than pursuing commercial trade, and therefore the town never developed a strong merchant class. Lawyers and innkeepers dominated commercial life while ship builders, for example, were conspicuously absent. The town's physical environment still reflects its tradition of comfort and urbanity.[10] By the American Revolution, approximately one thousand people lived here, and the first decade of the next century saw the population grow by another 25 percent. New Castle flourished from 1780 to 1840. The town had derived its plan from an earlier time and now enhanced it with elegant buildings. Many of the town's Georgian and Federal houses exhibit the spirit of these years.

Fig. 9.4. This perspective, and others by Benjamin Latrobe (1804), of the courthouse and Green aided twentieth-century preservation efforts (Delaware Public Archives).

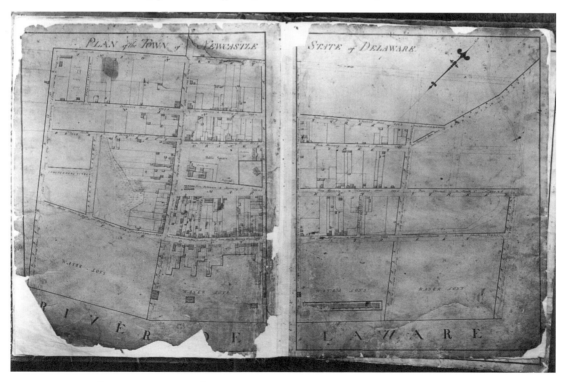

Map 9.3. In 1804 the town commissioned Benjamin Latrobe and his assistant, William Strickland, to recommend drainage improvements for this low-lying settlement. They produced these and other plans of the area (Delaware State Archives, ca. 1804).

Fig. 9.5. *During the seventeenth century, the river's edge was near the Strand, or Front Street. Later the river silted this area, and property owners built wharves, filling in to create additional land on which to build houses (1990).*

Tiring of the increasingly boisterous commercial life on the Strand, the town gentry relocated north of the Green. Lawyers built stately houses along Third Street, overlooking the Green and the nearby courthouse. Others preferred upper Delaware Street.[11] Wealthy builders favored large corner lots, locating houses close to street corners, which left the middle of the blocks to be subdivided for smaller houses. Builders on these lots then clustered houses together, making them appear similar in scale to the larger single-family houses on the corner lots. Residents built both types of houses in stages, starting with the main house and adding wings, porches, walls, and outbuildings, usually to the rear where land was available.[12]

Rapid growth after the American Revolution prompted the town to reevaluate its street plan because of problems with poor drainage. In 1804 the town commissioned Benjamin Latrobe and his assistant, William Strickland, to prepare a physical survey. Their recommendations affected every street, raising and lowering some by as much as one-half story relative to buildings along the streets' edges.[13] Latrobe and Strickland left New Castle not only an enlarged and better-drained town but also a beautifully recorded one, producing maps and drawings which later aided twentieth-century restorations.

The danger of fire was a major physical threat for this town, as it was for others that used wood as the dominant building material. In 1824 a major fire swept through the river side of the Strand, jumping across a street to burn more houses until stopped by the masonry construction of the George Read House and the firebreaks provided by long backyards. The memory of this fire influenced subsequent town building practices. Builders thereafter constructed in brick and stucco, using wood primarily for details and special features.

A Small Town with Grand Public Spaces

The central precinct, which combines civic grandeur with comfortable informality, is the most remarkable physical feature of New Castle. Overall, it measures 650 by 400 feet, an immense area compared to other civic spaces.[14] Freestanding buildings within the central area subdivide it into a complex of smaller spaces. Thus, the precinct can be viewed as a large space or a collection of smaller ones. On the southwest side is a space formed by the New Castle Court House, dating from 1732, and the adjacent town hall, dating from 1823. Set

Map 9.4. Clustered private buildings sit on narrow lots close to the street. The Green, with its complex of public buildings, is in the center. The corners of the central precinct are open, allowing views of public buildings (Sanborn map with buildings rendered black, 1912).

back from Delaware Street, these public buildings align with each other and, together with the commercial buildings opposite and buildings on Second and Third Streets, create a public space large enough for ceremonial occasions yet pleasant for individuals at other times. Views south down Second and Third Streets terminate in buildings, reinforcing the sense of spatial enclosure.

North of this space is the Green, with its expansive lawns and overarching trees. The Old Arsenal, built in 1809, separates the Green from Market Square. Further north, the Old Academy (established in 1798) groups with Immanuel Church (dating from 1704) to form a precinct similar in size to the space in front of the courthouse but different in mood. The courthouse space is paved, bustling, and commercial, while the area around the academy is landscaped, quiet, and contemplative. Free-standing and angled on its site, Immanuel Church contrasts with its surrounding buildings, which conform to the street grid. It remains distinct, separate, and sacrosanct, while the courthouse actively engages the town.

Buildings within the central area asymmetrically relate to other buildings and adjacent exterior spaces. They are free-standing in a town of row houses. These and other public buildings around the Green, especially the Presbyterian church on Second Street, built for the old Dutch Reform Congregation in 1707, have identifying roof features—cupolas, spires, and belfries. The surrounding houses and stores on Third, Harmony, Second, and Delaware Streets provide backgrounds for the prominent public buildings on the Green. Further emphasizing the importance of this area, the corners of the central precinct are open, unlike those in the residential areas, to encourage distant views of public buildings.

Immediately south of the historic district is the Battery, where, in the mid-seventeenth century, artillery guns stood to ward off Spanish raids and where,

Fig. 9.6. The present courthouse (built in 1732), town hall (built in 1823), and surrounding buildings create a space sufficient for public occasions yet pleasant for individuals (1990).

Fig. 9.7. Each of the public buildings around the Green has a distinguishing architectural feature and roof profile (1990). Top left: the town hall (1823). Top right: Immanuel Church (church, 1703; steeple, 1820). Bottom left: the Old Arsenal (building, 1809; cupola, 1852). Bottom right: the courthouse (building, 1732; cupola, after 1765).

during the War of 1812, the federal government again stationed cannons for defense. While no invasion occurred, these installations initiated public use of the area. The town filled marshes and leveled land. By 1828 the New Castle and Frenchtown Railroad had reached here, which in turn encouraged small industries—a gasworks and iron factory—to locate in this area. However, the land was still relatively open and perceived as public space, particularly along the shoreline. With the dismantling of the rail link in 1858, residents enjoyed the renewed openness of this area near the river, which, because of its low-lying topography, remained largely marshlands and woods.

In 1939 the trustees of New Castle Common bought this land, filled in the marshes, created a park with playing fields, river walks, and picnic facilities, and then gave it to the town. Offering sweeping river views and seemingly endless lawns, the park complements the intimate and formal spaces of the town. Indeed, a pleasant walk takes one from the Green and the landmark spire of Immanuel Church, down Harmony Street and within view of the river, along the Strand with its elegant townhouses, through a narrow lane such as Packet Alley (which runs from the Strand to the river and the location of the once bustling port) or through other passages that allow views into the many small and exquisite private gardens, and finally to the expansive riverfront park and its paths winding along the water. One can then return across the spacious fields of the park through other lanes to the space in front of the courthouse and its civic formality. In recent years, outsiders as much as residents have enjoyed these walks and the other recreational pleasures of Battery Park.

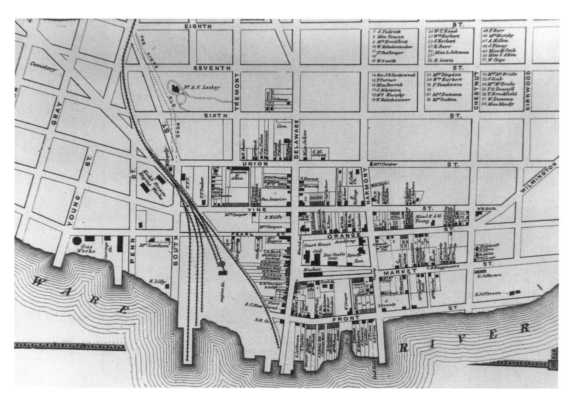

Map 9.5. In this 1868 map of New Castle, long linear lots dating from the town's Dutch settlement still characterize the town pattern. Rail lines extended to the waterfront and promoted industrial growth. In 1939, the industrial area became Battery Park (D. G. Beers, Atlas of the State of Delaware, *Delaware Public Archives*).

Fig. 9.8. Battery Park, south of the town center and overlooking the Delaware River, is now used for its playing fields and paths. In early colonial times, marshes covered the area; later, cannons on this site guarded the coast; and, in the nineteenth century, rail yards and industries occupied it (1990).

The Trustees of New Castle Common

In the early Dutch Colonial period, residents recognized the area surrounding the town where they cut wood and pastured cattle as community land. In 1704 William Penn, the English Quaker who founded Pennsylvania and was one of the Lords Proprietors, surveyed approximately one thousand acres there and confirmed its status as common land. Following years of poor land management, Penn's agents in 1764 chartered a group of wealthy citizens as the "Trustees of the Common," with terms for life to administer the lands "for use, benefit and behoof of the inhabitants of the town."[15]

This organization still exists. Acting independently of the municipal government, today's thirteen trustees, elected to twelve-year terms by property owners, manage trust-owned real estate within the town as well as in the greenbelt and surrounding area, a total of six hundred acres. As the town expanded, trustees sold land to create an endowment and leased other properties to gain income. Until 1850 the town had no municipal tax because trust lands provided sufficient income. In recent years the trust has focused on "enrichment" opportunities, usually physical improvements, that the municipal government could not otherwise support. With their holdings and influence, the trustees constitute a second level of municipal government. Regrettably, they have recently permitted strip commercial developments on properties along surrounding highways, an action that has compromised the quality and prominence of the greenbelt. For the most part, however, the trustees have wisely managed their land holdings.

Industrialization, Decline, and Stagnation

During the mid-nineteenth century, when factories began to appear along the Delaware River, the area around New Castle changed dramatically. Several factories located immediately south of town, one of which, the Tasker Iron Works, employed more than nine hundred workers. To accommodate managers and workers, the factory owners built houses that respected existing building patterns within the town. Workers themselves cast many elegant iron details that still grace the public spaces of the town.

In the latter part of the nineteenth century, New Castle stagnated, particularly compared to nearby Wilmington, which profited from its location along the seaboard rail line at a point that offered abundant water power and port capacity. New Castle relinquished state and federal courts to Wilmington in 1881.[16] As its old ambitions to become a city of consequence faded, New Castle came to rely economically on its role as an agricultural market center and fishing town. During the First World War, the munitions industry and the DuPont Company, as well as shipbuilding and foundry facilities, brought prosperity to the general Wilmington area. However, after the war, the heavy industries declined, and, while DuPont's chemical plants spread to new locations along the Delaware River near New Castle, the company's managers and scientists primarily resided in the hilly, bucolic countryside north of Wilmington.[17]

Before major pollution of the Delaware River occurred, many New Castle residents had earned their livelihood from the water. Indeed, New Castle was once known as "Fishtown." Herring, sturgeon, and, especially, shad spawned upriver every spring. Fishermen were very much part of the town, often seen drying their large nets in Battery Park and frequenting the local taverns and stores.[18] By the 1920s, as industrial wastes accumulated with that of humans, the river became significantly polluted and fishing noticeably declined. By the 1930s, fishing in New Castle was virtually nonexistent. During these decades, New Castle was an economically depressed town. People survived on what few jobs existed, and, as the Great Depression deepened, many had to look elsewhere for work. The streets and houses of New Castle deteriorated into shabby decay. To some people, the town even seemed to have become disreputable. It was a working-class, even poor, community, whose cultural heritage generally went unappreciated during these hard times.

Because change was slow to occur and the town's economy remained depressed during the first half of the twentieth century, New Castle was able to preserve its older buildings and adjust gradually to new pressures. One of the forces of change was the introduction of new forms of transportation. As early as 1897, a trolley connected New Castle to Wilmington, allowing people to commute more easily to jobs, schools, and stores in the larger city.[19] The old town became less of a self-sufficient community and more a "street car suburb." Before the state created a highway department, in 1916, county roads in the surrounding areas were not much better than they had been in the Colonial period.[20] As roads improved, people ranged more widely and comfortably, first in buses and then in automobiles. From 1925 to 1951, a ferry operated at the foot of Chestnut Street, near the location of old Fort Casimir, to transport cars traveling along the eastern seaboard across the Delaware River. The traffic passing through New Castle did not overwhelm the town, but it was enough to sustain the local economy. In 1951, the Delaware Memorial Bridge opened five miles north of town, to serve as the conduit between the New Jersey Turnpike and Interstate 95. In retrospect, if the increased bridge traffic had been routed through New Castle, it would have devastated the town.

World War II restored industrial activity in the New Castle region. Steel mills and defense contractors operated at capacity, providing full employment for residents and attracting outside workers. With the Coast Guard also active, even maritime life returned. New Castle revived as a prosperous working-class town. After the war, many workers remained to find peacetime employment in the chemical and automobile industries in this part of the region. However, land-use regulations in the surrounding county were minimal at best, permitting commercial strips and crude housing developments.[21]

Gentrification

Gradually, people came to appreciate New Castle for its traditional qualities, and the town slowly changed from a community of mixed uses and social classes to a more sedate residential enclave. This new respectability began to take hold in the mid-1920s, when the Laird family moved to New Castle and bought properties on the Strand, including the George Read II House, the great Georgian mansion originally built by the son of a signer of the Declaration of Independence. In their ambitions for the town, the Lairds and their friends restored some buildings, demolished others, and altered still others.[22] With their cousins, Irénée and Felix du Pont, the Lairds also constructed a yacht basin and tennis courts along the river and filled additional river frontage to create additional private land.[23]

In the 1930s the Lairds, along with Daniel Moore Bates and another cousin, Louise du Pont Crowninshield, discussed other possible improvements to New Castle. They consulted with the Boston architectural firm Perry, Shaw, and Hepburn, who had previously guided the restoration of Williamsburg, Virginia, and requested that the firm prepare a preservation plan for New Castle. Initially the

Fig. 9.9. Since many of the blocks are long and run parallel to the river, midblock lanes evolved to connect residential areas to the Green and the riverfront (1990).

Lairds wanted to buy the entire historic area of New Castle, as Rockefeller had done with Williamsburg, but they were unable to raise sufficient funds. Perry, Shaw, and Hepburn then convinced the group that the town would ultimately be more interesting if it was owned by many people who could all contribute to its vitality, not held under central control of a few, as was Williamsburg. The Lairds agreed, although World War II forced a postponement of their improvements.[24]

Left: *Fig. 9.10. A gate leads to one of New Castle's many secluded private gardens (1990).*
Right: *Fig. 9.11. Throughout the town, railing details recall New Castle's industrial past (1990).*

In 1946 the Lairds hired the Boston firm to conduct an architectural study of the town. The architects addressed not only issues of preservation but also those of tourism. They cataloged the existing historic town, preparing plans of the general area and detailed surveys of important buildings. They also proposed new developments such as hotels, one of which they sited in Battery Park, and parking lots for tourists. However, the Lairds did not consult with other residents before initiating the study. When the town voted on the proposals in 1948, older residents rejected them, fearing town control by a small elite who might impose unfair property restrictions based on an "official" architectural style.[25]

It took a flagrant violation of unwritten standards—in the form of a new building near the Strand—to galvanize the whole town into realizing the dangers of inappropriate design. In 1951 the town adopted a zoning ordinance and established a planning board, although it did not create its Historic Area Commission until 1968. By the early 1960s, the town was noticeably changing. Wealthy outsiders bought the larger, old houses inland from the Strand. Yet local families also remained, particularly in the smaller, working-class housing beyond Fifth Street, the current boundary of the historic district. New and old residents continued to dispute preservation policies. On the one hand, members of the gentry prided themselves on their taste and their maintenance of property values through architectural standards. On the other hand, the local, less wealthy families contended that preservation standards (for example, the need to duplicate traditional wood details when restoring a house) were an expensive burden to bear for appearances' sake. These different attitudes remain today. The

Historic Area Commission, charged with enforcing these standards but having no specific guidelines until 1990, has been the focus of these disputes.

In the last forty years, the town has lost many businesses that once served local needs. The shoe stores, barber shops, theaters, gas stations, seafood stores, butcher shops, and pool halls are now gone. Old stores have been converted to townhouses or replaced by businesses catering to tourists—primarily restaurants and gift shops clustered around the space in front of the courthouse.[26] Zoning restricts commercial activities to the west side of this space, although a few grandfathered businesses remain elsewhere in the historic district. The loss of these stores and services, once scattered throughout the town, has diminished town activity, as residents are now less likely than before to run their errands locally or as pedestrians.[27]

The town remains split regarding tourism. Merchants want to encourage more visitors and allow additional stores, restaurants, and overnight accommodations. Many even advocate capitalizing on the waterfront—for example, by opening a new marina. The gentry, who want to preserve the tranquillity of the community, have so far successfully resisted these efforts. Since Delaware is without a sales tax, New Castle's coffers would not directly benefit from more visitors, even though the town would need to provide maintenance and police services for them.

Nevertheless, compared to other historic coastal towns in this book, New Castle enjoys a remarkably good balance between competing economic and social forces. It welcomes tourists, to an extent, holding festivals and providing overnight accommodations; yet the town does not allow tourism to dominate. New Castle is now a prestigious residential community, but lower-income people still live here, on streets away from the waterfront and in houses not purchased recently. The community has lost many of its old businesses, but there are still employment opportunities and service facilities within the town, even if many of these are on the fringe. Considering its location, near Wilmington and Interstate 95, the main eastern seaboard highway, New Castle maintains a reasonable and sane balance between museum qualities, tourism, small-town character, and a livable, everyday, community environment.

Since World War II, New Castle has become, more than ever, an anomaly within the region. Industrial installations still border the quaint old town sitting on the banks of the Delaware. Across the river, huge refineries, each larger than New Castle itself, spread across the landscape. Supertankers ply the river, while, upriver, two suspension bridges arc across the Delaware River to carry endless streams of traffic. These gigantic constructions have transformed the Delaware River valley into an industrial landscape. Many farmlands with old and stately homes have disappeared, only to be replaced by acres of pipes, storage tanks, and endless suburbs.[28] New Castle stands in contrast to this new landscape, offering instead a life of intimacy and tradition in a place bounded by wetlands and within the sounds of church bells.

The town of New Castle, which has fulfilled many purposes since Peter Stuyvesant first built a fort here in 1651, also succeeds in its present role as a suburb. With its generous public spaces, prominently placed institutions, range of architectural styles, housing for people of varied incomes, and encircling open spaces, New Castle stands as a provocative model for the development of new communities and the adaptive change of old ones. Through the interaction of deliberate design, accident, and benign neglect, New Castle merged its special qualities into a singular settlement. So near to, yet separated from, the rush of contemporary life, this venerable town, once neglected and now carefully tended, offers a useful critique on many of the suburban developments we have recently built with such abandon.

South Atlantic Coastal Towns

RALEIGH●

Edenton, NC

Ocracoke, NC

New Bern, NC

Beaufort, NC

WILMINGTON

ATLANTA
●

Georgetown, SC

CHARLESTON
●

Beaufort, SC

SAVANNAH●

Darien, GA

Old Fernandina, FL

JACKSONVILLE
●

St. Augustine, FL

ORLANDO
●

Palm Beach, FL

MIAMI
●

Coral Gables, FL

Key West, FL

Map 10.1. Map of South Atlantic coastal towns discussed in Part III.
Towns in larger type are the subjects of individual chapters.

CHAPTER TEN

Overview

The barrier islands arc along the South Atlantic seaboard, first reaching out to Cape Hatteras, North Carolina, then bending progressively southwesterly, paralleling closely and finally merging with mainland North Carolina. The islands then separate again as they sweep into the waters off South Carolina and Georgia, where they reappear only to dissolve into a maze of river deltas. In Florida there are no alluvial rivers and thus no deltas. Instead, waves have built up a strip of sandy islands that shields the mainland for most of the state's length.

In North Carolina the barrier islands are long and narrow, and the few inlets there tend to shift and are treacherous to navigate. The impressive body of water behind these islands, comprising the Pamlico and Albemarle Sound complex, covers more than three thousand square miles, but because it is shallow it is impassable to all but small craft. Early colonists therefore settled from within, arriving not by the arduous sea passages but primarily overland from Virginia and South Carolina to take advantage of the cheap and fertile land in this region. Typically, the early settlements were on rivers—such as the Roanoke, Tar, and Neuse—that flow into the sounds, allowing colonists river access to interior resources, ocean connections to foreign ports, and land routes to other colonies. However, extensive flood plains and vast swamps fill the region (the Great Dismal Swamp alone covers more than 1,500 square miles), and even where dry, the land, though extraordinarily rich in nutrients, is often soft and peaty, greatly limiting habitable locations. While towns flourished during brief periods of prosperity, coastal geography thwarted their continued development and they receded into quieter times. Consequently, the towns today are still small and few in number, and the overall region is one of the more sparsely populated areas of the eastern United States.

Along the northern part of the South Carolina coast, powerful waves have caused the ancient barrier islands to join with the mainland, forming the Grand Strand. For more than sixty miles this broad, flat beach is uninterrupted by tidal inlets. Since World War II, this area has become a major playground for sun seekers. Seemingly endless resorts, hotels, motels, restaurants, golf courses, second-home developments, amusement and entertainment venues, and strip malls have arisen to serve these visitors.

Stretching from the midcoast of South Carolina through Georgia is a region of river deltas. Immediately south of the Grand Strand begins the Santee Delta, the largest on the East Coast. The Santee River and other river systems bring sediment down from the Piedmont into the mouths of the old, drowned river valleys. Because the energy of ocean waves dissipates crossing the shallow continental shelf, waves here cannot fully disperse the rivers' sediment, which instead has built up into a complex of islands. The seaward sides of these islands, washed by the Atlantic, have wide, flat beaches that sweep up into dunes anchored by sea oats and knotted with bent live oaks, while the mainland sides, worked by tidal action and river flow, are labyrinths of marshes that host a spectacular variety of wildlife. The climate of the islands is subtropical, and late summer and early fall sometimes bring hurricanes that tear through the region and shatter the tranquillity.

Some historic coastal towns are located within this complex of waterways, sheltered from the periodic fury of the open Atlantic but connected by the river systems to both inland plantations and the deep waters of the Atlantic. South Carolina was settled, for the most part, by people from the West Indies. As the geographer and historian D. W. Meinig states,

> Carolina was essentially 'the colony of a colony,' primarily an offspring of Barbados, a reaching out from the constrictions of that congested little island to the expansive possibilities of the continent . . . the most influential body came directly from that richest of English colonies, and they drew upon that successful experience in the hope of generating the same kind of sudden wealth on an even larger scale . . . in a broad sense, they agreed on the fundamental idea of a strongly hierarchical social and political system featuring a small landed gentry and a large subordinate body of laborers.[1]

Benefiting from a growing season that stretches to 290 days, along with the region's fertile soil and abundant rain, this system proved immensely rewarding for the dominating society.

The coastal geography of Georgia is similar to that of South Carolina. However, Georgia began with different leadership. In 1732 the English Crown granted James Oglethorpe and his associates an immense tract of land between the Savannah and Altamaha Rivers. Oglethorpe sought to create a refuge for English subjects unfairly treated by the country's penal system and for those suffering religious persecution. In granting Oglethorpe the land, the Crown also hoped to create new markets for home manufactures and set up a buffer against the Spanish forces in Florida. Although Oglethorpe's experiment lasted only until 1751, he founded several settlements which reveal his philanthropic interests in their town plans.

As early as 1513 the Spanish sailed north from the Caribbean Islands to explore coastal Florida. Here they established missions to control the Indians and a few outposts to protect their shipping routes to Europe. With the noteworthy exception of Saint Augustine, none of these early settlements survived, and the Spanish never successfully colonized Florida. Not until the early twentieth century did Florida significantly develop, but, since World War II, it has done so with such alarming speed that larger-scale planning has been difficult.

I selected three historic towns to represent the South Atlantic region: Edenton, North Carolina, possesses beautiful public spaces, particularly its Courthouse Green and lower Main Street area. It also combines a wide range of housing styles and types into a delightful set of neighborhoods. Beaufort, South Carolina, embodies the pride, even what some might call arrogance, of antebellum South Carolina. Today it offers an instructive model for other coastal towns seeking to revive their waterfronts. Saint Augustine, Florida, is a living lesson in Spanish Colonial town planning. It is overlaid with the architecture of succeeding generations, as well as the nostalgic legacy of one of America's great industrialists, Henry Flagler, a founder of the Standard Oil Company.

North Carolina

The Outer Banks

The transitory nature of the Outer Banks has directly affected the cultural history of North Carolina. Over the past four hundred years, storm surges and high tides have opened up at least thirty inlets through the barrier islands only to have them refilled as sediments collect from rivers draining into the sea. Among these, two historically important inlets closed during the early nineteenth century—the one at Roanoke, in 1811, and the one at Currituck, in 1828—both of which had provided shipping access to the northern coastal regions of Albemarle Sound. After these closings, trade shifted to Ocracoke Inlet, seventy-five miles south of Roanoke Inlet, and then, as that too silted, to Oregon and Hatteras Inlets, which opened in 1846 between the former inlets at Roanoke and Currituck. The shifting inlets resulted in corresponding population movements along the Outer Banks. Furthermore, because the different inlets gave access to different sounds and rivers to the west, one and then another of the mainland ports was favored, such that no one port retained significance for any extended period of time—except in the southern part of the state at Wilmington, which had continuing direct access along the Cape Fear River to the sea.

On the Outer Banks, the first successful permanent settlements were not established until the mid-seventeenth century. Colonists favored forested areas behind protecting dunes on the sound, particularly along the northern stretches of the barrier islands between the former Currituck and Roanoke Inlets. These settlers sustained themselves with the oil they extracted from beached whales, the lumber they cut from the live oak, cedar, and pine forests (which they soon depleted), and the livestock they grazed on the confined islands.

The first vacationers appeared here as early as 1750, and the first hotel rose on Nags Head in 1838. The hotel owners and those of the early cottages also located their buildings along Roanoke Sound rather than facing the Atlantic, because, like the early colonists, they feared the fury of ocean storms. After the

Civil War, families of merchants, planters, and professionals from the mainland began to construct cottages along the oceanfront.

For generations, their descendants returned to repair and enjoy those houses and watch the ocean's edge encroach. Along the shore and also in many inland locations, typical cottages, then as today, were set on tall wooden piles to raise them above storm tides, some of which wash entirely across the barrier islands. Remarkably, the present-day mile-long Beach Cottage Row at Nags Head, lined with weathered wood-shingled frame buildings wrapped in airy porches, still survives to recall this late-nineteenth- and early-twentieth-century era of isolation and exclusivity, although many other more recent developments in the region have not lasted so long.[2]

In 1928 a bridge was built connecting Nags Head and Roanoke Island; it was soon followed in 1931 by a bridge from Roanoke Island to the mainland. The Outer Banks, which previously were accessible only by water, were now open to oceanfront resort development and tourists in automobiles. Fearing the consequences of extensive development, particularly after a devastating hurricane in 1933 had destroyed many beach houses and opened new inlets, conservationists proposed government acquisition of land. This proposal finally became reality in 1953, when the Mellon family, with matching funds from the state of North Carolina, helped establish the Cape Hatteras National Seashore; comprising thirty thousand acres, the protected area includes most of the Outer Banks between Nags Head and Ocracoke Inlet, except for six previously existing villages in that area. In 1966, to continue the preservation effort, the Cape Lookout National Seashore was authorized, which reaches fifty-eight miles south, from Ocracoke Inlet to Beaufort, North Carolina. Currently inaccessible to cars, the shore remains largely in its natural state. The National Park Service administers these properties, as well as the Fort Raleigh National Historical Site, on Roanoke Island, and the Wright Brothers National Memorial, near Kitty Hawk Village.

Roanoke Island, known in early American history as the site of the Elizabethan Lost Colony, is eleven miles long and two miles wide. The island lies between the Croatan and Roanoke Sounds two miles west of the Outer Banks and four miles east of the mainland. On the northern tip of this island, protected by the Outer Banks from the harsh winds and surf of the open Atlantic, colonists in 1584 established the first English settlement in what would become the United States. Between 1584 and 1591, seven colonial expeditions, six of which Sir Walter Raleigh sponsored, sought to establish a colony here. When the last expedition returned from England in 1591 with fresh supplies, it found no trace of the 116 men, women, and children who had been left on the island. It was never discovered what became of the settlers, and the short-lived venture became known as the Lost Colony. The exact site of the settlement is unknown, although it probably now lies under the water of the Roanoke Sound. The earthworks of the island's small fort, however, have been reconstructed on the foundations of the original and are now part of the Fort Raleigh National Historic Site, established in 1941.

The town of *Manteo* (pop. 991) is named after one of the two Algonquin Indians who returned in 1585 to England from Roanoke Island with the initial English expedition. Situated three miles south of the Lost Colony fort, the town dates only from the 1870s, when a wooden courthouse was built on the shore of Shallowbag Bay to serve Dare County and became the nucleus of a small village. The current brick courthouse, built in 1904, remains a focal point, albeit of a larger community that has grown up along the road connecting the Outer Banks to the mainland. The courthouse, with a neighboring inn, shops, condominiums, a public pier, and a boardwalk along the marshes, forms a compact waterfront complex. From the boardwalk there are immediate views to the east of the Elizabeth II State Historical Site across the narrow bay, where the *Elizabeth II* (a replica of an Elizabethan ship built locally for the 400th anniversary of the Lost Colony) is anchored, and distant views beyond that to the Outer Banks, where long stretches of contemporary development line the shores of Nags Head.[3]

Although most of the land south of Oregon Inlet on Hatteras Island lies within the Cape Hatteras National Seashore, several communities of privately owned land exist within the national park and have become centers for vacation home development. Just south of the Pea Island National Wildlife Refuge are the adjacent villages of *Rodanthe* (pop. 270), *Waves* (pop. 120), and *Salvo* (pop. 190), which spread along the highway and across the sandy breadth of the barrier island. Further south, *Avon* (pop. 550) was once a thickly forested area, but intensive cutting for shipbuilding there in the early nineteenth century resulted in a sparse landscape dominated by vacation houses.

In *Buxton* (pop. 1,300), commonly called "the Cape" in the nineteenth century because it lies at the "elbow" of Hatteras Island, buildings group around sound-side docks and along the highway. To the west is an extensive maritime forest known as Buxton Woods or Hatteras Woods, where live oak, red cedar, and holly trees grow along dune ridges that once formed the old shoreline. Today approximately nine square miles of this forest are protected by the National Park Service.

East of Buxton on the oceanside and also owned by the federal government is the local landmark of the area and icon for the Outer Banks—the Cape Hatteras Lighthouse. Rising 208 feet, it is the tallest lighthouse in the United States. With a light visible twenty miles out to sea, it warned ships of the dangerous Diamond Shoals, a complex of shallow sandbars formed where the warmer Gulf Stream from the south meets the colder currents from the north. The shoals are also know as the "Graveyard of the Atlantic" owing to all the ships that have sunk in the area. A storm in 1980 washed away the last foundation remnants of the previous lighthouse, which, when it was erected in 1802, was presumed to be located at a safe distance from the coastline (one mile inland). The present lighthouse, built in 1870 at one-quarter mile from the sea, is now seriously threatened by the ocean, which has since crept to within one hundred feet of its foundations. The National Park Service has ambitions (although the plan is controversial) to move this old structure inland to higher and, at least for the near future, safer ground.

In *Hatteras* (pop. 1,000), southwest of Buxton, buildings spread across the wooded island and group along the highway, around the inlet off the sound, and near the Hatteras-Ocracoke Ferry landing and adjacent Coast Guard Station. This village, like those to the north, is rapidly changing as new developments are built in the few remaining enclaves of privately owned land. Yet under the pressure of unrelenting natural forces, the land is migrating and changing shape, challenging the wisdom of long-term investments there.

Ocracoke Village (pop. 650) is, to many, the most coherent, identifiable, and memorable of the Outer Bank communities. It is also the most remote, lying twenty miles off the mainland. Automobiles can access Ocracoke only by ferry. Unlike the developments further north that stretch along the highway, Ocracoke wraps around a small body of water known locally as Silver Lake. This seemingly stable setting is in the center of an otherwise precarious natural environment. The village, encompassing 775 acres, is on the sound side of Ocracoke Island, a sandy strip sixteen miles long that comprises a total of 5,535 acres and is part of the Cape Hatteras National Seashore. The village owes its existence to Ocracoke Inlet, one mile south—one of the three Outer Bank inlets that have been continuously open since the sixteenth century. It is the only one that, in the last two centuries, has allowed access to the central and northern ports of North Carolina.

While crews from Raleigh's Roanoke expedition landed at Ocracoke in 1585 to explore the island, subsequent settlers preferred the mainland rather than the wind-swept, storm-prone, and defenseless Outer Banks. An act of the Colonial Assembly in 1715, requiring pilots to navigate ships through the Outer Banks, encouraged settlement on Ocracoke, as well as on Portsmouth Island on the opposite side of the inlet.[4] Settlement, however, was slow. Pirates and crews from vessels sailing along the coast harassed the settlers and raided their livestock, which roamed free on the island. The 1790 census recorded seventy-five island residents; twenty years later the population had grown to 209, most of whom were still involved with piloting services. As coastal trade grew prior to the Civil War, shipwrecks also increased off the Outer Banks. Ironically, lumber intended for East Coast cities and the West Indies washed ashore and became construction materials for island houses and ships.[5]

In the late nineteenth and early twentieth centuries, as Ocracoke Inlet became shallower and coastal trade consolidated with the growth of railroad connections at the ports of Norfolk, Virginia, and Wilmington, North Carolina (both of which had more direct access to the sea than other North Carolina ports), Ocracoke came to rely less on piloting and more on fishing to sustain itself economically. However, World War II and the threat of German U-boats to shipping lanes along the coast brought transformations to the village. To accommodate patrol boats, the federal government, first in 1931 and then more thoroughly in 1942, dredged the tidal creek that ran through a marshy meadow in the center of town and reshaped the tidal marshes surrounding the creek into Silver Lake. The military brought in electricity and telephones and also built the first paved roads on the island—from the new deepwater docks along the lake to ammunitions dumps outside of the village. In 1959 the island saw its first regular ferry service to the mainland, and a road running the length of the island was paved. In 1977, to replace the cisterns that each house traditionally had maintained to store fresh water, the village built a central water system that, in turn, established an infrastructure for restaurants, hotels, and vacation cottages and helped shape the growing tourist economy of today.

Rimming Silver Lake today is a string of buildings that includes the U.S. Coast Guard Station, a National Park Service Visitor Center, the ferry landing, motels, restaurants, shops, condominiums, and cottages. Several of the new motels and condominiums rise decisively—and unfortunately—above the treeline, heights previously reached only by the lighthouse and water tower, allowing those two structures to serve appropriately as navigational and civic landmarks. Howard Street, on the east side of town, is still an unpaved, dusty lane edged with fences that enclose the sandy front yards of many typical one-and-a-half story houses. These homes are set on blocks and have trap doors, or at least holes in the floor, to allow floodwaters to rise through the houses rather than lift them off their foundations. With its thick canopy of live oak trees, Howard Street recalls the former, isolated, inward-oriented character of the village, so different from the character of buildings emerging around the lake.[6] Yet, surrounding them all are the shifting sands of the Outer Banks, which complicate long-range planning and cause many to question the wisdom of any further development on this remote barrier island.

The Mainland

Because of the navigational barriers of the Outer Banks and the changing inlets that endangered shipping, coastal settlements on the mainland of North Carolina, including those on the rivers flowing into the sounds, became, over time, a dispersed constellation of towns and villages of more or less equal importance. Even today, no one major city dominates coastal North Carolina, making the region particularly atypical among others on the Atlantic.

Until recently, the remote locations of many North Carolina historic coastal towns have saved them from the ravages of tourism, although not always from the impact of industrialization. However, today's improved highways and the Intracoastal Waterway are bringing more visitors to the old towns dotted along the tidal rivers, creeks, and bays of the state.

Located on the Pasquotank River on the northern side of Albemarle Sound,

Elizabeth City (pop. 14,292) was incorporated in 1793, the year in which construction began on the nearby Dismal Swamp Canal. The town's present building character dates from the 1880s to the 1920s, when the community prospered as a regional commercial and social center. Platted on twenty-five-foot-wide building lots, Elizabeth City has an unusually high density for a southern coastal town. It also has an excellent inland harbor and is in the process of developing a waterfront park along its river.[7]

West of Elizabeth City is *Hertford*, (pop. 2,105), a courthouse town incorporated in 1758 that sits on a slight rise of land bounded by the meandering Perquimans River. Settlers from Virginia, other colonies to the north, and England migrated here. A prominent group among these seventeenth-century settlers were the Quakers, although many of them left after the American Revolution as slavery became a contentious issue. Hertford has glorious tree-shaded streets, which complement its enviable collection of antebellum houses.[8]

On the southern side of Albemarle Sound is *Plymouth* (pop. 4,328), an old port town that was laid out in 1787 on the Roanoke River. Severely damaged during the Civil War and, more recently, transformed by a nearby paper mill and an outlying commercial strip, the town still has its magnificent Washington County Courthouse, a hauntingly beautiful church (designed in the Gothic Revival style by Richard Upjohn and built in 1860–61), the impressive New Chapel Baptist Church (built in 1924 for the African American community), and the Roanoke River, in all its quiet grandeur.

Further east, on the south bank of the Scuppernong River, lies *Columbia* (pop. 836), which dates from 1791 and is the seat of Tyrrell County, the least populous county in North Carolina. A fishing and lumbering village, Columbia now has a new boardwalk, stretching more than a half mile across its waterfront and along the edge of an adjacent park and marsh.

West of Pamlico Sound, where the Tar River widens to form the Pamlico River, the town of *Washington* (pop. 8,418) was laid out in 1775. During the next several decades, it thrived by shipping naval supplies to the West Indies, becoming an official port of entry with its own custom house. Much of the town, however, was destroyed during the Civil War and then rebuilt in the late nineteenth and early twentieth centuries. Although its waterfront is now covered with parking lots, the nearby business district boasts a rich collection of turn-of-the-century commercial and civic buildings.

Further east of Washington is *Bath* (pop. 154), which is currently only a hamlet but was North Carolina's first incorporated town (1705) and a former province capital. Still within its boundaries are many of its eighteenth-century buildings, and the community retains much of its old village charm.

New Bern (pop. 17,363) rests on a low bluff at the confluence of the Neuse and Trent Rivers, thirty-five miles from the Atlantic Ocean. In 1710, a Swiss baron led a group of German Protestants in founding the town, which, for defensive as well as religious reasons, they laid out in a cruciform plan, with one street connecting the two riverfronts and the other running from the rivers' junction into the wilderness. For most of the period 1765–90, New Bern was the colonial and then state capital of North Carolina. Built in 1767–70, the Governor's Palace, or Tryon Palace, as it is known today, was one of the grandest public buildings in the southern colonies.[9] Destroyed by fire in 1798, it was meticulously rebuilt in the 1950s and has again become an important feature of the community and is open to the public.

Spared during the Civil War, New Bern also avoided the destruction that industrialization brought to the historic qualities of many towns. The region's lumber industry flourished from the 1870s to the 1920s and attracted considerable wealth, which helped grace the town with remarkably fine architecture. Today New Bern arguably contains North Carolina's richest, albeit eclectic, collection of historic urban architecture. Building examples range from stately Georgian brick mansions to humble clapboard cottages.[10] Regrettably, in the late 1960s and early 1970s extensive waterfront areas were cleared and have been rebuilt at a larger scale with motels, parking lots, and boating facilities. The disconnected riverfront now appears to belong more to the passing tourists and yachtsmen than to the town that was once so intimately related to its beautiful rivers.

Although it possesses an excellent natural harbor, *Beaufort* (pop. 3,826), unlike New Bern, has not had the benefit of a major river to access inland resources. Laid out in 1722, the town remained isolated, grew slowly, and enjoyed no periods of great wealth. It lacked a road connection to the mainland until 1927, and neighboring Morehead City, across the harbor, absorbed most of the industrial and transportation facilities that gravitated to the region. However, Beaufort's isolation and slow growth protected it. Today the main highway from the bridge connecting it to Morehead City does not infringe upon the historic district. The waterfront was rebuilt in the 1960s, when rotting buildings were cleared and replaced with a riverfront boardwalk, new commercial activities, and pockets of parking. Across a narrow waterway and immediately adjacent and parallel to the waterfront is an island marine sanctuary created by the U.S. Army Corps of Engineers' dredging operations. This island complex is a nature conservancy and a rich habitat for birds on the Atlantic flyway. Its quiet beauty and natural features are a delightful contrast to Beaufort's waterfront. A marvelous range of natural and historic environments now coexist.

In the southern part of the state, just inland from the coast, are two more historic towns. The old fishing village of *Swansboro* (pop. 976) was settled around 1770 at the mouth of White Oak River, near an inlet from the Atlantic Ocean. The community has an unusual compactness for a tidewater town, and the topography slopes up unexpectedly, allowing buildings on the higher ground to overlook the roofs of those farther seaward. *Southport* (pop. 2,824), established in the late 1740s, became home to the pilots who have traditionally guided ships up the Cape Fear River to Wilmington. In recent years, a nuclear power station has overshadowed the town.

Settlers began to venture into the Cape Fear River area around 1665, although they did not establish *Wilmington* (pop. 55,530) until 1730. Located at the junction of two branches of the Cape Fear River, thirty miles inland from its mouth (but only eight miles west, overland, of the Outer Banks), Wilmington was considered part of the Port of Brunswick; authorities at that time designated an area as a port rather than a specific settlement.[11] Throughout Wilmington's early history and until the railroads arrived, in 1840, linking it to the growing interior cities, the river was the corridor of communication between this town and its region. The Cape Fear River had the advantage of being the only major river in North Carolina that flowed directly into the ocean, an early benefit for Wilmington as well as for other settlements along the river. However, riverborne sediment, exacerbated in part by farming and urbanization, accumulated at the river's mouth to form the treacherous Frying Pan Shoals, which, along with the narrow river channel, inhibited the passage of larger ships and thus prevented Wilmington from growing into a major port.

Now a booming small city, Wilmington has at its heart a historic district with the qualities of a coastal town. This district steps up the steep eastern slope of the narrow river valley to form a community defined by its topography and its tidal river orientation. Graceful streets are enhanced by a rich collection of buildings, most of which survive from the town's period of prosperity, 1840 to 1910, when it was the largest city in North Carolina. Although architectural styles vary, the town is unified by its common details of brick paving, ironwork, and statuary, and by the softening landscape of the region, in which subtropical live oaks, oleanders, Spanish moss, and even palmetto palms mix with the pine forests of the Piedmont.

South Carolina

As far back as 10,000 years ago, Paleo-Indians lived along the South Atlantic coast and inhabited the region that would become South Carolina. While they and their descendants created a distinct culture here, waters inundated many prehistoric settlements as melting glaciers raised the sea level and flooded the coastline thirty to sixty miles inland.[12] By the late seventeenth century, soon after the arrival of European colonists, the Indians in the region—those of Siouan stock to the north of the Santee River and those of Muskhogean stock to the south—were greatly reduced in number and even approached extinction. However, the names these Indians gave to the river and surrounding places—Coosaw, Combahee, Pocotaligo, among many others—still survive to record their presence here and evoke the character of the region.

The European attempts at colonization and control brought first the Spanish, then the French, then the Spanish again, and finally the English to South Carolina. In 1521 Lucas Vasquez de Ayllon of Toledo, Spain, arrived with five hundred colonists at an undetermined location, possibly near the mouth of the Savannah River or St. Catherine's Sound, Georgia (the settlement did not last through the following winter).[13] In 1562 Jean Ribaut and a party of French Huguenots sailed north along the coast, naming rivers and bodies of water—one of which still retains its French-given name, Port Royal, identifying the place Ribaut and his men came ashore.[14] The party landed on present-day Parris Island (this name belongs to a much later owner) and built Charlesfort, a 160-by-130-foot encampment.[15] Although it survived less than a year, Charlesfort became the site of the second Spanish attempt at settlement, Santa Elena, established in 1566 by Don Pedro Menéndez de Avilés, who a year earlier had founded Saint Augustine, Florida. The Spanish presence in South Carolina lasted until 1587, when the Spanish retrenched to Saint Augustine as English influence grew in this region.

After the Restoration, with Charles II's advancement to the throne in 1660, the English aggressively pursued their territorial ambitions along the South Atlantic coast, basing their claims to all of North America on John Cabot's 1497 landfall in Nova Scotia. In 1663 the king granted a land charter to eight Lords Proprietors who had supported his claim to the throne. These grants included territories along the southern coast of the mainland and some of the Caribbean islands, most notably the strongly royalist Barbados and, later, the Bahamas. In 1663 Captain William Hilton, who would later give his name to Hilton Head Island, sailed into St. Helena Sound and explored part of South Carolina. In 1670 William Sayle, a leader of the Bahamian colony, founded Charles Towne on a low bluff overlooking the Ashley River north of today's Charleston. The nearby Oyster Point, a more strategically located peninsula in the Charleston Harbor bounded by the Ashley and Cooper Rivers, however, became the site of the colony's major city. Anthony Ashley-Cooper, one of the Lords Proprietors, in 1672 gave instructions for the layout of the town in this location.

The eighteenth-century town that developed here as *Charleston* (pop. 80,414), which essentially comprises the old section of the present-day city, has impressed visitors with its gracious livability for generations. Although its plan emphasizes civic features such as the waterfront promenade and park, known since the War of 1812 as "the Battery," and St. Michael's Episcopal Church (dating from 1752), it is the unique house type that evolved there to meet urban living conditions in this subtropical climate that cumulatively unifies the community.

The Charleston "single house," the most pervasive type in the community, is one room wide and two rooms deep, with a bisecting stair and hall. The narrow gable ends of these houses are turned flush to the street, and the rooms open to walled side-gardens. The houses are sited on the side property line, either to the north or to the east depending on the block location, to capture prevailing southwest winds and maximize enjoyment of the garden spaces. Piazzas—open porches or galleries—line the houses on the garden sides and serve as functional interfaces between the interior and exterior spaces of the house. The formal entrance does not lead directly into the house but, through a door off the street, into the piazza or garden. Typically three stories high, the houses sit on elevated basements that provide ventilation, an area for services, and protection from water in this flood-prone region. This house type lends itself to dense but livable urban residential patterns that support civic activities, helps establish beautiful streets that feature the alternating rhythms of house fronts and walled gardens, and offers comfortable, well-ventilated houses.[16]

Charleston dominated the social, cultural, and commercial life in South Carolina more than did any other city in any other American colony. Several other coastal communities in South Carolina nevertheless developed as smaller centers of trade and shipping and also served as places where planters could escape the tropical afflictions of their swampy coastal properties to enjoy, if Charleston was too distant, the social and political life of, at least, a small town community. Of these, Georgetown, McClellanville, Rockville, Beaufort, and Bluffton are notable.

Georgetown (pop. 10,144) lies at the head of Winyah Bay, into or near which five river systems flow, funneling the trade of 80,000 square miles into its port.[17] Established by the English in 1721, the small port thrived on exports of indigo and especially rice (around 1850 it was the largest exporter of rice in the world). However, shifting sand bars restricted the size of ships entering the bay and thwarted the port town's growth. Today the original grid plan, with five broad streets running parallel to the Sampit River, still orders the town. A new boardwalk along the river behind the buildings that face Front Street has revived the waterfront, while a range of buildings dating back to approximately 1740 reflects the community's long history. Perpendicular streets terminate in small parks along Front Street and extend into the nearby residential areas, where churches at street corners mark the centers of neighborhoods. To the southeast, a huge paper pulp mill processes the rich timber supplies of the region, providing employment but depreciating the town's historic qualities.

South of Georgetown and surrounded today by the Francis Marion National Forest is *McClellanville* (pop. 366*), which began in the early 1850s as a summer community. Numerous houses with double-tiered verandahs to catch the cooling breezes are casually set under giant live oak trees along the main street, which ends in a little park at the water's edge. The natural wood, Gothic Revival style Episcopal Church and the early-twentieth-century brick school are the most recognizable architectural features in this town otherwise consisting of white-painted clapboard houses.

Originally the site of an old plantation on a bluff overlooking Bohicket Creek, *Rockville* (pop. 160*) was laid out as a community between 1809 and 1824. It also served as a shipping transfer point for cotton being transported to Charleston and as a way station for planters making that same journey, and it flourished as a summer retreat for these same gentlemen and their families. Today, sandy streets wind among live oak trees hung with Spanish moss, leading to the houses that, though varying in size, are unified by spacious porches, raised foundations, and large central halls that alleviate the summer heat. Two antebellum churches within the village have long served as centers for the community, while a newer yacht club on the town's edge is a more recent focus of activity.

Other nineteenth-century rice and cotton planters brought their families to *Bluffton* (pop. 541) to enjoy the refreshing breezes and social life in this small village. It was built on the cove-indented banks of the May River and has structures dating from around 1815 and a road pattern from the 1830s and 1840s. The ravages of the Civil War left two-thirds of the village destroyed, but steamboat service and eventually roads revived the community. Today, small-scale vernacular wood buildings, highlighted by a Carpenter Gothic style church that survived the Civil War, spread out under the deep shade of live oak trees.

Georgia

The 150-mile coastline of Georgia is split by four major rivers—the Savannah, Ogeechee, Altamaha, and St. Marys—which flow to the southeast and fan out to embrace wide deltas at their mouths. On the way to the Atlantic, their waters thread through great expanses of sea marsh and around sizable barrier islands, the best known of which are Ossabaw, St. Catherine's, Sapelo, St. Simons, Jekyll, and Cumberland. Hugging the coast, these islands are densely forested with longleaf pines, moss-hung oaks, magnolias, palms, palmettos, cypress, and cedar trees. Although swampy, this tidewater region has supplied naval stores and supported the growth of rice, indigo, and the prized Sea Island cotton. Georgia retained the aspects of a border country even as its way of life merged with that of South Carolina. Comparatively few coastal towns developed in Georgia, although the few that did are notable for the philanthropic, even utopian, intents on which they were planned.

The English acquired the colony's land from the Indians in a series of three treaties, the first of which came about in 1733. General James Oglethorpe, who earlier had gained prominence as the head of a Parliamentary investigation of England's squalid prison conditions, established a group to found a colony for imprisoned debtors. In 1733 the Crown granted Oglethorpe a twenty-one-year trusteeship of land in the newly acquired territory. Using this opportunity, Oglethorpe and his group oversaw the planning of five main towns there: Savannah, Darien, Augusta, Frederica, and Ebenezer. While the last two were largely destroyed during the American Revolution and soon thereafter became "dead towns," Savannah, the first to be settled, became a model not only for the other towns organized by Oglethorpe but also, after the first royal governor arrived in

1754, for later colonial towns in Georgia. Regrettably, Savannah did not become a model for subsequent American town planning because, unlike New York City and Philadelphia, it did not lie along the route of national expansion.[18]

General Oglethorpe and his followers selected the site for *Savannah* (pop. 137,560) on a bluff along the Savannah River eighteen miles inland from the Atlantic. The former location of an Indian settlement, this site had the benefits of a deepwater port and flat, drained land on which to develop a community with generous public open spaces, one that would be an opposite to the crowded, unsanitary conditions Oglethorpe witnessed in English prisons.[19] By setting the town on a bluff, Oglethorpe also disengaged the life of the town from that of the waterfront, where the warehouses, wharves, and waiting ships dominated activity.

Drawing on Georgian town planning principles, the Olgethorpe plan incorporates a systematic set of landscaped public squares, each 315 by 270 feet, tied together by a hierarchy of streets that defines locations for different types of buildings.[20] Broad, central streets enter the four sides of the squares, around which are located major buildings—churches, civic buildings, and mansions. These streets encourage pedestrian and visual connections between neighboring squares. Secondary streets pass along the sides of the squares and provide sites for row houses.[21] Running between pairs of squares are through streets, which permit uninterrupted passage through the city as well as locations for services. Finally, alleys pass behind the blocks of houses, allowing service to them. In Savannah, Oglethorpe established a unique town pattern that was commodious, intimate, versatile, and expandable. It set the pattern for other towns in Georgia, particularly those along the coast.

Overlooking a branch of the Altamaha River, near its mouth, *Darien* (pop. 1,731) rests on a bluff where Indians had a village and, it is believed, Spaniards had a mission-presidio in the sixteenth and seventeenth centuries.[22] Settled by Scottish Highlanders in 1736 and initially named New Inverness, Darien served as a buffer against Spanish encroachments from Florida. In the early nineteenth century the town was the state's most important shipping center for lumber and naval stores. After damaging fires in 1824 and 1825 and with the growth of better inland roads, Darien, which lacked a good harbor, lost trade to Augusta and Savannah. During the Civil War, the entire town was burned down by Union soldiers, a calamity from which it never fully recovered. Today it is a sleepy town with sandy streets. The Oglethorpe ideas, however, remain apparent in its plan. Three squares still exist, one of which centers on a church, but none have the density of Savannah to define spatially the character of the square. Ruins on the waterfront are reminders of the warehouses, shops, and taverns that lined the shore during the early nineteenth century. A public stair down to the waterfront and a boardwalk along the river once again make the waterfront a feature of the town.

Brunswick (pop. 16,433) is noteworthy as the last town the British established in their colonization efforts. It was laid out in 1771, and, similar to Darien, it was based on the town planing principles of Savannah. Unlike Darien, however, Brunswick had an excellent harbor on a small river and prospered in the latter part of the nineteenth century because of its railroad connections. Broad streets, some with landscaped medians, that serve as through routes similar to those in Savannah, are lined with palm and oak trees. The squares of the Oglethorpe-inspired plan, however, have lost their integrity, and many no longer exist at all. Public buildings such as City Hall and the Glynn County Courthouse occupy two of the squares, and in the residential area streets bisect the squares rather than purposefully passing around their sides, as in Savannah. Along Newcastle Street, the improvements of the public right-of-way and the adjacent buildings are reviving the old main business district and offering an alternative to the parking lots that otherwise have dominated the center of town in recent years.

Situated on the river of the same name, *St. Marys* (pop. 3,596) lies on the southern border of the state near a location where Indians previously had a village. Established in 1787, the community prospered as a sea town and provided wood for shipbuilding centers. Osborne Street, the main commercial street, features a rich mixture of buildings, including the First Presbyterian Church, built in 1808, and Orange Hall, built in the years 1829–33. Osborne Street passes through the center of town, to end at a public pavilion that overlooks the shrimp and pleasure boats in the harbor and the river activity on the waterfront. The town is now the Atlantic coast headquarters of the Trident Submarine. Fortunately, the naval base and a paper mill are located sufficiently beyond the historic district such that they do not compromise the character of the old town.

Florida

Geologically more akin to its southern neighbors, the Caribbean Islands, than to the North American mainland to which it is attached, Florida was the first of the states to be explored by Europeans, yet it was the last region along the east coast to be settled. First sighted by Juan Ponce de León when he sailed north from Puerto Rico in 1513, Florida had long been inhabited by Indians who had settled there probably as early as 5,000 B.C. The Spanish established a chain of outposts along the coast for their Caribbean empire, although, with the outstanding exception of Saint Augustine, little evidence of those settlements exists today. Throughout the nineteenth century, Florida remained remote and thinly settled. In the 1880s Henry M. Flagler began building his East Coast Railroad and, with it, a string of luxury hotels south along the coast. He introduced tourism to Florida, and development soon followed.

Within a brief period of time, the Florida real estate boom of the 1920s had attracted an influx of people into the state, which prompted the dredging of marshes and bays to create more land for development. After having abruptly ended in 1926 with the first wave of the Great Depression, the migration of people from the north, many of them retirees, revived after World War II and continues today. The growing population has also been reinforced in recent years by immigrants from the Caribbean. Because of its recent settlement and the accelerated pace at which this settlement has occurred, few historic towns exist in Florida today. Those that do, however, are remarkable for the variety they represent.

Old Fernandina (pop. 100*) and its larger offspring one mile away, *Fernandina Beach* (pop. 8,765), are on Amelia Island, in the extreme northeast corner of Florida across the St. Marys River from Georgia. In 1686 the Spanish built a small fort and mission near the site, which had an excellent natural harbor close to the Atlantic. Long a part of territorial disputes, Old Fernandina was destroyed by a British force from South Carolina in 1702. The British established a new settlement at this location in the 1760s, but the area did not grow until the 1850s, when rail lines were built to ship yellow pine from the interior to this port. Rather than expand Old Fernandina, which was surrounded by marshes, railroad managers laid out Fernandina Beach in a grid plan, and the town grew out from the depot and the docks. The new town prospered with further extensions of the railroad, although after the Civil War it was eclipsed as a regional center by Jacksonville, thirty-two miles to the south. Fernandina today has one of the best collections of nineteenth-century architecture in Florida, as well as another legacy from its past, the pulp factories that still process pine wood brought from the interior.

Approximately one hundred miles south of Fernandina and fifty miles south of Saint Augustine is Volusia County, where the towns of *Ormond Beach* (pop. 29,721) and *Daytona Beach* (pop. 61,921) lie adjacent to each other along the Halifax River, which separates the mainland from the barrier island to the east. Eight to ten thousand years ago, Timucuan Indians lived in this area and left burial mounds, still evident but little noticed today. By 1587 Franciscan Friars had established missions in this area, but these ruins have not survived. Successive attempts to raise indigo, rice, and sugarcane also failed. However, one of the planters, James Ormond, a Scotsman from the Bahamas, is remembered in the community's name. The major impetus for land development came in the late 1880s when Henry Flagler's East Coast Railroad extended south to this area. Flagler coordinated railroad building with hotel development, purchasing and enlarging the Ormond Hotel in 1890. As in Saint Augustine, Flagler attracted the wealthy to the pleasures of wintering here. John D. Rockefeller, Flagler's former partner, particularly appreciated the area and its low-pollen atmosphere. In 1918 he purchased "the Casements" and made it his winter residence for the remaining twenty years of his life. Today, this house is a cultural and civic center and an architectural feature of the town.

In 1871 Mathias Day from Ohio bought an old plantation and laid out the town of Daytona. While the railroad also spurred development here in the 1880s, it was the automobile that later defined the character and image of the town. Because the beach is five hundred feet wide and tides have packed the gentle white sandy slope into a hard surface ideal for racing, cars have raced on it since 1902. The downtown area is now a federally designated historic district.

Sixty miles south of Daytona Beach are Cape Canaveral and the Kennedy Space Center. Since 1950 the U.S. Air Force and, subsequently, the National Aeronautics and Space Administration (NASA) have launched long-range guided missiles and space explorations from here. NASA's installations are surrounded by approximately 200,000 acres of wilderness area in the Merritt Island National Wildlife Refuge and the Canaveral National Seashore, where over five hundred animal species, some of which are endangered, have been protected from the extraordinary growth in the region as the Cape became the focus of international attention.

Palm Beach (pop. 9,814) is on a narrow island never more than three-quarters of a mile wide, which is connected by three bridges across Lake Worth to *West Palm Beach* (pop. 67,643). Palm Beach's relative remoteness on the lower east coast of Florida discouraged early settlement—the first resident here was a draft dodger from the Civil War—but its tranquil isolation encouraged Henry Flagler in 1893 to select this location to develop an exclusive resort community. He routed his rail line through West Palm Beach and sited support facilities there, including quarters for servants and gardeners, while he focused on transforming the palm-covered island across the lake into an exclusive playground for the very wealthy.

In the 1920s the architect Addison Mizner, with the backing of Paris Singer, heir to the sewing machine fortune, fashioned a style of architecture that was partly drawn from Saint Augustine but had Moorish and Gothic influences, among others, added. He employed this style, loosely termed "Mediterranean," in the design of fanciful houses in Palm Beach for members of high society and in Via Mizner, an exclusive shopping precinct on the island. Palm Beach remains a community of extraordinary luxury, while West Palm Beach has become more diversified as a regional commercial center with an international airport.

While it is the most recent of all community examples in this book and is no longer a small town, *Coral Gables* (pop. 40,091) is a landmark in Floridian, if not American, town planning. A product of the land boom that swept Florida in the 1920s, Coral Gables melded the historic Mediterranean imagery developed earlier in Saint Augustine and Palm Beach with the needs of automobiles, whose enormous potential to shape a new scale and offer new pleasures of movement, as well as to threaten the environment, was then just emerging in American society. Although called a "Master Suburb" by George Merrick, its founder, Coral Gables offered a wide range of activities that few suburbs then or since have provided, and Merrick purposefully marketed his community to people from a broad economic spectrum, something that Flagler did not do in his developments.

In 1898 the Merrick family came from Massachusetts to South Florida for health reasons, just as Flagler was routing his East Coast Railroad to that area. George Merrick's father, a Congregational minister, bought 160 acres of pine land three miles southwest of the then small town of Miami. George Merrick inherited this land, acquired more, and in 1921 began to build a new community. He employed a full range of professionals, architects, landscape designers, artists, artisans, and prominent salesmen, including William Jennings Bryan, to market his development.

Merrick and his collaborators planned and designed Coral Gables across a range of scales, from houses with beautifully tiled loggias to broad, spatially defined avenues, some as wide as two hundred feet; from the residential streets along which houses were related through gradations of pastel colors and individualized through fanciful awnings to the bridle paths and canals that connected the community to Biscayne Bay (Merrick advertised Coral Gables as having forty miles of waterfront). He also included ethnic-themed villages within the community—Chinese, Italian, American Colonial, French Normandy, and Dutch South African, among others—and developed a commercial district that is still thriving along Ponce de Leon Boulevard. Possibly the most notable features, however, are the entrances—those to the city itself, through grand architectural gates, and those to individual houses through elegant, crafted doorways; the numerous plazas, many of which have been built for automobiles and are framed by thick rows of palms and live oaks; the unified variety of buildings of unusually high architectural standards (even houses with similar plans often have varied roof lines); and the fabulous Venetian Pool, a pit from which coral rock was initially quarried to construct the community's buildings and which was later filled with water to become a recreational fantasy land and, when periodically emptied, is transformed into a site for operas and plays.[23]

By 1926 Coral Gables was a city covering sixteen square miles, with a population of more than 7,500. A hurricane that year halted construction, and the Great Depression subsequently deterred the previous pace of development. Since then, greater Miami has swelled around Coral Gables, yet the community has matured and remains an enviable place in which to live. One of the tragedies of twentieth-century development in Florida, as well as in the rest of the country, is that little attention has been paid to this early seminal example of town planning that graciously incorporated the automobile into the fabric of everyday lives.

Near the end of the Florida Keys, 150 miles southwest of Miami and ninety miles north of Cuba, *Key West* (pop. 24,832) spreads over a small subtropical island approximately three and a half miles long and one mile wide. Settled in 1822 as a United States naval base, the town was laid out in 1829 by William

Whitehead, who established a grid of streets that aligned with the shore, containing blocks that ranged from 425 to 500 feet on a side. During the first half of the nineteenth century, the town prospered on fishing and—a more lucrative but less predictable source of income—salvaging cargo from the ships that wrecked on the treacherous coral reefs and sand bars that lay offshore. The town's strategic location attracted military installations and prompted economic booms, first during the Spanish American War and again during World War I, when protecting the newly opened Panama Canal became a concern.

Although periodic fires have destroyed sections of Key West, residents have rebuilt each time in wood. Today the historic district of approximately 160 blocks has within it over 3,100 wooden buildings, the largest and most important collection of wooden buildings in Florida.[24] Notable exceptions to the prevailing wood construction are masonry public buildings, including the former U.S. Custom House, the Monroe County Court House, the former Key West City Hall, and the old post office, although these are not featured as focal points in the town plan. By far, the greatest number of buildings are residential in character, even though they may serve other purposes. These vernacular buildings typically have verandahs to allow outdoor living and cooling ocean breezes. Casually relating to one another with no clearly defined system of setbacks or pattern of yards, these structures and the erratic building placements reflect the relaxed style of living for which Key West is known. Located in relative isolation from the mainland, Key West has historically been influenced by diverse cultures, and the combination of these has made Key West today an active tourist center.

Conclusion

Historic southern coastal towns more typically were planned settlements, reflecting the power of centralized authorities and their desire to maintain control. The Lords Proprietors in Beaufort, South Carolina, and the Spanish military in Saint Augustine, Florida, for example, imposed plans and supervised development according to preconceived physical layouts. Towns in the South Atlantic coast, however, developed less intensively than those of the Mid- and North Atlantic regions. The agrarian economy of the South encouraged population dispersal rather than concentration in towns and cities, which was the common pattern in New England. Also unlike that region, few deepwater natural harbors exist along the South Atlantic coast, and the treacherous conditions created by shifting inlets through the Outer Banks further thwarted commercial trade. Although notable coastal cities and towns did develop, life in the South revolved around plantations and farms. Southern towns thinly inhabit the coast, and even within the towns themselves buildings are separate from one another. As the nation grew in population and in commercial activity, the vast swamps and innumerable streams in the South impeded land connections between coastal towns and regional transportation networks, also hindering development.

Because topography along the South Atlantic coast is usually flat, albeit often poorly drained and susceptible to floods, topographical concerns were less of a determinant in laying out towns and shaping their character. Other aspects of the region, consequently, gained importance for town planners. Notable among these were climatic conditions, adaptations to which are evident at the civic scale in the public spaces of Saint Augustine and Savannah, as well as at the domestic scale in the porches, shading, and ventilating features of houses throughout the region. The mazelike configurations of land and water along the coast also produced finite land areas that limited the growth of towns, and can be seen in retrospect as forces that helped preserve the historic integrity of many southern coastal towns.

Rendering by Peter Lorenzoni, after a drawing by the author.

Edenton, North Carolina

Fig. 11.1. Street section of Edenton, North Carolina.

Fig. 11.2. The old downtown business district along Broad Street runs perpendicular to the water. The bucolic park on the east waterfront (right) contrasts with the once busy shipping area that formerly filled this site (Forest Aerial Photo Surveys Co. Inc., 1990).

The Town of Edenton, North Carolina, lies at the head of a shallow bay on the northern side of Albemarle Sound, well inland from the treacherous Outer Banks. The Chowan and Roanoke Rivers, which empty into the sound several miles west of the town, gave settlers access to inland resources. Edenton flourished as a major port during the Colonial period even though surrounding creeks and swamps restricted convenient land connections. The difficult passage through the Outer Banks and the arduous trip up Albemarle Sound at first provided protection, but after the American Revolution towns with more accessible harbors and better land transportation surpassed Edenton in importance. During the first half of the nineteenth century, Edenton languished in isolation. In the late nineteenth and early twentieth centuries, however, its economy revived to sustain its tradition of town building and architectural quality.[1]

Edenton has always related to its waterfront. The town's orderly grid pattern, its main commercial street, and, most notable of all, its Courthouse Green, a swath of lawn reaching one block inland, all connect functionally and visually to Edenton Bay.[2] Streets perpendicular to the shoreline offer, even from well inland, distant views of the glistening water. Main Street, also called Broad Street, terminates at the head of Edenton Bay in an expansive waterfront overlook. The Courthouse Green terraces from the bay up to the eighteenth-century courthouse, which rests on a slight rise of land that provides an unobstructed view of the bay.[3] Unpretentious yet dignified, the Green integrates the near and intimate with the far and expansive. Today, a quiet park along the water's edge spreads across land where there was once a bustling waterfront full of wharves, fish houses, and rail yards, which focused town activity. Large old houses along Water Street now form a monumental edge to the bay.

Colonists settled the town in a dispersed pattern, and later residents infilled buildings. Georgian, Federal, Greek Revival, Gothic Revival, Italianate, Colonial Revival, Queen Anne, Neoclassical Revival, and Bungaloid style houses are frequently found on the same street. This inclusive building vocabulary resulted in a variety of building setbacks, colors, massings, rhythms, and materials that gives the town an unusual visual richness.

The Founding

When English settlers first ventured into the western reaches of Albemarle Sound in the late sixteenth century, they found Indians of the Weapmeoc tribe

Fig. 11.3. The Chowan County Courthouse sits at the head of the Green,
a public space established in 1712.

Fig. 11.4. The view from the courthouse across the Green to Edenton Bay (1990).

living in a series of villages near present day Edenton.[4] Not until the mid-
seventeenth century did Virginians, searching for cheap and fertile land, gradually move into the area. The primary road from Virginia, forty miles to the north,
ended here on the sheltered bay, making it a logical place to house the previously
itinerant court that served the region. Other settlers came from Scotland, the

Fig. 11.5. Large houses now form a monumental edge to the east side of the waterfront
(1990).

West Indies, and Bermuda.[5] An act of the colonial assembly in 1712 formally established the town, providing not only accommodations for the court but also, through the sale of house lots, a means to defray construction costs of the courthouse building. In 1722 the General Assembly mandated that most of its sessions should occur in Edenton, and until 1746 it followed this policy, although, apparently, it did not have a specific building constructed for this purpose.

The original town centered on the southeastern quadrant of the Sauthier Plan of 1769.[6] The town was platted into half-acre lots, sixty-six feet wide and 330 feet long, with two acres each designated for a courthouse, church, jail, schoolhouse, and other public structures.[7] The deep lots extended from street to street, permitting settlers to keep stables in the town while comfortably separating the main houses from them, a pattern which must have given the town a clustered, farmlike appearance. Under threats of forfeiture, settlers had to build within a year and meet minimum house sizes (approximately fifteen by twenty feet in area and eight feet high). They built first along the water's edge and set houses close to the street. Over time residents rebuilt most of their houses and moved them back within the lots.[8] They sited the courthouse one block inland at the end of the Green. Around it were clustered inns and taverns to serve court visitors.[9]

In the 1720s and 1730s, New England merchants began stopping at Edenton to load forest and agricultural products to trade in the West Indies for rum, molasses, and salt.[10] The English also needed raw materials to construct ships for their rapidly expanding navy, and here they could find large quantities of

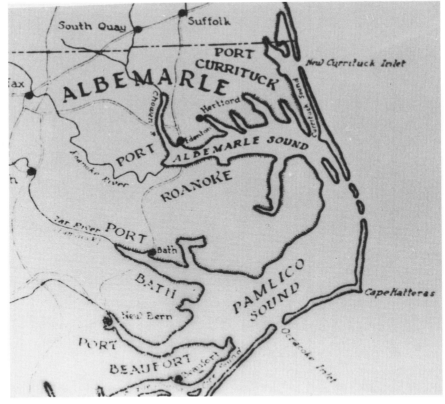

Map 11.1. Regional map of the Carolina coast (1770). Town settlement occurred in the far reaches of the sounds so that residents could benefit from coastal access yet also capitalize on inland resources. Edenton lies at the mouth of the Chowan River, where the road from Suffolk, Virginia, terminated (North Carolina Division of Archives and History).

lumber, tar, and pitch.[11] As settlers pressed inland, those in the southern and western counties of North Carolina successfully lobbied in 1747 to have the capital moved to New Bern. Yet Edenton continued to flourish, mainly because the Earl of Granville maintained an office in Edenton to administer his property domains, which included much of the northern half of present North Carolina. His agent occupied the Cupola House, still an important landmark on lower Broad Street.[12]

With its advantageous location, Edenton prospered and grew in size. By the 1730s the western blocks along the waterfront were laid out, and in 1757 the "Governor's pasture" on the far western side was divided and sold. Town leaders employed the same pattern used on the east to organize the western side, thus relating both sections of town. On the Sauthier Plan of 1769, paths, fence lines, gardens, orchards, and open land lay along the eventual rights-of-way that became streets perpendicular to the bay. The grid pattern that emerged was extraordinarily large, 330 feet wide and up to 800 feet long. There are approximately twice as many east-west streets as north-south streets, suggesting settlers anticipated more movement in the former directions. Because of the town expansion, Broad Street, which earlier formed the western edge of town, ran through the middle of it by 1769. At ninety-six feet in width, it indeed was the most expansive street. East-west streets were typically fifty-six feet wide, and other north-south streets were usually about sixty-six feet wide. Broad Street became the primary route into and out of the town. Commercial activity gravitated here, particularly along the three blocks closest to the water.

The town that emerged in 1769, as illustrated in the Sauthier map, consisted of clustered houses and outbuildings separated by open land. Settlers valued even a slight rise of land in this flat, poorly drained landscape. Avoiding water drainage areas, they built first on higher land and used lower areas for animals and crops. Later residents filled in and built around these early clusters. Consequently, neighborhoods today contain houses from different periods.

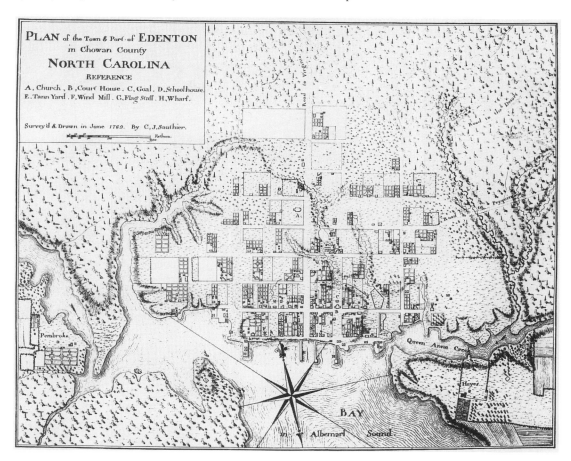

Map 11.2. The Sauthier Plan of Edenton. Scattered development filled in the plan and accommodated drainage through this flat site (map surveyed and drawn by Charles Joseph Sauthier, 1769, Library of Congress, Geography and Map Division).

Edenton's period of glory was from 1750 to 1775, when it was an active, prosperous, and even cosmopolitan community. Ships from New England bound for the West Indies regularly stopped here.[13] Shingles, tar, corn, fish, tobacco, and deerskins were the primary exports, while rum, molasses, sugar, salt, and linen were the primary imports. As the English increased taxation on colonial trade in the 1770s, Edenton's merchants and ship owners grew increasingly hostile to the royal government and the town became one of the centers of rebellion in North Carolina. Joseph Hewes, a leading local merchant, was one of the signers of the Declaration of Independence.

The town remained important throughout the revolution. In 1786 Edenton had a population of 1,112; approximately half of this number represents slaves who worked as fishermen, artisans, and laborers.[14] However, as the nineteenth century neared trade increasingly bypassed the town, and in 1795 a hurricane closed Roanoke Inlet through the Outer Banks. New, larger ships had difficulty navigating the Outer Banks and making the long voyage through the shallow waters of Albemarle Sound. Rutted trails and unreliable ferries frustrated overland travelers.[15] Although fishing improved from 1810 to 1850, Edenton suffered a disastrous economic setback with the opening of the Dismal Swamp Canal, in 1805, which connected eastern North Carolina to Norfolk, Virginia.[16] Prosperous international trade shifted to Norfolk, and Edenton entered a long period of stagnation.

During the Civil War, Edenton residents supported the Confederacy. However, the isolated town was of little strategic importance and suffered no damage when Union forces easily occupied it in 1862. After the war, Edenton, along with the rest of the South, was faced with economic depression. Large surrounding estates were subdivided and sold or lay unattended. Freed black slaves, along with the newly impoverished tobacco and cotton planter families, fled the area. From 1860 to 1870, Edenton lost twenty percent of its population, leaving fewer residents than the town had had in 1820.[17] It remained cut off, served by poor roads and distant from coastal shipping routes.

Late-Nineteenth-Century Diversification and Revival

After Reconstruction, a new generation of civic leaders and entrepreneurs, both from within and from outside the community, emerged to expand the economy in Edenton. They improved transportation and access to the town, the lack of which had crippled development for most of the century. Although earlier leaders had envisioned a rail line to Edenton in the 1830s, trains did not arrive until 1881.[18] Avoiding expensive central commercial property, railroads entered on the east and west sides of town to service waterfront wharves and warehouses. Rail line placement limited subsequent town development in these directions, fostering instead a corridor of commercial growth north along Broad Street. The railroads efficiently served Edenton's productive fisheries, lumber

Map 11.3. *Long streets parallel to the waterfront characterize the town. At the time of this map, railroad lines served both sides of the waterfront (Sanborn map with buildings rendered black, 1893).*

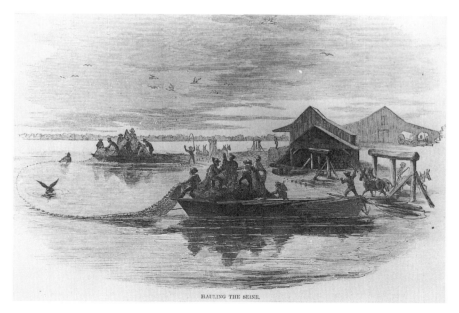

HAULING THE SEINE.

Fig. 11.6. *Using large seine nets, fishermen hauled huge quantities of fish from Edenton Bay. In the late nineteenth century, fish were transferred to nearby freight cars for shipment to northern cities (Harper's Weekly, 28 September 1861, 620).*

industries, and agriculture and also attracted manufacturers seeking available labor and raw materials. The Branning Company, founded by two brothers from Pennsylvania, was foremost among these manufacturers. Started in 1888, by 1895 the company employed nearly half the people of Edenton in a complex of cotton gins and grist, shingle, planing, and saw mills.[19]

Left: *Fig. 11.7. Numerous sawmills operating in the Edenton area produced a remarkable variety of wood architectural ornaments (1991). Right: Fig. 11.8. This crafted wood porch detail celebrates the 1910 passing of Halley's Comet over Edenton (1991).*

Large fisheries based in Edenton thrived in the late nineteenth century. Using seine nets one mile long, fishermen caught in excess of 500,000 fish with each haul.[20] Later the pound net, an adaptation of Indian techniques, allowed two men to haul large quantities of fish efficiently. After cleaning and salting, workers loaded their catch onto ships and boxcars waiting at the waterfront to ship the seafood north; Philadelphia was a major destination for Edenton's harvest. Five sets of rail tracks covered more than eight hundred feet along the waterfront, and a 750-foot pier for ferry service stretched into the bay.[21] Industries also located east, and then in the early twentieth century they began to move north of town. The Edenton Cotton Mill, organized in 1898, still operates on the east side. Its adjacent village, comprising workers' houses, a playing field, and a church, remains virtually as it did seventy-five years ago.[22] By the early twentieth century Edenton was a regional trading center, sustained by old ties and developing new ones. It had established a diversified economy based on lumbering, agriculture, fishing, local banking, and manufacturing. This new period of prosperity was marked by a range of buildings constructed in the eclectic styles of the late nineteenth and early twentieth centuries. These buildings, many of which have ingeniously fabricated wood details, contribute significantly to the character of the town today.

With the growing use of automobiles, Edenton spread more rapidly beyond its eighteenth-century core. The first bridge across the Chowan River, completed in 1927, and another across Albemarle Sound, in 1938, made the town more accessible to a wider region.[23] Agricultural methods, peanut production in particular, improved with the adoption of crop rotation, deep cultivation, and modern farm machinery. Manufacturing continued to prosper in the area surrounding the town, leaving the historic core intact. Outlying warehouses and business, accessed by trucks and automobiles, developed in loosely organized patterns that contrasted with the rectangular plan of the old town. During World War II, the U.S. Marine Corps Air Station, located several miles east of the town, brought large numbers of military personnel into the community. Developers subdivided large, old houses in town and built new, detached housing to accommodate the recent arrivals. The town further expanded and adopted suburban street patterns unrelated to its early-eighteenth-century plan.

Post—World War II Changes

Since World War II, residents of Edenton have become increasingly conscious of their town's history and have sought to preserve the buildings and environments that embody its past. At the same time, Edentonians have continued to emphasize traditional issues, particularly improved transportation and economic development. Public debate and civic action have focused on resolving these at times conflicting goals.

The main coastal road, U.S. 17, passes through the center of Edenton. As traffic along this route grew, it threatened Edenton's historic character. Responding to local concerns, state authorities completed a bypass on the north side of the town in 1977. While the bypass relieved traffic pressures from the historic area, it further promoted suburban and commercial development, making cheaper land in larger parcels more accessible. There are now six interchanges in Edenton, an extraordinary number for a town this size. The main interchange at Highway 32 has been the focus of commercial development; several shopping centers and the regional hospital are now located near this interchange. Consequently the town has become binodal, with this new locus of activity based on highway orientation, economies of scale, and large parcels contrasting with the historic district, which is pedestrian based, smaller-scaled, and water oriented. The two commercial districts, one and a half miles away from each other, are too distant for a convenient walk. The outlying shopping centers first competed with downtown merchants, but highway-oriented areas soon came to dominate local retail trade.[24] As a result, downtown merchants increasingly depend on specialty retail shops and tourism.

Meanwhile, the waterfront has changed more profoundly than has the business district. The old port has disappeared. The eastern section of the waterfront is now a quiet park, and the western side is a mixture of scattered public facilities, industrial areas, and vacant land. Fishing declined after World War II owing to the extensive overfishing by foreign offshore fleets and the pollution of Albemarle Sound from agricultural runoff and the point source discharge of factories.[25] With the demise of maritime activity and the concurrent rise of suburban shopping centers, land along the water lost commercial value and the few remaining fishhouses were removed. Town leaders set about searching for a new waterfront identity. In 1952 the Barker-Moore House, displaced by new construction on Broad Street, was moved three blocks south to a site created from landfill in the bay, where wharves and warehouses once stood—an improbable location for a house once surrounded by gardens and auxiliary buildings, but a prominent one for its new role as a visitors' center. With the Cupola House one block up Broad Street, this new visitors' center now forms an arrival area for tourists.

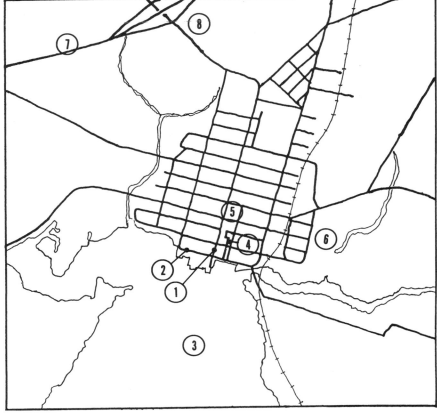

Map 11.4. Location Map of Edenton, North Carolina (redrawn
from current U.S. Coast and Geodetic Survey maps).
1. Broad Street; 2. Water Street; 3. Edenton Bay; 4. Old Courthouse; 5. New Courthouse;
6. Edenton Cotton Mill; 7. U.S. Route 17 Bypass; 8. New Shopping Centers.

Fig. 11.9. Historical view of lower Broad Street, from the water tower at the foot of the street
(Peoples' Bank Scrapbook, ca. 1890).

Fig. 11.10. *View from Cupola House of lower Broad Street and Edenton Bay. Lower Broad Street provided a central and convenient location for the old business district. In the distant center is the Barker-Moore House, which was relocated from the business district to the location of a former wharf (1990).*

Public sanitation improvements initiated in 1966 meliorated the water quality of the bay and encouraged residents to reconsider new opportunities for the waterfront. Property owners in adjacent neighborhoods immediately began house renovations. In the early 1970s the local historical society opposed a plan to develop condominiums on the east waterfront and, with funding from private donations, persuaded the town to purchase the property for use as a public park.[26] Consequently, the eastern waterfront, once filled with rail yards and warehouses, has gradually become a sedate residential area with a park open to all and no major activity to attract outsiders. The park provides a beautiful transition between the bay and the row of large houses that edges Water Street. Recognizing the advantages of this park, the town bought additional land on the western waterfront for recreational purposes. It built a small dock, which has not been intensively used other than by local people, as Edenton is several hours journey by boat from the Intracoastal Waterway. The town has periodically considered commercial development proposals for this area, with the hope that tourist facilities would support the nearby business district. Yet the future of the western waterfront remains unresolved. It requires a comprehensive plan that will relate the area physically as well as economically to the eastern half of town and the adjacent historic district.

Public actions have supported the historic town center. After World War II, the old courthouse, dating from 1767, could no longer house expanding services, so in the early 1970s the county government decided to construct a new facility. It initially proposed building near the highway bypass, but Edenton residents objected, arguing for a location on the north edge of downtown, and proceeded to clear a site there to facilitate new construction. The county built the new courthouse on this downtown location, and court visitors now continue to support downtown business, just as they have since early colonial settlement.

Edenton enacted land-use zoning in 1969 and has been a historic district on the National Register of Historic Places since 1973. In addition to its historic ordinances, Edenton has a jurisdictional zone that extends one mile beyond town limits. The county currently controls this land but encourages the town to plan jointly for the zone's future. The county expects the town eventually to assume authority over this land and to be responsible for public services in it. Edenton is also considering a greenbelt approximately a half-mile in width, which would comprise the swamps and wetlands that wind through this area. The town also initiated development of the former U.S. Marine Corps Air Station located several miles beyond its limits in the county. When the station closed in the 1950s, a citizens' group organized to reuse these facilities, develop the land, and attract light industries. The town soon annexed this county land into its tax base even though it was not contiguous with town boundaries.[27] The airport is now public and serves the region, while the industrial park has allowed the town to diversify its economic base.[28]

Because it is relatively remote from major metropolitan centers, Edenton traditionally has not been a tourist destination but rather a place to pass through while visiting the general region.[29] An estimated 54,000 visitors came to Edenton in 1989, a small number compared to other coastal towns in this book but a significant increase over past years for Edenton.[30] While there is no beach in the area for swimmers, visitors come to enjoy Edenton's history and its pleasurable town qualities. The town continues to debate whether or not it should encourage tourism. Those who seek a diversified economy believe tourism should grow "naturally" and be a supplemental activity to support downtown business. Others argue that the town should actively promote tourism. They note the difficulty of attracting new business and, if new employers do come, the possibility that competition would raise labor rates throughout the area. Tourism, on the other hand, has already demonstrated strength in Edenton and requires few public incentives. Both sides of this debate welcome retired people, particularly those from northeast states, who find Edenton to be a quiet, safe, small-town environment. They relocate here for its comparatively low-cost housing, benign climate, and medical facilities. Edentonians appreciate retirees because they make few demands of the community, willingly volunteer for civic activities, and support the economy, including downtown stores.[31]

With the major exception of fishing, Edenton today relies on its traditional economic activities—agriculture, lumbering, cotton milling, and peanut production—but it also welcomes new business and increasingly benefits from tourists and retirees. Edenton values its traditional town environment and the social and physical relationships fostered by its historic pattern. Having grown slowly and in relative isolation, the town avoided many of the scarring intrusions of the late twentieth century. By contemplating growth alternatives and promoting different options, Edenton has tried to blend a variety of uses and not allow any single economic interest to dominate its direction. The town's future has increasingly come to lie with its past. Fortunately, Edenton has been able to preserve that past and retain its leisurely charm. With effort, wisdom, and foresight, it will continue to foster the diversity that generated the original town.

Rendering by Peter Lorenzoni, after a drawing by the author.

CHAPTER TWELVE

Beaufort, South Carolina

Fig. 12.1. Street section of Beaufort, South Carolina.

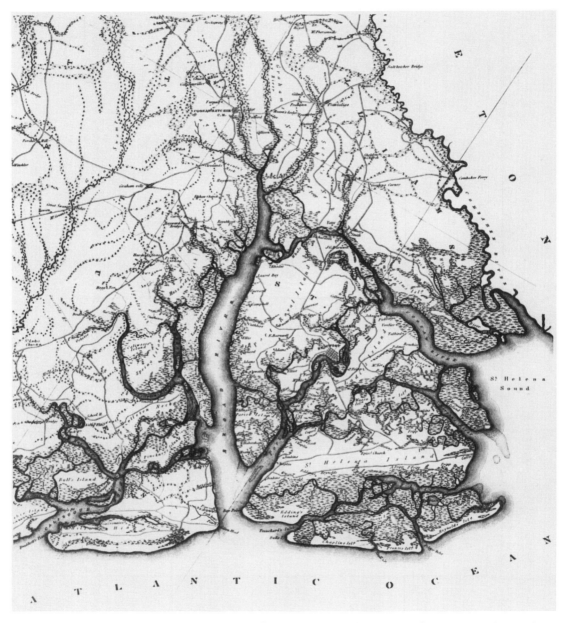

Map 12.1. *The only significant settlement in the area, Beaufort orients south toward Port Royal Sound. Rivers snake through the tide-dominated deltas of the region* (Atlas of the State of South Carolina, *by Robert Mills, 1825*).

Beaufort lies in the lush, serene landscape of the Carolina Low Country, where tidal rivers and creeks wind through a maze of grassy marshes and sandy islands to form one of the most intricate patterns of land and water in the world. The region is suffused with a mystery partly reflected in its place names—Ashepoo, Calibogue, Coosawhatchie, Daufuskie, Dahtah, Huspah, Little Pon Pon, and Tuckassa King. The town of Beaufort rests on Port Royal Island, the second island east of the mainland, roughly midway between Charleston and Savannah where the Beaufort River wraps around a point of land. From Beaufort there are commanding views downriver into Port Royal Sound and the best deepwater harbor on the South Atlantic coast.[1]

Beaufort became the sublime expression of a proud and privileged class. Colonists grew rich first on indigo, then on rice, and finally on the high-quality cotton that thrived in the fertile saline soil of the region. With the immense wealth gained from these crops (which were worked by Gullah slaves brought from West Africa), a landed aristocracy created in Beaufort a community of elegant mansions to complement their otherwise isolated plantation lives. They transformed Beaufort from a small colonial trading post into a leading social, resort, and intellectual center of the Old South. Avoiding destruction in the Civil War, Beaufort passed the late nineteenth and early twentieth centuries in economic depression and geographic isolation. Only recently has it emerged to confront the pressures and opportunities of late-twentieth-century life. Now vast truck farms transport vegetables to northern cities, while tourists and retirees descend upon the Sea Islands to enjoy the benign climate and play golf on transformed plantations. Beaufort remains one of America's great treasuries of antebellum architecture and culture.

The original eighteenth-century plan still orders the town. Until recently, town expansions simply extended the colonial street pattern. Distance from the water determined street importance and social status. Bay Street in particular, with its crescent of vaulting oaks and belvedere mansions overlooking the bay, conveys the aristocratic essence of the town. Adjacent to the mansion area and immediately south of Bay Street, the public can now enjoy the waterfront in a new park that stretches across four blocks. This park symbolizes a period of renewed activity for this traditionally conservative community.

The Lords Proprietors' Trading Post

In 1562 the French seized control from the Spanish and briefly held the area; they chose the name "Port Royal" for the island on which Beaufort is now

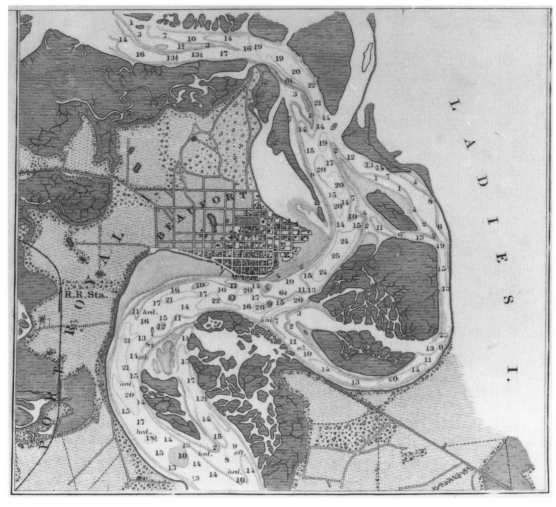

Map 12.2. In this map, the town is seen clustered on the knob of land surrounded by river channels and marshlands. Unlike most towns, Beaufort was not reached by the rail line, seen on the left (U.S. Coast and Geodetic Survey, 1886).

Fig. 12.2. The Beaufort River wraps around the edge of Port Royal Island and the town of Beaufort. The town's grid pattern contrasts with the intricate water channels twisting through saltwater marshes and tidal sediment deposits (U.S. Geological Survey, 1989).

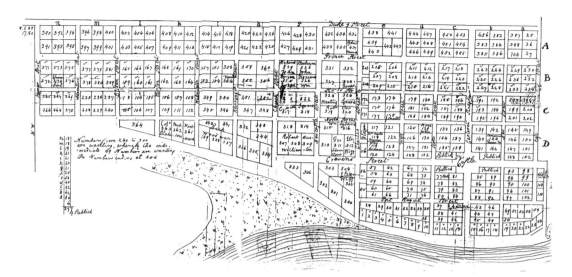

Map 12.3. *Colonial Map of Beaufort (1760). Earliest settlement occurred along the waterfront to the east (right) (Beaufort County Library).*

located. Not until the English dislodged the Spanish from the region in 1702, however, did European settlement start. English colonists, many from Barbados, arrived to lay out plantations and establish an outpost at Beaufort to guard this point along the inland waterway. As traders and Indians gathered here, Beaufort emerged as a small commercial settlement. In 1710 the Lords Proprietors whom King Charles II had earlier designated to colonize the area agreed to build a town there.[2] They named the settlement after Henry Somerset, Duke of Beaufort, who was one of their group, and authorized the preparation of a town plan.[3]

The layout was undistinguished, with a typical street block being a square with 350-foot sides, platted with sides in a north-south and east-west direction. The organizers assigned 379 lots for development and designated for public use four lots grouped around a space noted on the colonial map as "Castle," at the intersection of Carteret and Craven Streets. Today public buildings, including the town library, are still at this intersection, although a sense of civic space is not noticeable there. In the 1760 plan most of the rectangular blocks east of Carteret Street are each subdivided into six to ten lots, and those west of Carteret, into four to six lots. The largest lots were in the western section overlooking the river, where planters later built great mansions. Twenty-four small lots on the north side of Bay Street along the water's edge became the central business district.

Between 1711 and 1717 Indian wars disrupted colonization, but in 1717 town settlement began in earnest and seventy lots were recorded within a month. The first buildings rose in the New Street vicinity, on the eastern side near the water. To encourage development, the colonial government required settlers to either build or forfeit their land. Fortunately, the economy boomed. By the 1750s, planters were cultivating rice in freshwater swamps and growing indigo for English textile manufacturers. Shipbuilding also prospered because oak, used for frames, and cypress, used for planks, grew abundantly nearby. With this economic activity, Beaufort residents began to construct larger houses. Influenced by buildings in the West Indies where they traded, a region that also had a similar climate, townsfolk erected houses with main floors raised above the ground and airy front porches to provide generous shade. These early houses, although comparatively spartan and conservative, established themes that later generations refined into elegant mansions.[4]

Early in the American Revolution, British troops seized Beaufort. Fortunately, they spared the town the destruction they wreaked elsewhere in South Carolina. After the revolution, Beaufort declined in political importance (district courts moved in 1781 to the mainland) and in commercial significance (Charleston and Savannah soon attracted much of Beaufort's cotton business and foreign trade). Beaufort flourished, however, as a social and cultural center for Sea Island planters.

Some of the enormously wealthy South Carolina planters had residences in Charleston and Savannah and only infrequently visited their properties, which could be quite distant from those two cities. Others in the Beaufort vicinity who wanted to be closer to their holdings yet have some relief from the isolation and heat of the country came to Beaufort and the smaller coastal villages in the region to enjoy the cooling breezes. These planters came from their plantations to Beaufort in April, after crops had been planted, and stayed through spring and summer. With the first frost, families left to spend Thanksgiving and Christmas at their plantations. They sent their children to school in Beaufort during the summer, reversing the traditional yearly schedule, and the town prided itself on having some of the finest educational institutions and libraries in the South.[5] Beaufort College was among the outstanding schools of the time, and its main building, constructed in 1852, is now part of the University of South Carolina at Beaufort. Inevitably, the town became a major center for the southern intelligentsia, including leading secessionists.

A Truly Wealthy Society

The area prospered with the cultivation of Sea Island cotton. The slaves who endured the arduous, unhealthy, and undesirable agricultural labor turned this region into one of the most intensively cultivated parts of the world and brought enormous wealth to the area. By delegating management responsibilities to overseers, plantation owners could profit from their land while living elsewhere. In Beaufort they enjoyed a more active social life and a benign climate. By 1819 a steamboat line connected Beaufort with Charleston, Savannah, and Augusta and contributed to the growth of Beaufort's resort life. Cotton booms in the region meant mansion building in Beaufort, first from 1795 to 1820 and then, most magnificently, from 1852 to the outbreak of the Civil War, in 1861.

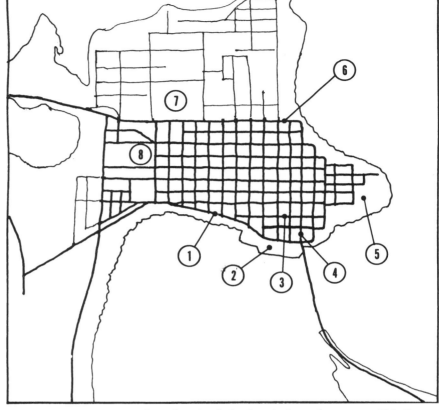

Map 12.4. Location Map of Beaufort, South Carolina (redrawn from current U.S. Coast
and Geodetic Survey maps).
1. Bay Street; 2. Waterfront park; 3. Craven Street; 4. Carteret Street; 5. The Point;
6. Boundary Street; 7. National Cemetery; 8. New county building.

Fig. 12.3. On the Point, the Edgar Fripp House, known as "Tidalholm" (built in 1856), faces
south and benefits from cooling water breezes (1990).

Left: Fig. 12.4. In homes with multilevel verandahs, the upper porch provided outdoor sleeping space, the main-floor porch extended the living level of the house, and the bottom area allowed for working and storage (1990). Right: Fig. 12.5. Front porches respect common architectural themes while also expressing individual ownership (1990).

Beaufort flowered during this later period. Building in the Neoclassical style, planters erected colossal mansions to assert their significance in a society they hoped would be timeless. They concentrated their mansions in two areas—first on the western side of town along the crescent of Bay Street and, later, on the east side of town in an enclave known as "the Point." Residents platted the eastern section in 1809. While the street grids of the Point and the main part of town do not align, the Point is still clearly part of the town. Indeed, an important characteristic of Beaufort is the manner in which its mansion districts bracket the main business area.

Beaufort's mansions are a remarkable assemblage. They derive from the plantation house type, a design originally intended to sit in splendid rural isolation but which soon gathered together in Beaufort as a collective. Unlike residents of Charleston and Savannah, who built more densely, developers in Beaufort erected free-standing houses with verandahs or porches facing the street and generous front and side gardens. The "Beaufort style" is a loose term embracing a set of architectural elements frequently used in these houses that reflects adaptation to local conditions, especially coastal climates. Buildings in the Beaufort style have five essential characteristics: southern orientation, raised foundations, porches or verandahs on the south side, low-pitched roofs, and T-shaped plans.[6]

Originally, visitors to the mansions arrived by boat and therefore approached

Top: *Fig. 12.6. On the edge of the business district, mansions with typical two-level porches front the street (1990).* Bottom: *Fig. 12.7. Several blocks inland from the waterfront mansions, much smaller houses are still free-standing and also have front porches and raised main floors (1990).*

from the waterside. Central entrances up broad, gracious stairs are common on this end, although main entrances may also be on the verandah ends. Houses typically sit on masonry foundations of brick or "tabby"—a cementlike mixture of crushed oyster shells, sand, and lime. Foundations or podiums, especially those constructed on piers, aided ventilation by raising main floors above damp grade levels.[7] Not incidentally, living quarters are also above flood levels in this hurricane-prone area. On the upper floors builders used wood, usually the locally plentiful live oak and cypress. Ceiling heights are as high as eighteen feet on the main floors to promote circulation and relieve summer heat.[8]

Verandahs stretch across the south facades and often wrap around the sides of the house to shade the interior and to provide space for exterior living during the hot summer season. Usually there are two porch levels: the lower, more public one for entertaining and family living and the upper, more private one off the bedrooms for sleeping. In homes with low-pitched roofs, the main roof plane may extend over the verandahs, which are the most carefully proportioned, detailed, and crafted part of the house exterior.

The T-shaped house plan allowed builders to gain more rooms while maximizing ventilation; the rooms often have windows on three sides. Typically, these mansions have four rooms and a central hall and stair on each floor, but within the general Beaufort house type there are innumerable variations, since residents built these houses from the early Colonial to the late Victorian periods. Throughout these periods, however, the basic constituent elements were incorporated into both small and large houses, as well as in commercial, institutional, and residential buildings, thus giving the town a visual unity.

The Consequences of War

Beaufort's grand style of living abruptly ended with the Civil War. Hoping to open a military front in the heart of the South, Union forces avoided heavily defended Savannah and attacked Beaufort. When Union soldiers arrived by sea in November 1861, most white residents fled to the mainland, leaving behind mansions, slaves, and virtually all their belongings. A northern newspaper reporter noted the irony of a defiant South Carolina being "attacked in the exclu-

Fig. 12.8. Drawing of the Beaufort waterfront during the Civil War, when Union troops occupied the area (Harper's Weekly, 14 December 1861).

Top: *Fig. 12.9. View of waterfront during the Civil War, showing rear yards of Bay Street businesses (the Samuel Codley Photo Collection, Parris Island Museum, ca. 1864).*
Bottom: *Fig. 12.10. During the Civil War, Union photographers extensively recorded Beaufort and the surrounding military installations. In this example, on the left is a Bay Street mansion and in the distance are the main business district and docks (Beaufort County Library, ca. 1862).*

sive home of the most exclusive few of that most exclusive aristocracy . . . the concentrated essence of first-familyism."[9]

The federal government confiscated plantations and Beaufort mansions for delinquent taxes and declared Beaufort slaves "contraband of war." The government resold the property, portions of which were bought by black freedmen who had pooled their small savings, but most of which went to northerners, who bought the property at enormous discounts from its prewar value. Union officers also used mansions for offices, staff quarters, and hospitals, preserving the houses themselves but often discarding the furnishings. The federal government resurveyed the town, increasing the potential density by assigning six lots where there had been four and four where there had been two.[10] Yankees introduced town improvements such as a new pier on Bay Street and tried, albeit unsuccessfully, to change street names from those honoring southern heros to letters of the alphabet and ordinal numbers, after the plan of Washington, D.C.

As federally occupied territory and headquarters of the U.S. Army, Department of the South, Beaufort and Port Royal Island became staging areas for military raids into the Confederacy. The area also became the focus for northern abolitionists determined to reconstruct the South through a reform movement known as the "Port Royal Experiment." Willie Lee Rose writes that the

> Port Royal Experiment would encompass political and social changes to equal the transition from slavery to freedom. The decadent South, with its antique civil arrangements, would be regenerated by the vigorous institutions of New England, the public-school system, 'liberal Christianity,' and even the town meeting, if possible. But most of all, its sponsors thought the Port Royal Experiment would prove that the fundamental precept of classical economic progress through enlightened self-interest was altogether color-blind. Much was expected of the Negroes at Port Royal.[11]

Following in the wake of General Sherman's destructive 1864 "March to the Sea" campaign from Atlanta, thousands of fugitive slaves sought freedom and Union protection in the Sea Islands. On 16 January 1865, Sherman issued his Field Order Number 15, declaring all abandoned and confiscated lands in the Sea Island region and coastal lands thirty miles to the interior exclusively for freedmen settlement. Each freedman was to have possessory title to forty acres of land.[12] Many ex-slaves became property owners for the first time. These titles, poorly recorded at the time, have confused land transfers ever since and deterred subsequent real estate development.[13]

Following the Civil War, freedmen built houses in the northwest section of the town, which was until then largely underutilized land. They were joined by newly arriving northerners and a few returning (now impoverished) planters, but it was mostly freed slaves that occupied the old houses. With the area's entire social structure uprooted and little post-Reconstruction guidance, many mansions became tenements and some would continue to shelter poor families until after World War II.

After 1870, the cotton economy revived and phosphate mining began. Truck

Map 12.5. Among the evident town patterns are street rights-of-way to the water, street corners typically occupied by buildings, mansions located near the business district, and industries next to houses on the east side (Sanborn map with buildings rendered black, 1899).

farming also emerged as a profitable business, being well suited to the soil, climate, and smaller landownership patterns. Workers in these and other industries built modest houses in Beaufort on vacant property and on lots created from the breakup of old mansions. They and the growing merchant class preferred house styles popular nationally at the time, such as the Queen Anne and Eastlake styles (1860–1900) and the Bungalow style (1880–1925). Townsfolk renovating old mansions favored the Colonial Revival style (1880–1920), often adding picturesque features such as bay windows.[14] Yet, until at least 1900, most builders retained the distinctive two-level front verandahs traditional to Beaufort.

Bay Street, between Carteret and Charles Streets, developed more commercial uses. By 1884 buildings grouped into blocks lined both sides of the street, in marked contrast to the free-standing houses of adjacent neighborhoods. Only street rights-of-way opened to the water. By 1899, twelve grocery stores, eleven clothing and shoe stores, three hardware stores, and three furniture stores, along with a post office, custom house, tin shop, and cotton gin, had Bay Street addresses. Typical of a pattern that may seem incongruous today, a wood mill operated on the edge of downtown amid antebellum mansions. There was a jumble of activities and people, of the proud and the humble.[15]

A Long Depression

Beaufort declined in the late nineteenth and early twentieth centuries. Natural disasters first took their toll: In 1893 a devastating hurricane came ashore at high tide, killing at least a thousand people in the region. In 1907 a fire burned down sections of Beaufort and destroyed the local phosphate industry. The boll weevil arrived in 1918 to ravage cotton crops.[16] By the 1930s, Beaufort residents barely noticed the Great Depression, they had for so long endured their own. Beaufort had become a backwater town with an impoverished economy and little outside trade. Yet it was this very economic decline that preserved Beaufort. People simply did not have the resources to change it.

Beaufort also avoided many of the environmentally destructive forces of the twentieth century which altered the surroundings of many other towns. There has been no significant industrial development in Beaufort, primarily because of its poor accessibility. Although the first railroad arrived in 1876 as a spur from the main coastal line, it had little effect on the economy. The first automobile bridge to the mainland finally opened in 1926, but streets remained ankle deep in sand until after World War II. Only recently have automobiles shaped the town, and this has occurred primarily on the fringe. The increasing traffic through town to cross the Woods Memorial Bridge is, however, a growing and alarming problem.[17]

With World War II Beaufort became more enmeshed in American national life, the armed forces again serving as catalyst. Between 1941 and 1945, more than two hundred thousand recruits trained at the U.S. Marine Corps base on Parris Island, ten miles south of Beaufort.[18] Inevitably, these outsiders changed Beaufort's way of life. Old mansions became apartments for military families. A town that for generations lacked a professional class now had one in the medical and legal officers assigned here. More noticeably, the commercial strips, shopping centers, garden apartment complexes, and single-family residential developments common throughout the country now appeared on the western and southern fringes of town. The pace of life quickened. Beaufort residents adapted to new values and new ways of life, though they refused to relinquish completely those familiar to them.

After the war, many military personnel remained and others later returned to retire here and enjoy the tranquil Sea Island life. Activity first focused on nearby Hilton Head. Begun in the 1960s, development here was initially emblematic of a "design with nature" approach, and the island has since become one of the nation's major winter resorts, growing almost 10 percent each year in the 1980s. Its suburbanlike developments offer contemporary versions of plantation life for the upper middle class—gate houses, privileged and sequestered living, and houses nestled in the landscape, often organized around golf courses placed on land where indigo, rice, and cotton once grew. More recently, Beaufort, with its quiet setting, architectural qualities, and small-town life, has presented an alternative to those home buyers initially attracted to Hilton Head. With the exception of military personnel, Beaufort has become more a community of full-time residents.

A major hurricane in 1959 marked the start of the most recent wave of

Beaufort restoration. The trauma of this storm forced residents to consider their community's future. In so doing, they realized the value of their past and sought methods to preserve it. In 1969 the central area became a historic district on the National Register of Historic Places, and in 1974 it was named a National Historic Landmark District. Professional preservation efforts began early, first in 1972 with Russell Wright and Carl Feiss, whose work formed the basis of the first zoning ordinance and the creation of a board of architectural review. Later, in 1979, John Milner and Associates completed an inventory of historic buildings and a preservation manual.[19] The 1980s brought major investment in Beaufort's old housing stock, and the previously approved preservation controls guided these changes. Today, most building improvements have respected Beaufort's architectural traditions, but housing costs have escalated beyond commercial expectations. Indeed, old houses that were long ago converted to businesses are now being converted back to residences, the current favored use. Understandably, Beaufort's lower-income citizens find it increasingly difficult to live in a designated historic district, with its escalating property values and stringent building improvement guidelines.[20]

A Revitalized Town

The Beaufort downtown waterfront—known as the Henry C. Chambers Park, named in 1979 after the mayor who guided its development—reflects the town's new uses and constituencies. What was once derelict land is now a town asset. It is a well-designed park with diverse activities that welcome residents and tourists, including those arriving by car and foot as well as by boat. Town leaders had first suggested a waterfront park in the 1930s, with the hope of gaining more parking for downtown business.[21] However, Beaufort's commercial district turned its back on the water to face Bay Street. The town's fortuitous decision to build a wastewater treatment plant marked an attitude change in the community. While discussions for this plant started in 1945, Beaufort was not able to build it until the mid-1970s, when federal funds became available to eliminate sewage discharge into the bay.[22] Town leaders then realized they also had the opportunity to improve the waterfront. Again with federal assistance, they assembled twenty-two parcels of land extending 2,700 feet along the waterfront south of Bay Street. They developed a master plan, erected a long bulkhead, and proceeded to build the park to high standards.

Inclusive, attractive, and accommodating, the park is remarkably successful. There are places within for individual and group activities, as well as for the thousands of tourists who jam Beaufort during its annual water festival in late July. The park also presents an inviting entrance to the town for the growing water traffic. It connects to downtown streets and business areas, allowing people to filter through passageways and stores from Bay Street. The waterfront has something for nearly everyone, with thirty-two different planned settings for

Fig. 12.11. Crowds now gather in the new waterfront park (established in 1979), an area that was once the rear lots of Bay Street businesses (1990).

activities including promenades, outdoor theater, and a marina. Planners placed parking, hidden behind attractive landscaping, at either end of the park, making the maximum walk one and a half blocks to the farthest store.[23] Stores along Bay Street now face the park and overlook a sunken lawn area in its middle that can hold gatherings of up to a thousand people. A stage that is part of this composition can address crowds of six thousand assembled around the central lawn. Still, the park retains an engagingly human scale. Robert Marvin, the landscape architect, clustered trees together knowing that the foliage would resemble that of a single tree but the numerous trunks would enrich the scale.[24] Park developers extensively used an exposed oyster-shell aggregate concrete, similar in appearance to the traditional local tabby construction, for details such as benches, bollards, drains, and pavers to unify the complex.

The waterfront park and cleaner water, as well as the successful preservation efforts and new zoning ordinances, have changed the image citizens hold of their town and how they portray it to outsiders.[25] These accomplishments have also sustained the downtown business community. Owners of suburban shopping centers did not oppose downtown development, as the malls were then outside the town's boundaries. Beaufort has since incorporated the outlying areas into its jurisdiction and tax base.[26] The old business district on Bay Street has increasingly focused on specialty trade, offices, and restaurants, as mass merchandising has shifted to the outlying shopping centers.

Throughout the development of the park, various groups feared that one particular group might take control of the area. This has not happened, in part because the design of the park makes everyone feel welcome and safe. However, a subsequent proposal in 1989 to link further the park to the town did not succeed.[27] This plan recommended the establishment of a "cultural corridor" to connect the park to the new arts and professional activities and existing university complex.[28] The plan also suggested increasing the amount of middle-income housing close to the business district. However, Beaufort's African American community and other nearby downtown residents blocked this proposal, fearing it would infringe upon their neighborhoods and contradict the town's historic plan.[29] Nevertheless, aspects of such a cultural corridor have been achieved. For example, the library has expanded within the central area, and the city hall and the post office have also remained downtown. Yet, the county offices have relocated to the edge of town, taking with them activity that otherwise would have reinforced central business and the waterfront park.

Beaufort is now becoming a tourist destination in its own right. While it does not have a beach, it is directly on the Intracoastal Waterway and therefore serves as a convenient stop for boats, yachts, and even cruise ships. Retirees, many of them from the North, are the most rapidly growing group of new residents. Businesses serving tourism and the retirement community have joined the mili-

Fig. 12.12. View west on Boundary Street, around 1930 and 1991. These views, photographed from the same position, show the changes over the past sixty years. In the 1930's rows of palm trees lined the narrow entrance road to Beaufort (photo ca. 1930, South Caroliniana Library). Today, on the right the U.S. National Cemetery, one of ten established by President Lincoln in 1863, still remains. However, the rows of palm trees have been eliminated, the road has been widened, and a commercial strip has been built on the left (1991).

Fig. 12.13. Along Bay Street, a "window on the water" opens vistas to the wetlands and the central business district (1991).

tary and truck farming as the main economic supporters of the community. Unlike in the past, this new and more diversified economy has been relatively immune to recessions. New residents, having made their money elsewhere, are choosing this area for its setting and the quality of life here. Not surprisingly, friction between newcomers and old-time residents does occur, as each group wants to sway the town to its perceived advantage and its accustomed ways.[30] Yet Beaufort continues to support a broad range of income groups living within the historic area.

Beaufort today retains much of its traditional charm and serenity. Its landscape, often noted as having an otherworldly beauty, is still intact. With airconditioning the climate is now tolerable for northerners even during the hot, humid summers. Yet the increasing press of tourism threatens. The approach to Beaufort, which once threaded through expansive marshlands and rows of palm trees, has become a typical commercial strip. Further development and the widening of roads, deemed necessary, will harm the fragile environment. Bridges, particularly those that would arc high above the waterways (sixty-five feet of clearance is required), could disrupt the tranquil, low-lying landscape. Crude waterfront development could irreparably scar the delicate and convoluted boundary between water and land. In partial response to such threats, the city has zoned many areas and the Beaufort County Open Land Trust has purchased critical land parcels to preserve views of marshlands and the bay from main roads.[31]

Three themes underlie the history and character of Beaufort: the agricultural fecundity of the region, its popularity as a resort and cultural center, and the periodic presence of the federal military. Common to all, though for different reasons, has been the extraordinary setting of the Carolina Low Country, a unique environment whose ambiance pervades the town. The architecture of the town has traditionally captured the qualities of this environment, and the town planning, particularly the waterfront park, has more recently realized new opportunities. With conscientious attention, the fragile beauty of Beaufort's natural setting, which has had such an enduring appeal for so many, will not be lost in the quickening pace of life.

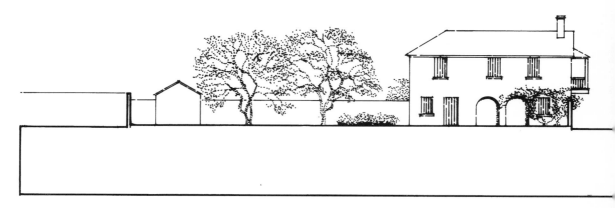

Rendering by Peter Lorenzoni, after a drawing by the author.

CHAPTER THIRTEEN

Saint Augustine, Florida

Fig. 13.1. Street section of Saint Augustine.

Fig. 13.2. Castillo de San Marcos National Monument, with Saint Augustine in the distance. The fort has had a long and varied career, having once served as a prison for Indians and, more recently, as a golf course for summer visitors (1991).

Saint Augustine is situated on a sandy peninsula, one of many low ridges formed as sediment driven shoreward shaped the northern Florida coast. To the east, barrier islands protect Saint Augustine from the open sea and edge the Matanzas River as it broadens into a lagoon in front of the town. Until a century ago when it was partly filled, the Maria Sanchez Creek on the west continued the near circle of water around the town, present on all sides except the north, where the Spanish built Castillo de San Marcos to guard the land approach and narrow sea inlet.[1]

Founded by the Spanish in 1565 as an outpost to defend vital shipping lanes from New Spain to Europe, Saint Augustine grew into a town of strategic imperial, although marginal commercial, importance.[2] Its peninsula location, shallow channels, and shifting inlets initially provided security from marauding enemies, but these same features subsequently impeded economic development. Guided by Spanish town planning principles, these first colonists built a compact and organized community here, which they controlled for more than two hundred years.[3] In 1763 the English gained control, but by 1784 the Spanish had recovered the area. They held it until 1821, when the Americans finally claimed the area. With the political changes came people of different cultures, each of whom contributed to Saint Augustine's character.

Under American control in the early nineteenth century, Saint Augustine slowly gained a reputation as a health resort. Not until Henry Flagler, Rockefeller's Standard Oil partner, discovered the town in the late nineteenth century did it become popular however, attracting a fashionable society it had not seen before and would not know again. Flagler's legacy in Saint Augustine would nevertheless influence subsequent growth throughout Florida. Once the northern outpost of Spanish culture, in the early twentieth century the town became the gateway to southern pleasures for vacationing Americans from the North. While the old street plan survived, fires, raids, and occupations destroyed most of the buildings from earlier periods. In recent years the city has reconstructed and celebrated its Spanish colonial past, at times to the exclusion of other traditions. Saint Augustine is, after all, a blend of different cultures, a fascinating yet often overlooked quality of the town.

Settlement

In 1565, fifty-two years after Ponce de León had claimed Florida for Spain, Don Pedro Menéndez de Avilés established a settlement at Saint Augustine to

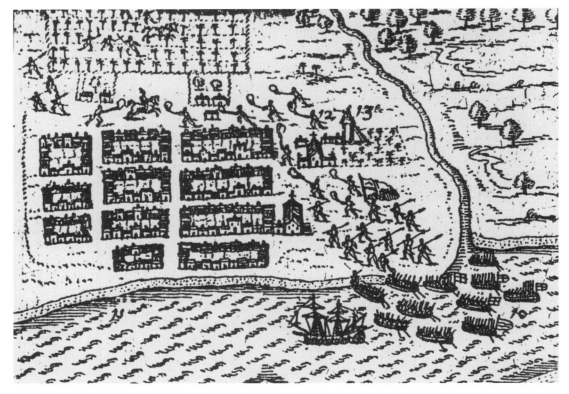

Fig. 13.3. This 1586 detail from the Boazio engraving, the earliest existing illustration of Saint Augustine and of any American settlement, depicts Sir Francis Drake's raiding party. Initial town settlement began south of the plaza, shown to the right in this drawing, where troops are firing on the settlement (Saint Augustine Historical Society, 1586).

thwart French ambitions in northern Florida and to protect Spanish treasure ships. After initially locating about a mile north of the present site, the Spanish established a community at the present location by 1571. Unlike subsequent Spanish settlements, which typically had one colonial purpose, Saint Augustine had three. It was not only a military base (*presidio*) but also a civic trading center (*pueblo* or *villa*) and a religious outpost (*misión*).[4]

To guide expansion in the Americas, Spain began in the early sixteenth century to develop regulations eventually codified in 1573 as the Laws of the Indies.[5] In accordance with these evolving principles, the Spanish sited Saint Augustine on the eastern bank of the river to catch the morning sun, placed its main plaza at the port landing in the center of the town, and made the plaza rectangular in shape.[6] This plaza was an all-purpose public gathering space, used by merchants for markets and by the military for parades. The Spanish planned civic and religious buildings to surround the plaza, with shops and dwellings filling in to complete the central space.[7] Principal streets led out from each corner of the plaza.[8]

While the codes did not specify the rectangular town plan, in many Spanish colonial towns this occurred spontaneously because streets had to connect to central rectangular plazas. In Saint Augustine, the long peninsular shape further encouraged a rectangular street pattern. The Spanish built houses close together to shade narrow lanes and to make the yards and corrals behind as large as possible. Spanish towns built according to the Laws of the Indies were flexible and expandable, largely because the town center contained the important civic buildings while the town periphery, with buildings of unspecified function, could change. However, Saint Augustine's peninsula location, coupled with the necessity for the fort at one end and the existence of a monastery at the other, constrained its growth. Since Saint Augustine lacked abundant natural resources and never had a large exploitable native population, the Spanish had to continue to subsidize its development for strategic purposes.[9]

Spanish Colonial Period

The settlement of Saint Augustine began south of the planned plaza, on the highest ground available. According to a map drawn by a member of Sir Francis Drake's party, who raided the settlement in 1586, there were eleven rectangular blocks of varying size. In the early seventeenth century, most development remained south of the plaza. In the late seventeenth century, building activity shifted to the northern area between the plaza and Castillo. The town grew in spite of attacks from the British, the French, and pirates. After the British

Fig. 13.4. In this relatively new Saint Augustine house, constructed in the old style, a loggia enlarges the building, which faces south to a garden courtyard through which one enters (1991).

burned Saint Augustine in 1702, the Spanish constructed a series of defense positions and fortifications north, west, and south of the settlement.[10]

During the seventeenth century, residents were relatively poor and typically lived in small one-story, two-room houses. After 1672, they built houses with thick masonry walls to protect against fire and to shield living spaces from chilling northern winter winds and hot summer sun. A loggia, or piazza, often increased the size of the house. Preferably, the loggia faced south or east to a garden or courtyard. Entrance to the house was through the garden or courtyard, not directly from the street.[11]

English, Second Spanish, and American Periods

With the Treaty of Paris in 1763, Spain relinquished Florida to the British, producing maps that would later aid twentieth-century preservationists, who came to view this time as the preferred date for restoration purposes. During the American Revolution, British refugees who fled to Saint Augustine from South Carolina and Georgia introduced the Anglican church and altered the landscape of the Spanish plaza to appear as a Georgian square, with a lawn and shade trees. They also built fireplaces and chimneys and added second stories to the Spanish houses. On these upper levels, residents enjoyed comfortable overhanging balconies where they could relax in breezy shade, watch activity in the street below, and converse with friends on neighboring balconies.[12]

In 1784 the Spanish regained control of Saint Augustine and remained until 1821, when Spain ceded East Florida to the United States. During these shifts, Saint Augustine added to its population mix. Historian Patricia Griffin comments on this diversity: "Possibly no small town on the North American continent has ever had such a diverse population. In the span of the thirty-seven years

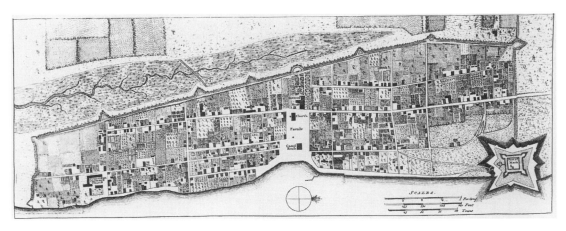

Map 13.1. Drawn in 1764, this map has guided recent restoration in Saint Augustine because it depicts the town at the end of its first Spanish period.

Fig. 13.5. *Street balconies, featured on residential, commercial, and civic buildings in Saint Augustine, thematically unify the town (1991).*

of the second Spanish period, Spaniards, Englishmen, Americans, Minorcans, Italians, Greeks, Swiss, Germans, French, Canary Islanders, Scots and Irish rendered the little town cosmopolitan."[13]

The Spanish built a new and larger church in 1796. They constructed substantial houses and more definitively established a Spanish Colonial Domestic style of architecture. Abandoning the old defensive line, the Spanish created a

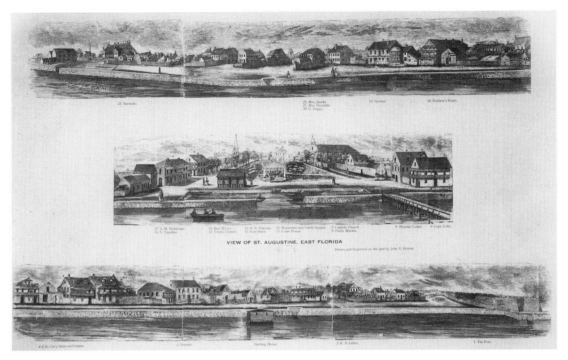

VIEW OF ST. AUGUSTINE, EAST FLORIDA

Fig. 13.6. View of the east side (waterfront) of Saint Augustine in 1855, as drawn by John S. Horton (Saint Augustine Historical Society, 1855).

three-quarter-mile swath of cleared land north of the city gates in which they allowed only temporary wooden structures, an area in which today large open spaces still exist for playing fields and tourist parking lots.[14]

With the Americanization of Saint Augustine during the early nineteenth century, visitors came to enjoy the town's old-world charm and explore its fort, now more romantic than defensive. Wealthy northerners escaping cold winters retreated here for the benign climate, sea breezes, and abundant fruits and vegetables. Invalids, particularly tubercular patients, found Saint Augustine restful and recuperative. During the 1830s and 1840s several hundred visitors came each year, usually lodging in private homes.

After federal forces easily took control of Saint Augustine in 1862, they rested troops here and organized a hospital and convalescent center, activities that added to the town's reputation as a health resort.[15] The military continued to sustain the economy after the Civil War, while tourism grew slowly. Saint Augustine was no longer only for consumptive invalids seeking relief—visitors increasingly came for the town's old-world charms, sunny climate, hunting, and sport fishing. Gradually the town expanded outside its historic boundaries, though it still lacked good overland transportation, forcing most visitors to come by sea. Finally, in 1883, rail connections were extended from Jacksonville. With links to the North, Saint Augustine now had new opportunities for development.

Henry Morrison Flagler

Henry M. Flagler was one of the first to recognize the development possibilities of Saint Augustine, and he had the resources to realize them. Having retired early as the enormously wealthy partner of John D. Rockefeller, Flagler first visited Saint Augustine in 1883. Captivated by the town and sensing Florida's development potential, Flagler decided to create a society resort here comparable to Newport, Rhode Island.[16] By 1885 he had purchased the railroad to Saint Augustine and bought a forty-acre tract of orange groves and swamps west of the old town wall.[17] He hired two young New York City architects, John Carrère and Thomas Hastings, to design first the Ponce de Leon Hotel, then the Alcazar Hotel, and eventually other buildings in Saint Augustine.[18]

In developing these projects, Flagler and his architects altered the landscape but respected the Spanish Colonial town plan. However, they did not choose hotel sites from which guests could enjoy ocean views. Instead they selected inland property immediately west of the colonial plaza, three blocks from the water. To prepare the site for the hotels, they filled in the headwaters of the Maria

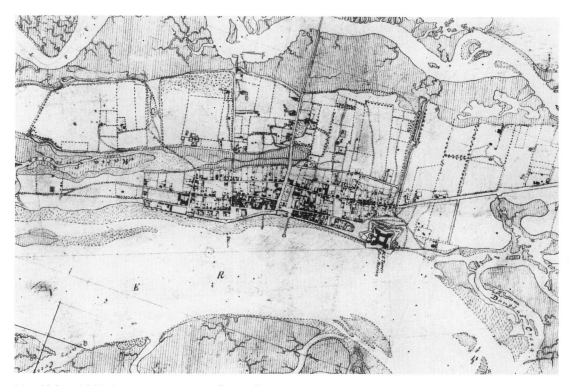

Map 13.2. In 1860, Saint Augustine was still a small town, lying primarily within its old Spanish boundaries. Wetlands edge the west side of the community, where Flagler later built his hotels in the 1880s (U.S. Coast and Geodetic Survey, 1860).

Fig. 13.7. Looking east, the original Flagler hotels are in the foreground grouped around the
Alameda. Beyond them is the plaza, now filled with trees, fronting on the Matanzas River
(Flagler College, ca. 1990).

Sanchez Creek, the wetlands that historically had protected the town's western
flank.[19] On this reclaimed land they created a new public space, approximately
two hundred by three hundred feet, around which they sited the hotels. They
designed it as an alameda, a formally landscaped park, as opposed to the all-
purpose, open plaza.[20]

Carrère and Hastings sited the Ponce de Leon Hotel to allow guests entering
the town from Flagler's railroad station on the western side views of the main
cathedral to the east.[21] Opposite the Ponce de Leon and across the Alameda,
Flagler built his second hotel, the Alcazar, which had a recreation casino and
boasted the world's largest indoor swimming pool. He also bought a neighboring third hotel (the Casa Monica, which he renamed the Cordova) from a failing
developer. Remarkably, Flagler's hotel complex, potentially threatening in size
to the old city, successfully related to the smaller-scaled existing buildings
through skillful site planning, landscaping, massing of buildings, and architectural detailing.

From 1885 to the early 1900s Flagler dominated the town. He widened and
paved public streets around his developments and laid out a subdivision further
west of his hotel complex. He also built churches, his winter home, a hospital, a
municipal government building, a public market, a firehouse, courtrooms, a

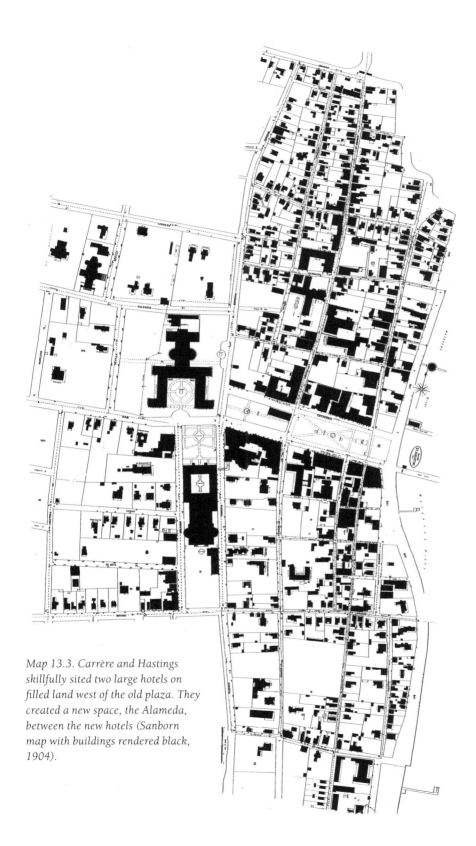

Map 13.3. *Carrère and Hastings
skillfully sited two large hotels on
filled land west of the old plaza. They
created a new space, the Alameda,
between the new hotels (Sanborn
map with buildings rendered black,
1904).*

Top: *Fig. 13.8. View of the Flagler hotel complex from the Ponce de Leon (before the summer of 1891). Carrère and Hastings designed the Ponce de Leon (foreground) and the Alcazar (on the right) across the Alameda. Flagler bought the Casa Monica (middle distance) to complete his hotel complex.* Bottom: *Fig. 13.9. View of the former Ponce de Leon Hotel (Special Collections, University of Virginia). Designed by Carrère and Hastings and completed in 1888, this once exclusive winter resort is now part of Flagler College (1991).*

waterworks, an electric plant, and a jail. In these structures, as in the hotels, his architects recalled Spanish architectural themes.[22] Most notably, Carrère and Hastings invented the "Spanish Renaissance Revival style," which subsequently became associated with Florida's twentieth-century development.[23]

With fashionable guests arriving to spend the four winter months, the town prospered and more than doubled in year-round population, to 4,742, during the 1880s. Flagler brought vitality to Saint Augustine, but he also encountered local opposition. Residents resisted paying additional taxes for the improvements he sought.[24] Ironically, the poverty and conservatism that had preserved the town's charm, thereby attracting Flagler's attention, now frustrated him.[25] Losing interest in Saint Augustine in the late 1890s, Flagler looked to southern Florida, where weather was warmer and development more controllable. While he retained ownership of the Saint Augustine hotels, Flagler extended his Florida East Coast Railroad to Key West and developed a chain of resorts along the route. Flagler's railroad continued to be headquartered in Saint Augustine and remained a major employer. However, the town lost its fashionable appeal after Flagler's departure. Saint Augustine became a stopover for tourists heading south rather than a destination in its own right. Flagler nevertheless left an extraordinary legacy, and his hotels still form a remarkable complex and are prominent features of the city's skyline.

Flagler introduced the concept of the theme park to Florida, even though this type of entertainment was already spreading throughout the country and the modern tourist industry. He and his architects reinvented Saint Augustine as a glamorous "Spanish" city, taking what had been an old, isolated, impoverished small town and, by altering it with new additions, creating an imagined, idealized life for vacationers seeking a designed setting and orchestrated events.[26] As the Disney Company would later do in nearby Orlando, Flagler integrated his hotels with his "theme park."

During the depression, hotel patronage declined. Increasingly, travelers came by car, not rail, and wished to stay in more convenient and informal accommodations along highways.[27] After World War II, the city encouraged businesses that had been displaced by Spanish Colonial style reconstructions to relocate to the unoccupied hotels around the Alameda. However, these businesses also preferred to join the suburban exodus. In the 1960s the city renovated a part of the Alcazar Hotel for municipal offices and allocated the rest to the Lightner Museum for its collection of art, antiques, and hobby artifacts. In 1968, St. Johns County purchased the Cordova Hotel for its offices and court facilities, and the Ponce de Leon Hotel became Flagler College. By 1997, however, the county had outgrown its facilities in the old Cordova Hotel and relocated to a new judicial center north of town. A new luxury hotel now occupies the Cordova, returning that building to its original turn-of-the-century use.

Saint Augustine's Preservation Movement

While Flagler boldly created a resort that capitalized on the city's traditional charms, others, working more cautiously and with less financial resources, succeeded him to address preservation of the town's antiquities. The Saint Augustine Historical Society became the forum for these interests.[28] Inspired by the restoration of Williamsburg, Virginia, which had begun in 1926, and with support from the Carnegie Institute, the society initiated building preservation efforts in Saint Augustine during the 1930s.[29] Abandoned with the outbreak of World War II, preservation was revived after the war and gained support thanks to the city's preparation for its quadricentennial, in 1965. In 1959 Governor Leroy Collins established a new state agency called the Historic Saint Augustine Preservation Board, whose recommendations significantly guided subsequent work. The board concluded that preservation should emphasize the period of the first Spanish occupation, focusing "at or near 1763," which was the end of the Spanish period and the beginning of the British Colonial period. It also encouraged citizens to continue their normal use of the city.[30] In retrospect, these were difficult goals to reconcile.

Although its preservation policies are controversial today, the board based them on legitimate concerns at the time. It realized Saint Augustine would have neither significant state funding nor a great benefactor such as Rockefeller in Willliamsburg to support its efforts. Instead, Saint Augustine had to appeal to a broad market and proceed carefully. Because of devastating fires, the most recent in 1914, the board argued that Saint Augustine did not have an outstanding intact building tradition to restore and was thus free to choose from the many in its past. By selecting Saint Augustine's first Spanish Colonial period, the board hoped to offer a unique environment that could follow but not compete with Williamsburg's successful presentation of British colonial life. Moreover, the Spanish and English had left detailed maps and other property records that proved useful in restoration efforts.[31]

Guided by these policies, the board initiated a master plan and created a nonprofit educational organization called Saint Augustine Restoration, Incorporated. This organization had a revolving fund derived from gifts, loans, and, later, rental income. In 1963 the board successfully lobbied the U.S. Congress to establish the Quadricentennial Committee to organize the forthcoming anniversary and to publicize the city's international role, particularly its Latin American relationships.[32] As its priorities, the board put preservation first, then restoration, and, if neither of these options were possible, authorized the reconstruction of buildings. However, since few historic buildings remained, reconstruction dominated. Nineteenth- and twentieth-century buildings were demolished to rebuild eighteenth-century Spanish style buildings.

However controversial, the restoration board presented a clear vision that unified the principles of preservation, reuse, and education.[33] Board members concentrated preservation efforts in the designated San Agustin Antiguo Restoration Area. They selected this northern section of the historic district along St. George Street because it had historic buildings, old foundations, and deteriorated existing structures that they could purchase for demolition using federal Urban Renewal funds. They envisioned St. George Street, the existing commercial street connecting the city gate and central plaza, reconstructed as a "typical eighteenth-century street," and encouraged tourist commercial uses and colonial life exhibits to open there. Pursuing this vision, the board solicited Spanish Colonial exhibits from outside sponsors, including the Spanish government (who built a Spanish Pavilion), some United States companies conducting business in Latin America (who constructed a Pan American Center), and the Florida Medical Association (who supported a Spanish hospital and pharmacy). Local merchants also operated exhibits in conjunction with shops.

The board viewed Charlotte Street, east of and parallel to St. George Street, as an access route and location for secondary uses such as services, offices, and residences. During the eighteenth century Charlotte Street served as the town's main street, connecting Castillo de San Marcos on the north to the plaza and barracks (which housed an old monastery) on the south. Residents used St. George Street primarily to reach outlying farms. By 1965 thirty structures had been restored or reconstructed in the restoration district, a significant achievement given the limited funding sources, multiple ownership of the area, and existing hybrid buildings. The resulting unified collection of buildings emphasizes the overall character of the district. At the same time these restorations are confusing, since all but the most knowledgeable observers walking along St. George Street have difficulty distinguishing authentic buildings from reconstructed or fabricated ones.[34]

The restoration board believed that the restoration of residences was desirable not only to maintain a "living city" but also because of the impracticality of restoring all buildings as historic museums. Many of the buildings sponsored through the federal Urban Renewal Program were conceived with shops below and housing above. However, combining tourism and residential life proved difficult. The architectural review board, established in 1974, insisted on specific activities and appearances in the historic district. Some people, though initially interested in living in the historic district, found the restrictions too inconvenient and decided not to purchase houses here. Wealthy retirees and second-home buyers have also not favored Saint Augustine, partly because they believe the mixed uses of the historic district would be too distracting as a living environment and because Saint Augustine lacks a collection of old, elegant houses to restore. Instead, retirees have preferred the convenience and security of the private, golf-oriented resort communities that have developed along the coast outside Saint Augustine.

Rebuilding slowed after 1968, when the governor appointed new preservation board members. Faced with reduced budgets, the board began to favor research rather than more reconstruction. While board members sought self-supporting retail sales exhibits (a weaver's shop, a coppersmith, and a blacksmith), they lost most education and interpretive programs for lack of funding.[35]

Archaeological work continued while tourist shops filled the vacant spaces, selling items often unrelated to Saint Augustine's history.

From today's perspective, the decision to focus preservation efforts on a specific period was questionable. Why should one period be more important than another? Indeed, should buildings of one era be demolished to allow simulation of a different time? Should Saint Augustine reinvent itself in terms of a romanticized past, or should it celebrate ongoing change, however tawdry, quixotic, and confusing that may be? Saint Augustine is remarkable not only for its Spanish heritage but also for the variety of cultural groups that have contributed to its history. It is a community that has grown and survived through the actions and beliefs of many people. For example, in 1777 Minorcans settled in what would become the restoration district. Regrettably, since they were not from the chosen period, the buildings of the Minorcans have not been featured in recent preservation efforts. While there are instructive exhibits on the variety in Saint Augustine's past, most notably the Gonzalez-Alvarez House (built ca. 1720–27), which documents three centuries of change in one dwelling, the richly diverse heritage of Saint Augustine is not well presented in the town's context.

Transportation for Tourism

Possibly of all the issues Saint Augustine has faced, the city has dealt most wisely with vehicular transportation. Initiated by different agencies over a long period of time and at different scales, these actions nevertheless have related to one another and have saved Saint Augustine from the destructive influence of automobiles that has damaged other towns. During the first half of Florida's twentieth-century development, East Coast tourist traffic passed through Saint Augustine. Travelers from the north drove down the coast on U.S. 1, called "the Dixie Highway," and then passed through the city gate and St. George Street to Saint Augustine's old plaza on their way to South Florida. In 1956 a bypass was built, saving Saint Augustine from traffic generated by Florida's subsequent extraordinary growth. Additional bridges and Interstate 95, six miles west, further protected Saint Augustine from unnecessary traffic.

As early as the 1930s, the city addressed local tourist traffic issues. With assistance from the federal Works Progress Administration, it built the Visitors Information Center, appropriately locating reception and parking facilities north of the old city, where most travelers arrive and where sufficient parking was available. After parking their cars in adjacent lots, visitors today can view an introductory film in the information center, walk to Castillo de San Marcos, which is the major regional tourist attraction, pass through the town gate, and walk down St. George Street to Cathedral Plaza.[36] Visitors can also ride trolleys from the information center to view historic sites. In 1997 there were over one million visitors to Saint Augustine.[37]

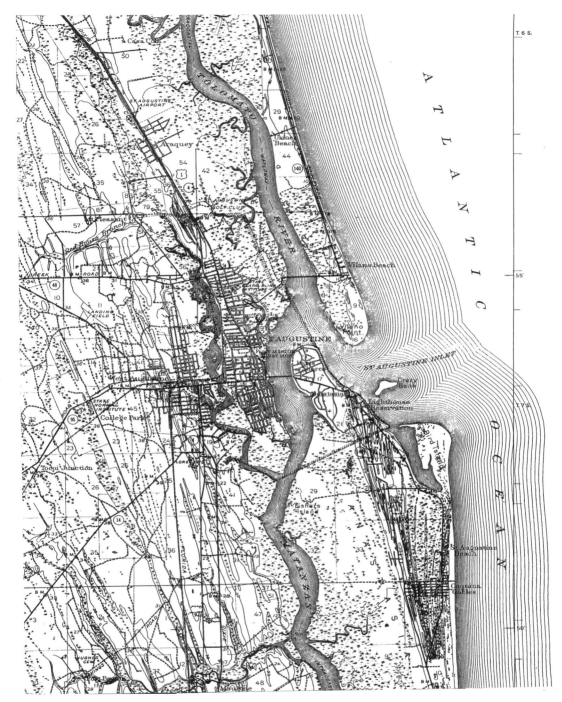

Map 13.4. Map of the Saint Augustine region (1943). Protected from the open Atlantic, Saint Augustine lies directly behind barrier islands in an intricate topography of rivers, bays, marshes, and sand bars. The coastal highway, U.S. Route 1, passed through the heart of Saint Augustine until 1956 (U.S. Coast and Geodetic Survey, 1943).

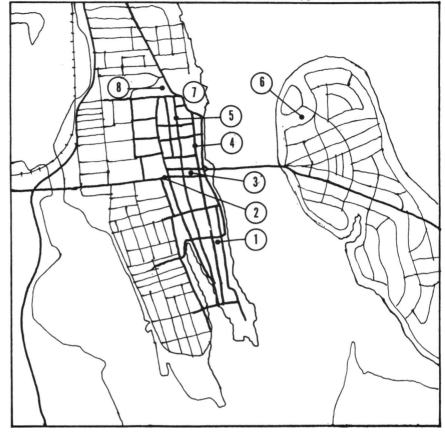

Map 13.5. Location Map of Saint Augustine, Florida (redrawn
from current U.S. Coast and Geodetic Survey maps).
1. St. Francis Barracks; 2. Flagler hotels; 3. Plaza; 4. Charlotte Street; 5. St. George Street;
6. Davis Shores; 7. Castillo de San Marcos (Fort Marion); 8. Visitors' center.

As part of its restoration efforts in the north section of the historic district, the
restoration board wisely placed parking for nearby property owners within the
middle of street blocks, where yards and corrals had been during the Colonial
period. Surrounded by walls, this parking now serves both St. George and
Charlotte Streets. In the 1960s, the board also persuaded the city to limit St.
George Street to pedestrians, one of the nation's first efforts to restrict cars on a
retail street. Here, with the narrow fifteen-foot-wide street connecting on either
end to the plaza and the Castillo, as well as the opportunity for cars to cross on
perpendicular streets, the strategy has been effective. Consequently, today cars
are convenient but not intrusive. Pedestrians still determine the character and
scale of the town.

Top: Fig. 13.10. *View of St. George Street, ca. 1900. A century ago this street was even more intimately scaled than it is today (Special Collections, University of Virginia).* Bottom: Fig. 13.11. *View looking south on St. George Street. Since the 1960s, the city has reserved this street for pedestrians, allowing tourists to walk easily from the old fort to the central plaza. The view of the Cathedral steeple on the plaza serves as a useful landmark along the walk (1990).*

Current Issues

Ironically, Saint Augustine, the country's oldest existing settlement and one based on specific town planning principles, did not have zoning until 1975 and only gained an official planning department in 1982. Until then, outside consultants and state agencies provided planning services. Today, the planning department considers the town "built out," with little room for new construction.[38] Planning instead focuses on the protection of existing resources and archaeological research. The city requires that all new construction in the colonial district reproduce either Spanish or British Colonial architecture. The planning department has also defined a conservation zone ordinance and willingly uses this legislation to approve or deny development proposals. Both the city and state have archaeological ordinances as well.[39] Saint Augustine now has a thirty-five-foot height limitation on buildings, wisely preserving its distinctive skyline.

With federal, state, and local governments, the Catholic Church, and Flagler College as major property owners, the city can tax only 49 percent of Saint Augustine's property. Consequently, the city depends on revenue from its sales tax and, ultimately, on tourists who pay the tax. Dependency on tourists can be a mixed blessing. Tourist stores, services, and exhibits, often only superficially related to Saint Augustine, line routes into the town, presenting a tawdry introduction. Meanwhile, the city seeks greater intergovernmental coordination with surrounding St. Johns County to compensate for the city's poor tax base and also to plan jointly for common traffic problems generated by new county development. The city and county have an agreement to review independently development along their common boundary. Saint Augustine and the surrounding county are becoming more economically diversified and less dependent on tourism, as several light industries have moved into the area. Tourism has also broadened. Today the city of Saint Augustine offers not only its antiquities but also a base from which to explore the surroundings—other archaeological sites, beaches and parks, and sports and amusement attractions.

Saint Augustine—marginally located, tenuously settled, disputed, flooded, burned, altered, reconstructed, and, now, commercialized—has nevertheless survived. With compelling reasons to fail, it has continued to adjust and recreate itself. With the notable exception of Henry Flagler's contributions, Saint Augustine is a town that favored simple, utilitarian means, that built incrementally according to a plan, and that featured a special site. It is a settlement that survived, although it would have benefited if the record of that survival, the curious twists and turns of events, the intermingling of different cultures, could have remained more evident in the town today. Even so, Saint Augustine is a richly informative place.

CHAPTER FOURTEEN

Conclusion: Threats and Opportunities

Historic coastal towns are in areas of dynamic change, where threatening natural and human forces converge and, in turn, generate controversial environmental and land-use issues. How these issues are resolved will affect not only the qualities of coastal regions but also those of inland areas. Coastal towns, which were the bases from which continental settlement in the east spread westward, are now emerging as catalysts for regional land-use management. In the past, isolated sites, local customs, and limited technologies shaped each historic coastal town independently. Today population pressures, transportation systems, and patterns of behavior spread rapidly throughout the country, reaching and influencing these communities at the same time, however remote they may have once been. Common solutions to coastal problems are possible, but ultimately the wisest solutions will address the specific conditions and characteristics of each town.

Coastal Population Growth

Since World War II, the United States has experienced major population growth in coastal areas. In 1996, 53 percent of the American people lived in coastal counties, roughly a fifty-mile-wide band along the coasts encompassing only eleven percent of the nation's land.[1] The population density of coastal counties is about 340 people per square mile, more than quadruple the national average. The Atlantic coastal counties alone constitute 23 percent of the nation's total population.[2]

Although not recorded in census figures, the growth of tourism indicates another intensifying human use of coastal areas. From 1975 to 1995, tourism-related industries (e.g., lodging, transportation, casinos, and restaurants) grew from 6.9 percent to 9.8 percent of all U.S. jobs.[3] Coastal areas hosted a high percentage of this activity. The nature of tourism is also changing. Americans today seek shorter, more convenient, and more intense vacations than they did a generation ago. Two-income families, especially, have more complex schedules and must coordinate responsibilities to find shared time. Historic coastal towns, particularly those near metropolitan areas, offer advantages of convenience. All nine towns discussed in this book are within a four-hour drive of a major urban center and are accessible to large numbers of people seeking weekend excursions.[4] Even a small influx of people noticeably affects these towns because of their limited size and fragile environments.

As more people frequent coastal areas, either as tourists for short periods, second-home buyers for summer seasons, or permanent residents seeking employment, they change these environments. They and the developers working for them have filled many wetlands and built in unstable and storm-prone areas. They have overloaded the community infrastructures of roads, water supplies, and waste treatment facilities and exacerbated runoff sediments and storm-water pollutants.[5] New arrivals also often increase the value of property, making it difficult for local people to afford housing. Too often suburban building practices that employ standardized lots, uniform setbacks, and automobile-oriented patterns have dominated new development, conflicting with the traditional, smaller-scaled, denser pedestrian environments of historic coastal towns. Such development also consumes the open spaces that have been integral to these towns. People come to enjoy the beauty of the coast, yet too often they ignore the collective problems they cause there. Officials in both the United States and other countries continue to debate the solutions to these problems, because their ramifications reach beyond national shores.[6]

Natural Forces of Change in Coastal Environments

Waves, tides, and winds are continually reshaping coastal environments. These forces transport sand and other materials through water and air to gradually alter landforms. Rivers bring deposits from inland sources to coastal estuaries. Biological life thrives in coastal environments and adds more organic materials. These forces cause landforms to build up, migrate, subside, and separate. Along the Atlantic coast, residents accept storms and hurricanes as inevitable events, but these are also major agents of change and threats to life and property. Coastal storms bring surges that can rise twenty feet or more above normal tides. Along the Mid- and South Atlantic coasts, surges are especially dangerous because they can sweep across the flat shores of these regions.

Through geological time, the oceans have risen and fallen across a vertical range of about a thousand feet.[7] While scientists and politicians debate the reality and effects of global warming, the sea level is currently rising. The last primary rise in the sea began about eighteen thousand years ago, occurring at a rate of one to two millimeters annually (about one foot per century) as indicated by tidal gauges around the world and documented in eroding beaches and receding glaciers. In the last century this rise has increased measurably, and there is growing scientific consensus that by the year 2100 the sea level could rise between 0.5 and 1.5 meters, depending on assumptions about global warming.[8]

Most land conversion to open water has been occurring in river deltas, but in the twenty-first century the problems of water reclaiming land will be more widespread. Scientists estimate that if the sea rises one meter it will inundate approximately 7,000 square miles of land in the United States—an area comparable to the size of Massachusetts.[9] The consequences of this shoreline migration would be further land erosion, flooding, destruction of property, saltwater intrusion into groundwater supplies, and damage to infrastructures such as roads and bridges.[10] Low-lying coastal towns, of course, would be the most vulnerable.

Efforts to Address Coastal Problems

The centerpiece of federal coastal policy in the United States is the Coastal Zone Management Act (CZMA), first enacted by Congress in 1972. Administered by the Department of Commerce, the CZMA seeks to address comprehensively the country's coastal problems. To gain federal funding as part of this legislation, states must prepare and implement coastal management programs. All the Atlantic states in this book have enacted CZMA legislation. Under these programs, local towns must develop and periodically update comprehensive plans according to state objectives. For these purposes, local governments may exercise their land-use planning functions of zoning, historic preservation, and subdivision regulations, as well as traffic management and disaster relief. The level of commitment and funding varies according to jurisdictions. For example, Saint Augustine, Florida, and Beaufort, South Carolina, have active planning staffs and programs and regularly employ outside planning and preservation consultants. Other towns rely for planning assistance on the larger jurisdictions of which they are a part. Several towns employ no local professional planners, nor do they have convenient, ongoing access to them in other jurisdictions. Instead, these towns rely on citizen volunteers to assume these responsibilities.

Other federal programs also affect coastal zone development. The Clean Water Act, by restricting fill and waste discharge into waters of the United States, has helped towns correct disposal problems and develop waterfronts for recreational purposes. The National Flood Insurance Program provides flood insurance coverage to owners of flood-prone land. Modifying this program, the Coastal Barrier Resources Act mandates that the federal government will not issue new flood insurance or postdisaster assistance for new development in environmentally sensitive areas. The government has also preserved through public acquisition and management important barrier beaches and associated ecosystems, and it has established seven National Seashores from Cape Cod to Cape Canaveral as well as additional wildlife refuges. Private organizations such as the Nature Conservancy have also been active in coastal land acquisition.

Particularly since the enactment of CZMA legislation and the introduction of more stringent federal and state laws, the loss of wetlands has diminished. Some states have required setback regulations and density stipulations for hazardous zones. Most have imposed significant limitations on development in tidal or saltwater wetlands. A few states are even beginning to include the sea level rise in their programs and provide incentives for relocating buildings to safer sites.[11]

At the heart of these efforts is a fundamental issue—the extent to which government should collectivize the risks of building in endangered coastal areas. For example, the National Flood Insurance Program offers subsidized insurance to owners of flood-prone property in participating communities. While only a quarter of those eligible elect to subscribe, the total federal financial liability is second only to that of social security.[12] In addition, the federal government, through its disaster assistance (the law mandates no less than a 75% federal payment for disaster assistance) and through its income tax code, which allows casualty-loss, interest, and property tax deductions for second homes, has further permitted and even encouraged hazardous development in coastal areas.[13] Many property owners in such areas view flood insurance as an entitlement and even a form of government approval for building in risk-prone areas. Government agencies should reconsider their subsidization policies along the coasts and instead limit these efforts to areas of significant public importance.

The Future of Historic American Coastal Towns

Historic coastal towns are living records of how the United States was first settled and has subsequently evolved. Situated in areas of change, these towns warrant public protection. While small in size, they carry great national significance. However, developers will continue to seek new opportunities, property owners will protect their individual rights, sea levels will rise and fall, and shorelines will migrate. Historic coastal towns will have to accommodate these realities while establishing policies to preserve their cultural legacies. The strategies and discussion that follow address these objectives:

- Encourage coastal growth in towns and not in surrounding open space.

Development should occur in existing towns and in new locations that are protected from storms and have transportation access, means for emergency evacuations, and freshwater supplies, not in open spaces. By combining population densities within towns and preserving the open spaces surrounding them, opportunities for public transportation and reductions in energy consumption, air pollution, and the number and size of roads are possible.

Coastal towns exist within patterns of regional activity. Historically, town residents were more self-sufficient as they locally harvested food, sought employment, schooled their children, and retired within these communities to pass on responsibilities to succeeding generations. Since World War II and the development of highway networks, residents have traveled increasing distances to work, shop, recreate, and socialize. Regional patterns should support these new linkages and associations. Not every town can provide sophisticated medical

Fig. 14.1. Lower Main Street, Edgartown, Massachusetts. Empty cars occupy this special location where Main Street ends at the water's edge (1992).

services to care for the elderly and infirm, land for industrial development to diversify the economic base and thereby expand employment opportunities, and oceanfront recreation access to benefit a wide range of people in the region. Residents of inland communities should be able to enjoy the amenities of coastal towns, while the residents of coastal towns should have access to the services, opportunities, and economies of scale that other areas can more easily accommodate. All must address the shared problems of pollution, traffic management, tourism, and a rising sea level.

• Support the public services and communal qualities of coastal towns.

Historic coastal towns offer people a common ground on which to gather because, more so than most other types of towns, they emphasize public features. Not only do they face and access the water, which is public property, but they often occupy strategic sites at the convergence of transportation systems.[14] As ports, many were official entry points into the country. Citizens developed buildings and spaces to serve the public. This public orientation should continue.

With the growing restrictions on coastal development, town waterfronts are becoming recognized as appropriate places to maintain water access. Fishing, warehousing, and industrial uses have declined, if not vanished, along most waterfronts. Mixed uses such as tourist retail shops, housing, offices, and recreation spread activities over the time of day and year and thus encourage more intense utilization. Priority now should be given to water-related uses that would enrich these locations. Large waterfront parking lots are single-use, overscaled misappropriations of critical sites. Beaufort, South Carolina, has rebuilt its waterfront to include an activity for virtually every interest group in the community. It linked these activities with a promenade along the water's edge and provided pockets of landscaped parking to serve nearby business. Arguably, Beaufort's waterfront now commands more of the town's focus than at any time in its history.

Besides having direct waterfront access, these towns should allow people views of the water from locations within. Although streets no longer end in wharves, old water vistas should remain. In Edenton, North Carolina, there are dramatic views down streets of the distant bay. In Ocean Grove, New Jersey, the "flaring avenues" effectively connect the body of the town to the water. Stonington, Connecticut, seeks to reclaim from private encroachments old pedestrian rights-of-way to the waterfront. In Beaufort, South Carolina, a land trust is purchasing critical shoreline properties to establish public "windows on the

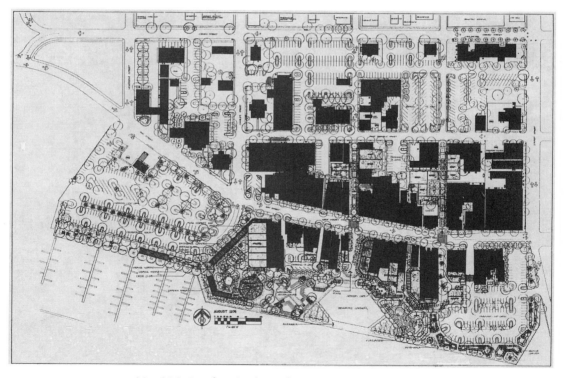

Map 14.1. Beaufort, South Carolina, Central Business District Plan, by Robert E. Marvin and Associates (1974). The new waterfront park replaced derelict wharves with a promenade along the river, a performance area, a marina, and landscaped parking areas. The park now presents a new and inviting "front" to Beaufort and connects successfully to the adjacent downtown business district.

Fig. 14.2. Beaufort, South Carolina (1991). Top left: the waterfront promenade and the marina in background. Top right: a bench-swing overlooking the waterfront promenade and river. Bottom left: the main public space in the waterfront park and the river beyond. Bottom right: the primary pedestrian connection to the old business district from the waterfront park.

water." These communities allow their water surroundings to be a visible part of everyday life.

The public importance of a building is often indicated by its height. In coastal towns this aspect is particularly important because people view the buildings from the sea as well as from land, often across large open spaces. Visitors and residents alike appreciate the overall town silhouettes. In the flat landscape of Edenton, North Carolina, the old courthouse sits on a rise of land to command its surroundings. The central public buildings in New Castle, Delaware, each with an expressive roof profile, comprise an impressive civic ensemble. Older buildings in these and other towns, having been built before the introduction of the elevator, are two and three and, occasionally, four stories high. Flagrant height violations remain a recurring threat because tall, newer buildings often disregard time-honored expressions and unduly emphasize mediocre design. In Saint Augustine, Florida, a massive bank building from the 1920s, although of some architectural merit, here intrudes upon and dominates an older skyline of spires and towers. Coastal towns should value their expressive profiles and distant views.[15]

Fig. 14.3. The massive block of a 1920s bank building now dominates the skyline of Saint
Augustine (1991). The city recently instituted a thirty-five-foot height limit for new
construction.

Within towns, civic environments support public life. Buildings shape spaces
that together form town identities. Public buildings in Edgartown, Massachusetts, sit prominently at the ends of streets; in Castine, Maine, they group around
a common; and in New Castle, Delaware, they accent the Green. The buildings
reflect pride and shared meanings. They shape spaces that are civic yet accommodating, large enough for public celebrations yet appropriately scaled for individuals. Private buildings serve as backgrounds, or "walls," for public buildings,
allowing the public ones to dominate.

• Encourage pedestrian use and scale.

Pedestrians are the measure of movement here, and therefore they influence
perception and experience in these compact towns. Through their pace, range,
and attention, pedestrians set limits to town size and encourage the creation of
places within, especially town centers. There are informal areas for casual encounters and more formal spaces for special occasions. Walking through these
settings from home to work, to stores, to church, and to schools, residents enjoy
a comfortable familiarity with a variety of activities. In recent years, however,
automobiles and trucks have endangered these spaces and activities. Automobiles alter the mood of the community and force activities away from streets
and into parking lots. Historic coastal towns should benefit from the convenience of automobiles but not allow cars to transform them. Too many essential
features of historic towns depend on pedestrians and the way they interact with
the environment.

Traditional towns grew slowly and incrementally. Local customs, restricted building materials, limited technical skills, and multiple ownership produced buildings that were similar to each other but also expressed individual taste and a human scale. Uncontrolled new construction of large parcels under single ownership can easily violate these traditional town qualities. Buildings derived from urban prototypes, in particular, can harm small towns. Recent large buildings at the Maine Maritime Academy in Castine, Maine, no longer continue the historic scale of the town into the new campus but instead overwhelm surrounding older buildings. In Kennebunkport, Maine, a motel over six hundred feet long blocks physical and visual access to the harbor and disregards the scale of the neighboring village. On the other hand, in Edgartown, Massachusetts, as new commercial development extends out from the historic district, modern construction retains traditional patterns—building setbacks, scale, materials— even as the buildings become larger in area and more convenient for automobile access.

• Restrict automobiles and trucks and encourage bicycle use within towns.

Automobile congestion is a growing problem for many historic coastal towns, particularly in popular tourist centers. Increased traffic often results in automobile services replacing historic structures, roads being widened, trees being cut down, and ill-defined parking areas taking over places where buildings once framed pleasant street spaces. At times, automobile traffic can overwhelm these towns. On an average summer day, some twenty thousand vehicles cross the narrow two-lane bridge into Dock Square in Kennebunkport, Maine. Many of these cars park randomly on either side of the road or in poorly managed lots. Out-of-town drivers indiscriminately enter and exit traffic, further congesting the flow. Coastal towns cannot accommodate such excessive and unmanaged traffic and still maintain their historic and pedestrian qualities.

Through traffic should bypass historic districts. Many towns founded on coastal trade, such as Castine, Maine, and Stonington, Connecticut, are on peninsulas or islands and thus primarily accommodate local traffic. However, highway and bridge improvements built after World War I that initially made towns more accessible have, since World War II, routed more and more vehicles through them, as has happened in Kennebunks' Port, Maine, and in Beaufort, South Carolina. Because heavy traffic damages historic environments, towns should seek alternate routes for through traffic that circumvent their historic districts. All towns also need clear signage to direct unfamiliar drivers who, having entered, then must exit the maze of streets and lanes without becoming lost and unnecessarily adding to congestion.

Within towns, street scale and preservation of town character are more important than the ease with which traffic moves. Local streets should primarily provide internal service and access needs, and they should be designed as instruments to protect historic character, a goal that should take precedence over

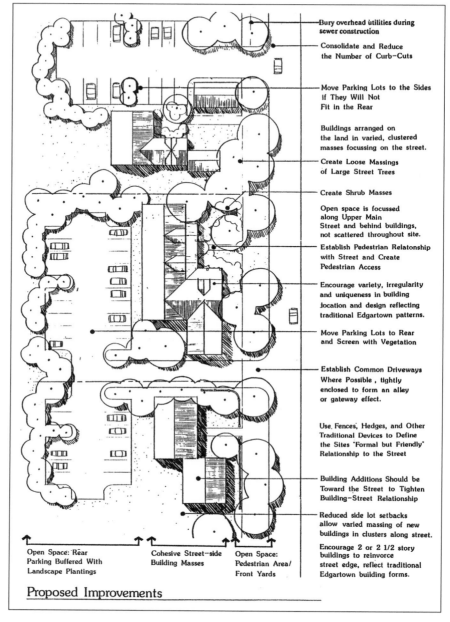

Bury overhead utilities during sewer construction

Consolidate and Reduce the Number of Curb-Cuts

Move Parking Lots to the Sides if They Will Not Fit in the Rear

Buildings arranged on the land in varied, clustered masses focussing on the street.

Create Loose Massings of Large Street Trees

Create Shrub Masses

Open space is focussed along Upper Main Street and behind buildings, not scattered throughout site.

Establish Pedestrian Relationship with Street and Create Pedestrian Access

Encourage variety, irregularity and uniqueness in building location and design reflecting traditional Edgartown patterns.

Move Parking Lots to Rear and Screen with Vegetation

Establish Common Driveways Where Possible , tightly enclosed to form an alley or gateway effect.

Use, Fences, Hedges, and Other Traditional Devices to Define the Sites 'Formal but Friendly' Relationship to the Street

Building Additions Should be Toward the Street to Tighten Building-Street Relationship

Reduced side lot setbacks allow varied massing of new buildings in clusters along street.

Encourage 2 or 2 1/2 story buildings to reinvorce street edge, reflect traditional Edgartown building forms.

Open Space: Rear Parking Buffered With Landscape Plantings

Cohesive Street-side Building Masses

Open Space: Pedestrian Area/ Front Yards

Proposed Improvements

Fig. 14.4. *Upper Main Street Master Plan, Edgartown, Massachusetts. The drawing illustrates ways to maintain the scale and character of historic towns in automobile-oriented developments. (Dodson Associates, 1989).*

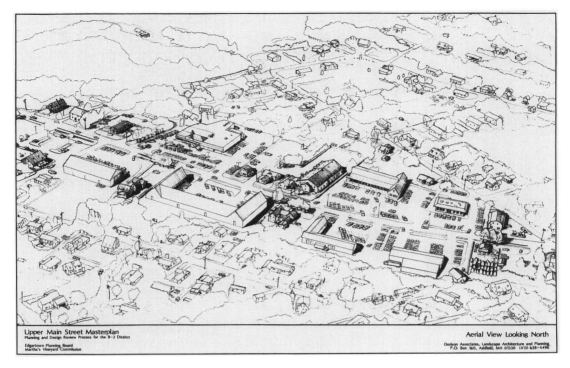

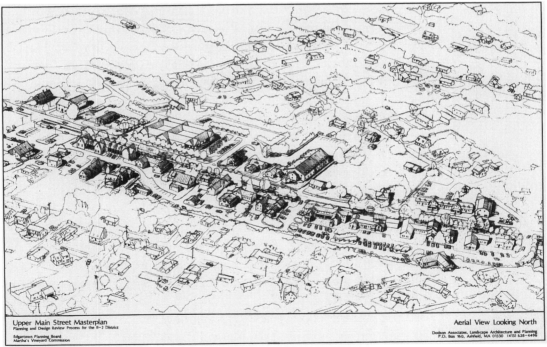

Top: *Fig. 14.5. Projected conventional development on Upper Main Street in Edgartown, Massachusetts (Dodson Associates, 1989).* Bottom: *Fig. 14.6. Development in Edgartown, Massachusetts, according to proposed guidelines on Upper Main Street (Dodson Associates, 1989).*

wider roads and higher bridges. Indeed, narrow roads and bridges, prominent landscaping, defined and generous sidewalks, and sharp turns with little room for maneuvering constrain traffic flow and thereby favor pedestrian travel. Since many towns have limited fiscal resources and are unable by themselves to construct major bypasses, maintaining and restricting road capacities may be one of the cheapest and most effective local ways of preserving town character.

Visitors gain their first and frequently most lasting impressions of towns as they enter. Therefore it is regrettable that many coastal town entrances have degenerated into cluttered and disorienting commercial strips. While providing services, these new corridors fail to be the informative and pleasurable routes that many once were. Entrance corridors are undergoing change because of traffic conditions and tourist needs, yet they are the least-controlled environments because they lie outside historic districts and extend over different political jurisdictions. Towns should coordinate with adjacent authorities to zone entrance corridors as special districts. They should encourage development along those routes to cluster buildings for greater transportation efficiency, safety, and the protection of natural environments.

Towns with heavy visitor traffic should provide peripheral parking areas and, ideally, locate them near tourist information centers. Visitors could then move from these parking areas to town centers on foot, on rental bicycles, or by using public transportation—trolleys, small busses, and even boats. Pockets of parking within towns, unobtrusively located behind buildings, can also offer convenience while still preserving existing town character. Coastal towns could establish more automobile-free pedestrian zones similar to those in Saint Augustine, Florida, or restrict automobile access during specific times as Ocean Grove, New Jersey, once did. Towns should determine their automobile capacities, deterring additional cars from entering once this capacity has been reached. While the amount of open space in towns has not always diminished, its quality has certainly been affected by the automobile age. Former work areas, storage yards, and open fields are now often asphalt parking lots.

Towns along the Mid- and South Atlantic coast in particular, but also many of those farther north, lie in areas of flat topography where, during clement weather, bicycles are an ideal means of travel. With them riders can gain access to points in town centers, enjoy the immediacy of these environments, and explore a variety of locales within the community, all without contributing to air pollution or destroying the character of the towns. Bicycle use greatly reduces the automobile-related problems of parking, noise, and pollution and offers, instead, the benefits of convenience and enjoyable exercise. Towns should support bike rental facilities and even consider the provision of "public bicycles"—ones that are communally owned and placed throughout the towns for the convenience of tourists and residents. Among cities, Copenhagen, Denmark, and Portland, Oregon, have provided public bicycles. Electronic tags or identifying colors on bicycles could reduce theft. Rights-of-way reserved for bicyclists

Fig. 14.7. Edgartown, Massachusetts. View of Upper Main Street, featuring a bike path to the historic district (1992).

would also contribute to the safety and greater acceptability of bicycle riding in these towns.

• Preserve the integrity and cultural continuity of towns.

In recent years many towns have become gentrified to such an extent that they have lost their traditional social diversity. Property values have risen to levels at which many local residents can no longer afford to live in these communities. Many older residents who wished to remain have reluctantly had to leave because they can no longer afford property taxes. Many town employees— teachers, police officers, and fire fighters—can no longer live near where they work. Historic coastal towns need to regain their former social diversity, and opportunities do exist to do so. Affordable housing can be linked to the tourist industry, for example, and site-planning solutions are possible. Underutilized second and third floors of commercial buildings could become year-round housing. Subdividing land into smaller parcels, a common traditional practice in these towns, would allow for more buildings, particularly in those towns with relatively low densities.

In historic coastal towns, details express a sense of place and history. These are the elements that people walk on, touch, lean against, and closely observe; they are measures of local civility and identity. In Stonington, Connecticut, granite provides boulders for sea walls and, after being cut and polished, details for public buildings. In Edenton, North Carolina, and Ocean Grove, New Jersey, fanciful wood scrollwork recalls craft traditions and evokes through its wavelike patterns the nearby sea. In New Castle, Delaware, elegant ironwork reminds people of the town's nineteenth-century iron industries. Such details should be protected and sympathetic new ones should be fostered.

Natural processes are fundamental qualities of these towns, tying them to their locales and expressing the larger contexts in which human communities exist. The flow of water across land, the succession of indigenous vegetation, and the migration of animals are among the many essential natural systems that should be accentuated and celebrated. At a more intimate level, the venerable trees, understory plants, ground covers, and accenting flowers shape individual spaces and create memorable streets, merging public and private properties into larger wholes. Trees beneficially modify climate as they grow and change with the seasons, adding a particularly poignant visual drama to these towns. Evident natural processes such as the harnessing of water power at river fall lines and the launching of boats with ebb tides link the human world to that of nature, allowing people to gather in communities while strengthening their connections to the natural environment. Historic ordinances should apply to the natural processes of towns as well as to the buildings within them.

- Protect towns from sea level rise.

It would be ecologically unwise and financially inconceivable to stabilize all parts of the coastlines. Instead, efforts should focus on coastal cities because of their high population densities and large capital investments and on historic coastal towns because of their cultural importance. To protect these areas, two basic strategies are available—methods using "soft" and "hard" devices. Beach renourishment or dune rebuilding efforts are described as soft devices. These solutions require frequent maintenance and replenishment because storms can readily alter them. Hard devices more directly armor vulnerable shores. Groins (wall-like structures running perpendicular to the shore into the water), bulk-heads and sea walls (vertical walls facing the sea), and revetments (units laid on a slope to reduce wave scouring) are commonly used hard devices. Other options are raising structures above threatening levels or relocating entire towns to the safety of higher ground. However, altering sites radically or moving communities to different locations would destroy the character and importance of these towns.

- Accept sea level rise and restrict development in
  environmentally sensitive areas.

As ocean levels rise, strategies will be needed for the orderly abandonment of coastal properties to allow for the impending conversion of lowlands to marshes. Where possible, existing structures should be relocated, and new ones should be built beyond endangered zones. Open space could also be assembled in co-herent patterns for agricultural use and recreation. In any case, by allowing shorelines to recede, the benefits of wetlands can be retained. They will continue to act as buffers against storms as well as absorb excess runoff during heavy rains and thereby help replenish towns' aquifers. Tidal marshes can continue to serve as sediment traps for erosion and habitats for wildlife. The other alternative is to squeeze wetlands between the rising sea and restraining dikes, providing more dry land but forfeiting those advantages of wetlands.

Through outright land acquisitions, the purchase of development rights, deed restrictions, view easements, land trusts, and gifts, these towns have preserved open spaces in the past. These strategies should continue, enabling towns to acquire future land reserves.[16] With proper state-enabling legislation and local planning commitment, towns can transfer development rights from unsuitable areas to sites more appropriate for building. An even more comprehensive strategy would be for public bodies to purchase options on wetlands to allow ecosystems to migrate inland.[17]

Further research, the establishment of broader criteria, the blending of a wider range of talents, and the coordination of more diverse groups of professionals and participants will be needed to achieve viable futures for historic coastal towns. Landscape architects, architects, and planners who are trained in ecological design and environmental planning and who have a knowledge of the geography and history of places will be valued leaders in these efforts. Underlying all, of course, will have to be greater public awareness of the issues and a willingness to address implications of long-term significance.

A Useful Past for Future Growth

Historic coastal towns have recorded their pasts and the variety of people who shaped their development. Rather than being presented as an idealized history, the record of that survival—the influence of different groups, the styles of succeeding periods, the unexpected fortunes and calamities of the local economy—should be evident in the built form and landscapes of these towns. Historic coastal towns should also remain open to the future, not frozen in time. Future generations should have room to leave their marks alongside those of the past. Architectural styles should not simply mimic old ones but be receptive to new conditions. Careful infill development should be possible, and selective demolition and reconstruction should also be permitted. The qualities of these towns have grown from each succeeding generation's respecting the past while contributing its own beliefs and values.

Historic American coastal towns, organized around centers, shaped by walking patterns, and bounded by nature, offer not a nostalgic and obsolete past but time-honored traditions and a perspective from which to evaluate how we live. As new generations influence future development, they should continue to honor the wise concept of individuals living in human-scaled communities in sympathy with the natural world.

Appendix

Quantitative Characteristics of Town Scale

Town	Gross Residential Density (Dwellings/ acre)[1]	Average Block Length	Average Residential Lot Width	Average Distance between Buildings across Street	Length of Commercial Activity on Main Street[2]
Castine, Me.	1.7	391	81	78	550
Kennebunks' Port, Me.	2.8	242	92	68	750
Edgartown, Mass.	4.25	314	59	48	520
Stonington, Conn.	5.7	199	37	48	1,310
Ocean Grove, N.J.	10.9	175	30	60	690
New Castle, Del.	8.6	390	29	50	900
Edenton, N.C.	2.5	460	84	74	970
Beaufort, S.C.	3.9	290	72	63	920
Saint Augustine, Fla.	5.6	293	53	36	1,800
AVERAGE	5.1	306	60	58	934

SOURCE: Data are derived from the Sanborn insurance maps used in this book. For dates of these maps, see Bibliography.

1. Gross residential area includes streets and public and commercial uses in predominantly residential areas but excludes areas of main commercial streets, waterfronts, and large open spaces.

2. Defined as the length of main street in which commercial activities dominate other uses.

Notes

Photographs not otherwise attributed are by the author.

Preface

1. *Kennebunks' Port* refers to the village of Kennebunkport and the lower village of Kennebunk, which lie on either side of the Kennebunk River.
2. Meinig 1986, 139.
3. Ibid., 174.
4. Ibid., 191.

O N E   *Lessons from the Towns Left Behind*

1. Hutchins 1967, 89.
2. Gary Nash elaborates on the scarce colonial populations of these coastal towns, stating, "None of the American port towns could compare with even the secondary commercial centers of western Europe such as Lyon, which had reached 45,000 in the 1530s, or Norwich, which had grown to 19,000 by the 1570s. Nor could they claim equal status with the cities of Spanish and Portuguese colonies to the south, where Bahia, Caragena, Potosi, and Mexico City . . . numbered 50,000 or more by the end of the seventeenth century." Nash 1979, 3.
3. Lee 1967, 25.
4. Douglas 1967, 47.
5. A port usually has a different hinterland for each trade in which it engages, adding up to not just one but a range of hinterlands; see Morgan 1959, 376–87.
6. Rubin 1966, 8; Bridenbaugh 1964, 30.
7. Hutchins 1967, 83.
8. Bridenbaugh 1964, 53.
9. On how the hills of Boston were leveled and the bays filled to accommodate city growth, see Whitehill 1971, 73–94.
10. Bridenbaugh 1964, 31.
11. Davison 1966, 74–75; Dorfman 1966, 151–52.
12. Dorsey 1966, 62–67.
13. Goldfield 1988, 13–16; Bridenbaugh 1964, 32.
14. Castine has land slopes at angles of between 5 and 10 percent. Land at a southern slope of 10 percent receives as much direct sun radiation as does flat land 6 degrees closer to the equator, a difference equivalent to the distance between Portland, Maine, and Richmond, Virginia. Lynch and Hack 1993, 52.
15. Summer houses in the North are often sited back from the roads, since snow removal is not a problem during those months.
16. Accommodating air conditioning equipment and satellite dishes is a growing issue in

historic towns. New England houses were traditionally oriented inward because of their small windows and doors, which minimized heat loss. Modern technical features have permitted newer homes to be even more so.

17. Railroad stations, for example, were centrally located on the waterfronts of Kennebunks' lower village, Stonington, and New Castle. On the other hand, the planters in Beaufort sought to avoid the smoke and noise of trains and located their station a safe distance outside of town.

18. Street blocks vary in size from 120 feet in Ocean Grove to 800 feet in Edenton.

19. Blumenfeld 1967, 216.

20. On the social problems of local residents due to cyclical employment, see Mazer 1976.

21. In an average street, people on sidewalks would be less than fifty feet from houses on either side. Hans Blumenfeld notes that about forty-eight feet is the distance at which a "portrait" of a person can be discerned. Referring to the work of H. Maerterns, he concludes that the distance of seventy to eighty feet is the "normal human scale" at which we can recognize a particular person. Great European urban plazas, meanwhile, rarely exceed 450 feet. At this distance, one perceives essential human characteristics such as age and gender. Blumenfeld 1967, 217–18, 229.

22. Lawrence Houston found a gross residential density of 1.25 dwellings per acre for New Jersey villages. To determine area in his ratio he included all streets, sidewalks, cemeteries, nonresidential structures, and recreation spaces. Houston 1988, 14–25.

23. In 1800, New Castle had an average median household size of 6.3 people; by 1990 this had fallen to 2.57 people per household.

24. J. C. Nichols used a minimum lot width of fifty feet in developing the country club district of Kansas City, one of the first successful automobile-based developments. He preferred a width of sixty feet and sold many with 100- to 200-foot frontages in his more expensive subdivisions. Worley 1990, 115.

25. Lawrence Houston suggests that a half mile is the determining distance, but the greatest density occurs within a one-quarter-mile radius. Houston 1988, 14.

T W O   *Overview*

1. Conkling 1995, 92–95.

2. The province of Newfoundland includes the island of Newfoundland as well as the mainland section of Labrador.

3. Wallace 1990, 178.

4. Numbers in parentheses indicate 1990 U.S. Census population; numbers with an asterisk are estimated based on information from local sources because the towns were not counted separately in the 1990 Census.

5. James 1996, 1–7.

6. Rees 1995, 71.

7. Curtis, Curtis, and Lieberman 1995, 69.

8. Federal Writers' Project 1937, "Maine: A Guide 'Down East,'" 225.

9. James L. Garvin, letter to author, 2 April 1996.

10. Candee 1992, 1–5, 19–24, 49–50.

11. Garvin and Merrill 1971.

12. Massachusetts Historical Commission 1985, "Yarmouth."

13. Massachusetts Historical Commission 1985, "Wellfleet."

14. Massachusetts Historical Commission 1984, "Provincetown."

15. Garland 1988, 17.

16. *Life Magazine* 1968.

17. Garland 1988, 161–63.

18. Weiss 1987, xi.

19. Rhode Island Historical Preservation Commission 1990.

20. Rhode Island Historical Preservation Commission 1980.

21. Rhode Island Historical Preservation Commission 1974.

22. Mallory 1954, 16–17. Up until 1870 the valley's population did not exceed 3,600. Since 1789, 869 vessels have been constructed in the Mystic Valley, almost all of them during the period up to 1870.

23. Epstein and Barlow 1985, 4–7.

24. Ibid., 64–65.

25. New York State Office of Parks 1987.

26. New York State Office of Parks 1986.

27. U.S. Department of the Interior 1994, "Sag Harbor Village Historic District."

28. New York State Office of Parks n.d., "Historic and Natural Districts Inventory Form."

THREE *Castine, Maine*

1. The general depth of the channel into Castine Harbor is 72 feet, and the mean range of tides is 9.7 feet. The population of Castine is 800.

2. The name *Castine* refers to the area both on and off the peninsula. Castine as a political jurisdiction dates from 1796, when it separated from the Township of Penobscot to the east, which included the present Brooksville and Penobscot jurisdictions.

3. Native Castinians still refer to people as those who live "on-neck," or in the village, those who are "off-neck," or within five miles of the village, and those who are from "away," or beyond approximately five miles of the village.

4. For a historical discussion of Castine's entrance roads, see Doudiet 1978, 12.

5. In 1942, the Maine Maritime Academy assumed control of the property of the former Eastern State Normal School, which was built in 1872–73.

6. In 1667 Baron de Saint Castin arrived, took as his wife the daughter of the local Indian chief, made a fortune through trade with Indians, and in 1701 returned to France, leaving his name to the settlement even though he did not live on the peninsula.

7. Doudiet 1978, 1.

8. Ibid., 25.

9. Ibid., 10.

10. Wasson and Colcord 1932, 89–190, as footnoted in Castine Planning Board 1979, 20.

11. Bourne 1989, 235.

12. Doudiet 1978, 22.

13. Phillip Perkins, interview by author, 21 August 1990, Castine, Maine.

14. Sea captains, by nature, were more adventurous than their fellow townsmen, and in their voyages from Europe to the Orient they encountered a range of cultures. They tended to be more permissive in allowing freedom of thought.

15. *Wilson Museum Bulletin* 1974, 1–4.

16. Ellenore W. Doudiet, letter to author, 31 August 1991.

17. Doudiet 1978, 10.

18. Ibid., 63–65.

19. Doudiet 31 August 1991.

20. Doudiet 1978, 38, 63–64.

21. *Wilson Museum Bulletin* 1990, 1–2.

22. Town of Castine 1945–49, 1991.

23. Doudiet 31 August 1991.

24. People from forty-three states now own property in Castine. While some fly in five or six times a year to "get-away," others reside in Castine for five to twelve months of the year. Joseph Slocum, telephone interview by author, 4 November 1997.

25. Eugene Angers, interview by author, 22 August 1990, Castine, Maine.

26. Perkins 1990.

27. Slocum 1997.

28. Ibid.

FOUR *Kennebunks' Port, Maine*

1. The term *Kennebunks' Port* refers to the old maritime community that lies on both sides of the Kennebunk River near its mouth. This community is part of two municipalities, the boundary between them being midriver. The town of Kennebunkport is north of the river and covers an area of 18.6 square miles. Kennebunkport village is the settlement within this town on the north side of the river. The town of Kennebunk lies south of the river and is 36 square miles in area. The lower village is the settlement within Kennebunk and immediately south of the river across from Kennebunkport village. Kennebunk's village, on the other hand, is on the coast road, U.S. Route 1, six miles inland. The lower village of Kennebunk developed lower down the river, thus the name. Cape Arundel and Cape Porpoise are the coastal areas of Kennebunkport, while Kennebunk Beach is in Kennebunk. Kennebunk was formerly a part of Wells, splitting off from it in 1820. Kennebunkport's names have changed from Cape Porpoise (still in use for the northeast section), Arundel (1719; still in use for North Kennebunkport), and Kennebunkport (1820). In 1916 Kennebunkport split into two municipalities, North Kennebunkport (now Arundel) and Kennebunkport. The name *Kennebunks* refers to Kennebunk, Kennebunkport, and North Kennebunkport.

2. The Lower River is approximately a mile long, ranging from one hundred to nine hundred feet wide. The mean tidal rise is eight feet six inches, and the tide moves approximately six miles upriver. Rosenfeld 1986, 11.

3. Butler 1989, 55–60.

4. Ruth Landon, letter to author, 28 October 1990.

5. For discussion of land grants and settlement, see Bradbury [1837] 1967, 16–18.

6. Butler 1984, 39.

7. Bradbury 27 June 1986, 5.

8. Landon 1990.

9. Butler 1984, 32.

10. U.S. Department of the Interior 1975, "Kennebunkport Historic District," 7.

11. Built in 1824, probably by carpenters who worked in the river shipyards, the South Congregational Church's construction reflected the shift of village focus from Burbank Hill to the river bank. Butler 1989, 39.

12. Joyce Butler, interview by author, 14 August 1991, Kennebunkport, Maine.

13. Butler 1989, 11.

14. This station closed in the early twentieth century as a result of the popularity of automobiles. The area became a boatyard again, and in the late 1980s it was converted into a small shopping mall. Part of the old station remains, moved a short distance to be incorporated into a storage building.

15. Drake 1875, as quoted in Butler 1980, 2.

16. Butler 1980, 2–3.

17. Butler 1984, 49.

18. Ibid., 35.

19. Ibid., 56–57.

20. Landon 1990.

21. Bachelder and Schauffler n.d., 30.

22. Kennebunkport *Annual Report* 1955, 5.

23. Thomas E. Bradbury, interview by author, 16 August 1990, Cape Porpoise, Maine.

24. Traffic management also provided profit for the town. In 1984, after the town had built the Dock Square parking lot, first-year income of $37,276 from this lot more than covered the construction and start-up costs of $15,000. Kennebunkport *Annual Report* 1984.

25. Kennebunkport *Annual Report* 1955, 94.

26. "'Decorative changes' are specifically excluded from its [zoning ordinance] purview . . . standards for mitigation of adverse impacts on significant scenic vistas and effect of a proposed design on adjacent properties lack clear enforceable standards." Lovejoy 1985, 115.

27. Lovejoy 1985, 116.

28. Kennebunk Comprehensive Plan Committee 1991, 90.

29. Rosenfeld 1986, 3–12.

F I V E   *Edgartown, Massachusetts*

1. The island of Martha's Vineyard is approximately one hundred square miles in area. The population of Edgartown is 1,138.

2. One indicator of Edgartown's international reputation is the circulation of the local island newspaper, the *Vineyard Gazette*, published in Edgartown and distributed to subscribers in every state and at least twenty-six countries abroad. The Chamber of Commerce attributes a significant part of the island's popularity to the celebrities who have vacationed there, the Chappaquiddick incident involving Senator Edward Kennedy, the filming of *Jaws* (1975) on the island, and, more recently, the vacation trips of President Clinton and his family.

3. Banks 1966, vol. 1, 181.

4. Edgartown was named after Edgar, son of the Duke of York (the brother of King Charles II). Edgar, unbeknownst to the settlers, had already died by the time this honor was bestowed upon him. Railton 1988, 2.

5. Banks 1966, vol. 1, 24.

6. Ibid., 81 and vol. 2, 36.

7. U.S. Department of the Interior 1983, "Edgartown Village Historic District," item 7, 2.

8. Ibid., item 8, 3.

9. Ibid., item 7, 4.

10. Hough 1936, 23.

11. Ibid., 26.

12. Ibid., 242.

13. Ibid., 271.

14. Allen 1982, 73.

15. For a discussion from islanders' perspective on the problems of seasonal work, high cost of living, and social disorders, see Mazer 1976.

16. Allen 1982, 113.

17. Robert J. Carrol, interview by author, 14 May 1992, Edgartown, Mass.

18. Railton 1988, 227.

19. Edgartown Planning Board 1990, 37.

20. Vacationers are defined as those who stay on the island for more than four days but less than a month; visitors are those who stay for less than four days. Not included in these figures are the "day-trippers." Ibid., 37.

21. Davis and Stutz 1991, 15.

22. Delbonis 1991, A1.

23. Dodson Associates 1989, 28.

24. Edgartown Planning Board 1990, 26.

25. In developments of ten or more units, the commission requires that either 10 percent of the units should be set aside as affordable housing or 20 percent of the assessed property value should be contributed to a fund for these purposes. Martha's Vineyard Commission n. d.

26. Martha's Vineyard Commission 1992, A16.

27. First-time buyers are exempt from such fees on the first $100,000.

28. Delbonis 1991, A1.

S I X   *Stonington, Connecticut*

1. Since its incorporation, in 1801, the community's official name has been Stonington Borough. Historically, however, people have referred to the settlement as Stonington Village. Its population is 1,100.

2. F. S. Gould, interview by author, 22 August 1989, Stonington, Conn.

3. Robert Jones, interview by author, 24 August 1990, Stonington, Conn.

4. Historians differ, but they estimate the populations as between six thousand and twenty thousand. Surowiecki and Tedone 1982, 3.

5. Palmer 1913, Ch. 1; and Surowiecki and Tedone 1982, 3–9.

6. Although the English and the Indians coexisted, they developed conflicts because they used the available resources quite differently. The English dammed streams for mills (inhibiting stream fishing for the Indians), insisted on using fallow land for crops, let livestock roam, and, most critically, consumed wood for construction and warmth—up to an acre of forest per house per year—which destroyed Indian hunting grounds. Generally, the English contractually purchased the land from the Pequots. However, the two cultures had totally different concepts of property rights, and the Indians did not always understand that they were relinquishing hunting and fishing rights with the sale of property. Surowiecki and Tedone 1982, 7.

7. In 1614, the Dutch captain Adriaen Block, after whom Block Island is named, sailed the Connecticut coast and ventured up the Connecticut River as far as the falls at Enfield, near the present-day border of Massachusetts.

8. Stonington was the first Connecticut town not to build a "center," in which houses clustered around a church and green. Stonington Planning and Zoning Commission 1989, A2–3.

9. Louise Pittaway, letter to author, 7 January 1992.

10. Haynes 1957, 11.

11. Stonington Planning and Zoning Commission 1989, A5.

12. Palmer 1913, 27.

13. Stonington Planning and Zoning Commission 1989 A4, quoting from an 1819 issue of the *Gazetteer of the States of Connecticut and Rhode Island*.

14. Borough of Stonington 1991, 5.

15. Surowiecki and Tedone 1982, 29–36.

16. Palmer 1913, Chapter 15.

17. Borough of Stonington 1991, 22.

18. Haynes 1957, 11.

19. "Census in 1910 gave the Borough a population of 2,500; was said to be in proportion to population the richest town in Connecticut." Palmer 1913, 102.

20. Ibid., 82.

21. New York City is 120 miles away, Providence and Hartford are each 50 miles away, and Boston is 100 miles away from Stonington.

22. Wojtas 1991.

23. Louise Pittaway, telephone interview by author, 4 October 1991.

24. In 1990 Connecticut passed a law mandating communities in which less than 10 percent of the housing is considered affordable to accept new developments that have a minimum of 20 percent affordable housing. According to state figures, 3.5 percent of the town's housing and less than 1 percent of the borough's housing is currently "affordable." Wojtas 1992.

25. Charles Storrow, telephone interview by author, 7 October 1991.

26. The Stonington harbor is considered the best port between New London, Connecticut, and Newport, Rhode Island. The Stonington fishing fleet is the last remaining commercial fleet operating in Connecticut, although it has been greatly reduced in size since the days before World War II. The fishermen drag trawl nets in nearby ocean waters, but, owing to efforts to restore the stock of fish, they are limited by the federal government in the quantity of their haul.

SEVEN *Overview*

1. Fischer 1989, 435.

2. Industrialization was also discouraged by English colonial policy, which favored transporting raw materials to England, where manufacturing would take place, and then returning finished goods to the colonies.

3. Allaback 1995; for discussion of railroad resorts, see 21–46; for religious resorts, see 47–68; and for the influence of the automobile on the coastal development, see 91–104.

4. Pepper 1965, 121–23. Numbers with an asterisk are estimated based on local sources.

5. After the War of 1812, New Castle, Delaware, became an important stop for steamboats going to Cape May, often carrying southerners who had traveled north on the Frenchtown and New Castle Railroad.

6. U.S. Department of the Interior 1976, "Cape May Historic District," item 8, 1–3.

7. Jordan and Kaups 1989.

8. U.S. Department of the Interior 1986, "Lewes Historic District," item 8, 1–8.

9. Bodo 1994, 6–10.

10. In 1689, after the Protestant revolution in England enthroned Mary and her consort, William of Orange, the colonial government came under royal control. Lord Baltimore retained ownership of his vast holdings but lost significant political power. These political changes also resulted in the adoption of *Maryland* as the state name and the shift of the capital to Annapolis from St. Mary's City, which was considered too remote and thought to be under the influence of Catholics.

11. U.S. Department of the Interior 1984, "Chestertown Historic District," item 8, 36–41.

12. U.S. Department of the Interior n.d., "St. Michaels Historic District," item 8, 15–19.

13. U.S. Department of the Interior n.d., "Cambridge Historic District," item 8, 4–18.

14. Miller 1986, 123–48.

15. Treasurer and Council for Virginia, "Letter to Governor and Council in Virginia," 1 August 1622, as quoted in Reps 1972, 46.

16. Meinig 1986, 146.

17. Issac 1982, 20.

18. West Indians had been raising tobacco, and the crop was already known in England. In 1586, when the Lane Colony returned to England with Sir Francis Drake from Roanoke Island, they brought with them tobacco as well as potatoes and corn. Lefler and Newsome 1973, 10.

19. Maneval 1990.

20. Reps 1972, 79–81.

21. Ibid., 86–87.

22. Ibid., 213.

23. Federal Writers' Project 1941, 379.

24. Ibid., 386–87.

E I G H T   *Ocean Grove, New Jersey*

1. More specifically, Ocean Grove was founded as part of the "Holiness Movement out of the Methodist Church." Bucke 1964, 612. The population of Ocean Grove is 4,818.

2. For a discussion of New Jersey's Victorian resorts, see Methot 1988.

3. Stephen Crane, whose father was a Methodist clergyman, often visited his mother, who had a house in Ocean Grove. He noted the "sombre-hued" gentlemen of Ocean Grove who arrived "with black valises in their hands and rebukes to frivolity in their eyes. They greet each other with quiet enthusiasm and immediately set about holding meetings." Brewer 1987, 26, quoting the *New York Tribune,* n.d.

4. For a discussion of Methodism and the Great Awakening, see Bucke 1964.

5. U.S. Department of the Interior 1976, "Ocean Grove Camp Meeting Association," item 8, 2.

6. Reverend Ellwood Stokes was also instrumental in the initial success of Ocean Grove. Reverends Osborn and Stokes embody two of the town's distinguishing characteristics, evident even today—religious fervor and organizational skill. Brewer 1987, 6–11.

7. Lots that sold for $86 in 1870 sold for as much $1,500 in 1890. Brewer 1987, 15.

8. In the 1877 season there were 710,000 tickets sold to this station. Brewer 1987, 17.

9. U.S. Department of the Interior 1976, "Ocean Grove Camp Meeting Association," item 8, 5.

10. The association banned not only traffic on Sundays but also fishing, swimming, sunbathing, and hanging out wash.

11. In comparison, Philadelphia has blocks four hundred feet by four hundred feet, and Manhattan, two hundred feet by eight hundred feet.

12. These tents are in two parts. The front halves are canvas stretched over wood supports, and the rear sections are permanent wood cabins that house utilities and are used for winter storage. Overall, the tents are usually about fourteen feet wide and twenty-eight feet long.

13. Weiss 1987.

14. Hutton and Boyd 1989, 11–18.

15. Craig 1987, 9.

16. Hand 1986, H1.

17. The state spends approximately $80,000 a year per patient in one of its psychiatric hospitals. When a discharged patient moves into a community, financial responsibilities shift from the state to the federal government, which permits $5,500 to $6,874 in annual payments to chronically ill people living alone. Nordheimer 1992, 31.

18. The local church, St. Paul's United Methodist Church, has instituted a Christian social outreach program to work with deinstitutionalized people. Wayne T. Bell, Jr., letter to author, 20 December 1991.

19. The case was appealed to the U. S. Supreme Court, who refused to hear it, thereby upholding the lower court's decision against the association.

20. In 1990 there were 4,173 people in Ocean Grove and 28,366 in Neptune Township. To secede, a majority in both the community and the township must approve. Not since 1920 has a town seceded from its township in New Jersey.

21. Hawkins 1989, ii-iii.

22. Martin Rakita, interview by author, 26 June 1992, Ocean Grove, N.J.

23. Ben Douglas, interview by author, 25 June 1992.

NINE *New Castle, Delaware*

1. My discussion focuses on the historic town of New Castle, which is part of today's city of New Castle, both of which are in New Castle County, Delaware. The town's population is 4,837.

2. Timothy Mullin, letter to author, 23 December 1991.

3. Cooper 1983, 5, 9.

4. The governor allocated riverfront lots to merchants and lots further inland to farmers. Heite 1986, 145. The Dutch laid out deeds from Second Street to the river's edge that at low tide was near today's Strand. Mullin 1991.

5. Heite and Heite 1989, 12–16.

6. Ibid., 4.

7. Ibid., 21.

8. New Castle, on the western bank, is on the opposite side of the natural river channel. Since before European settlement, the river had silted on New Castle's side. With the clearing of land and the local extinction of the beaver, natural flood control was lost and silt accumulated at a greatly increased rate. Mullin 1991.

9. Heite and Heite 1989, 31.

10. Cooper 1983, 127.

11. Heite and Heite 1989, 45.

12. In 1800, the median household size in New Castle was 6.3 members and single-person households were most unusual. Cooper 1983, 72. In 1990, the average household size was 2.57, reflecting the increase in space per resident.

13. The terrace on which the courthouse rests results from the surrounding streets being graded down. Mullin 1991.

14. For example, few squares in European cities exceed 450 feet. Blumenfeld 1967, 229.

15. Federal Writers' Project [1936] 1973, *New Castle on the Delaware,* 1936, 51.

16. Heite and Heite 1989, 18.

17. Hoffecker 1983, 53.

18. McIntire 1986, 83, 105.

19. Ibid., 122.

20. Hoffecker 1983, 53.

21. Ibid., 115–17.

22. Timothy Mullin, interview by author, 15 October 1991, New Castle, Del.

23. Since 1701, when water lots were granted to adjacent property owners, waterfront land remained private. However, two public rights-of-way leading to the water extend through the middle of the block owned by the Laird group.

24. Mullin 15 October 1991.

25. Ibid.

26. For example, the Gilpin house, 210 Delaware Street, has been a residence, a tenement, a tavern, a hotel, a store, a food market, and, most recently, a bank. Immanuel Episcopal Church 1989, 25.

27. John Klingmeyer, interview by author, 30 June 1990, New Castle, Del.

28. McIntire 1986, 126.

TEN *Overview*

1. Meinig 1986, 174.

2. For discussions of the ecological dynamics of the Outer Banks and the futility of stabilization efforts, see Pilkey, Neal, and Pilkey 1980 and Schoenbaum 1982.

3. Bishir and Southern 1996, 154–55.

4. "The opening of Oregon and Hatteras Inlets in 1846 resulted in the steady withdrawal of shipping traffic away from Ocracoke Inlet. By 1867, the town of Portsmouth was on a rapid decline. The population of that settlement had dwindled to 18 people in 1955, and, at present, no permanent residents live there, although numerous buildings remain intact." Dolan and Lins 1985, 20.

5. "Shipping lanes off the North Carolina coast always have been among the most treacherous in the world. The northward-flowing Gulf Stream and south-bound drift along the Virginia coast make travel in sailing vessels faster but also force ships to navigate dangerously close to the shore." Ibid., 18.

6. For a history and a personal account of growing up on Ocracoke Island, see Ballance 1989.

7. Federal Writers' Project 1955, *North Carolina Guide*, 190.

8. Bishir 1996, 111–118.

9. Sandbeck 1988, xiv.

10. Ibid., x.

11. The town of Brunswick, laid out in 1725, was located downriver from Wilmington, approximately fifteen miles from the Atlantic. Although once the seat of the royal governors, Brunswick was abandoned by 1825. Its building ruins have been preserved and it is now a state historic site.

12. Rowland, Moore, and Rogers 1996, 4.

13. Ibid., 18.

14. Port Royal Sound was of strategic importance, particularly for the Spanish, because it was the "deepest and most accessible harbor on the southern coast of North America . . . and on the westward flank of the route of their galleons transporting gold to Spain." Ibid., 20.

15. The recently rediscovered site is on the edge of the golf course at the U.S. Marine Corps training base at Parris Island. Wilford 1996, 2.

16. The "Charleston house" type dominated construction in the city after a devastating fire in 1740, and its popularity lasted until the Civil War.

17. Bridwell 1982, iii. Numbers with an asterisk are based on local sources.

18. Reps 1969, 258–60.

19. There is evidence that Gabriel Bernard, a native of Geneva and an uncle of Jean Jacques Rousseau, actually developed the plan for Savannah. Nichols 1957, 11–12.

20. The dimensions for the squares include the width of the streets that pass along their sides, which vary in width depending on the square.

21. The secondary streets that pass along the sides of the squares are only oriented in the east-west direction. Since another, more important parallel street enters the square between these secondary streets, unusually narrow blocks (approximately seventy-two feet in width) result. These narrow blocks force the houses that front on the middle street to open on their back sides to the secondary streets, an awkward condition in an otherwise elegant plan.

22. Vanstory 1956, 57–58.

23. For history and illustrations of Coral Gables, see LaRoue and Uguccioni 1988.

24. U.S. Department of the Interior 1982, "Key West Historic District," item 7, 1.

1. Edenton has a population of 5,268. It is part of Chowan County, which has a population of 13,538. In 1722, shortly after the death of Governor Charles Eden (1673–1722), the town was named Edenton.

2. John Reps speculates that the courthouse mall may have been related to another mall almost symmetrically located west of Broad Street, as illustrated on Charles Joseph Sauthier's plan, and that on inland streets the malls were possibly "intended to provide views to and from sites for important buildings that would have faced the Sound." Reps 1969, 232.

3. The terraces on the Green are recent, dating from the 1960s.

4. Butchko 1992, 2.

5. Ibid., 3.

6. Charles Joseph Sauthier was a French surveyor and draftsman who, as an employee of the British government, drew maps of five other North Carolina towns during the years 1768–70.

7. Butchko 1992, 3.

8. Elizabeth Vann Moore, interview by author, 13 July 1990, Edenton, N.C.

9. In 1718 the town leaders initially built a wooden building to serve as a courthouse, and in 1767 they replaced it with a brick structure across the street, which remains today.

10. Parramore 1967, 19.

11. Ibid., 10.

12. Ibid., 21.

13. Ibid., 26–27.

14. Butchko 1992, 5.

15. Parramore 1967, 43.

16. Ibid., 58, 66.

17. Ibid., 77.

18. A second railroad arrived in 1887. Ibid., 82.

19. Ibid., 83, 87.

20. Butchko 1992, 40.

21. Ibid., 43.

22. Ross Inglis, letter to author, 1 November 1991.

23. U.S. Department of the Interior 1973, "Edenton Historic District," item 8, F.

24. Large discount stores beyond Edenton and Chowan County are draining business from Edenton's shopping centers. John Dowd, interview by author, 12 July 1990, Edenton, N.C.

25. The fishing stock in Albemarle Sound is slowly reviving, although consumer tastes no longer favor the Sound's oily, dark fish—shad, striped bass, and river herring—which were popular in the nineteenth century. Since World War II, smaller outboard motor boats with trailers, requiring less onshore servicing and facilities, have replaced inboard motor boats.

26. Ross Inglis, letter to author, 1 November 1991.

27. Ibid.

28. The airport currently does not have regularly scheduled commercial passenger service.

29. Norfolk, Virginia, is seventy miles away, and Richmond, Virginia, and Raleigh, North Carolina, are both 135 miles away. The nearest interstate, Interstate 95, is ninety miles to the west.

30. The following visitors per year registered at the Barker-Moore House Visitor Center:

3,250 in 1970, 16,000 in 1980, and 28,500 in 1997. Estimates for the total number of town visitors are based on doubling these figures.

31. Dowd 1990.

T W E L V E *Beaufort, South Carolina*

1. Officially called "City of Beaufort," the town has a population of 9,576 and a land area of 3.67 square miles. Beaufort County has a population of 86,425 and a land area of 578 square miles, encompassing sixty-four major islands, including Hilton Head, and hundreds of smaller islands.

2. In 1663, after the Restoration, in 1660, King Charles II granted a charter for the Carolina lands to eight of his prominent supporters.

3. John Milner Associates 1979, 1.

4. Ibid., 2–7.

5. Rowland, Moore, and Rogers 1996, 379–82.

6. John Milner Associates 1979, 18.

7. The eastern end of the historic district, known as the Point, is on average two feet below the 100-year flood level.

8. Historic Beaufort Foundation 1985, 6.

9. Petigru Carson in the *New York Daily Tribune*, 15 November 1861, 413, quoted in Rose 1964, 11.

10. John Milner Associates 1979, 9.

11. Rose 1964, 38.

12. Ibid., 285, 327–28.

13. Sherman's Field Order Number 15 "reserved for Negroes the sea islands from Charleston to and including the lands bordering the St. John's River." Wallace 1951, 558–59. More than one hundred living descendants of a grantee may be involved with "heirs' rights." William Rauch, interview by author, 24 May 1990, Beaufort, S.C.

14. John Milner Associates 1979, 11–12.

15. Ibid., 9–11.

16. Rose 1964, 407.

17. Traffic volume on U.S. 21 at the Beaufort Woods Memorial Bridge has increased as follows: 5,000 vehicles per day in 1963, 13,400 vehicles per day in 1985, and 15,900 vehicles per day in 1994.

18. The U.S. Marine Corps Recruit Depot at Parris Island traces its history back to the Civil War, when Union forces seized the area from Confederates and transformed the installation into one of the largest naval facilities in the world. In 1915 the federal government converted the naval base to the Marine Corps Depot (Parris Island Museum Exhibit, Marine Corps Recruit Depot, 4 June 1991).

19. Russell Wright, Carl Feiss, and John Milner are architects who are nationally recognized for their work in historic preservation.

20. To alleviate this problem, the city has proposed a "Neighborhood Conservation Overlay District" for the northwest section of the historic area.

21. Henry C. Chambers, interview by author, 24 May 1990, Beaufort, S.C.

22. "In Beaufort all discharges were raw into the river; our rivers were classified 'C' (unfit for shell fish and recreation); it was a significant event when the first waste water treatment plant was constructed in that the classification of the river went from Class 'SC' to Class 'SA' (eligible) in a period of five years. We chose to remain Class 'SB' so that marinas and other water born activities could be accommodated." Henry C. Chambers, letter to author, 14 December 1991.

23. Initially, downtown merchants wanted the waterfront to be all parking and residents wanted it to be all park. Robert E. Marvin, telephone interview by author, 20 November 1991.

24. Ibid.

25. "The waste water plan . . . was the first significant action to bring about attitude change in our community . . . with few exceptions every vote cast within the City Council for the waste water treatment facility, the construction of the waterfront park, the revitalization of the downtown was a two vote against two vote for [resulting in a tie] with the Mayor breaking the tie in the favor of the projects. This included zoning in the historic district and will give you an idea of how difficult change comes in a small community." Henry C. Chambers, letter to author, 14 December 1991.

26. Henry C. Chambers, interview by author, 24 May 1990, Beaufort, S.C.

27. Marvin 1989, 30–36.

28. The "cultural corridor" was a proposal to link the waterfront to the University campus, approximately three-quarters of a mile to the north. Specialty shops, restaurants, and fine arts facilities were to be added along the route. Planners hoped that the town would thereby be revitalized without overcommercializing the historic district.

29. Cynthia Cole Jenkins, letter to author, 17 April 1992.

30. James Cato, interview by author, 23 May 1990, Beaufort, S.C.

31. John Trask, interview by author, 23 May 1990, Beaufort, S.C.

THIRTEEN *Saint Augustine, Florida*

1. The city of Saint Augustine has a population of 11,692 and covers approximately twelve square miles. It is the seat of St. Johns County, which has a population of 87,304 and an area of 617 square miles. Along the coast the mean tide range is 4.5 feet.

2. Saint Augustine is the oldest continuously inhabited community on the mainland of the United States.

3. The Spanish town planning principles, known as the Laws of the Indies, were developed during the Spanish colonization of the New World. "Literally hundreds of communities [in the Americas] were planned in conformity to their specifications—a phenomenon unique in modern history." Reps 1969, 41.

4. Ibid., 51.

5. The Laws of the Indies rank among the most important documents in the history of city planning, according to John W. Reps (1969, 45). While the evolving regulations appear to have influenced the planning of Saint Augustine, there is no absolute proof of Saint Augustine's connection to the laws. Manucy 1982, 4.

6. Crouch, Garr, and Mundigo 1982, 13, 35.

7. Reps 1965, 30.

8. Crouch, Garr, and Mundigo 1982, 14, 114.

9. Chaney and Deagan 1989, 174.

10. Scardaville 1980, 21.

11. Manucy 1978, 48–61.

12. Manucy 1982, 8–10.

13. Griffin 1983, 130.

14. Scardaville 1980, 22–23.

15. Graham 1978, 124.

16. Chandler 1986, 251.

17. Harvey 1980, 86.

18. Flagler hired his minister's son, Thomas Hastings, then aged twenty-four, who, with

John Carrère, started the firm of Carrère and Hastings. This firm subsequently became one of the outstanding architectural firms in the country. Most notably, they designed the New York City Public Library and the U.S. House and Senate Office buildings.

19. Graham 1978, 169.

20. *Alameda* literally means "a poplar grove."

21. The Ponce de Leon Hotel opened in 1888 with 540 luxurious rooms. In its early years it was regarded as the most exclusive winter resort in the nation. Graham 1975, 14.

22. Graham 1978, 84.

23. Crespo 1987, 248–68.

24. Graham 1978, 203.

25. Flagler wrote in 1906: "I have realized from the beginning that St. Augustine was a dull place, but it does seem as though twenty years would stir up some measure of public spirit." Henry Flagler to J. E. Ingraham, 24 April 1906, quoted in Blake 1976, 118.

26. Crespo 1987, 263, 322.

27. The Flagler interests opened the Ponce de Leon Motor Lodge on U.S. 1 north of Saint Augustine in 1958. Graham 1975, 26.

28. The Saint Augustine Historical Society was established in 1953. It developed from the Saint Augustine Institute of Science, founded in 1883, which was concerned with archaeology and natural history. The society became the repository of books, maps, photos, and other material relating to the history of Saint Augustine.

29. Earl Newton, telephone interview by author, 11 February 1992.

30. The board recommended the reintroduction of "as many of the primary physical features of Old Spanish St. Augustine" as possible, such as "shops and businesses . . . as well as the actual work of artisans carrying on the type of activities that have made Spanish cultural and economic life significant," a concern for historic details, such as "landscaping of plots and gardens, the bringing back of the dress and costume of the period," and the elimination of "ugly and inconsistent intrusions, that serve no good purpose and only clutter up the community." Upchurch 1959, 19–20.

31. Newton 1992.

32. The Quadricentennial Committee was not affiliated structurally with the other committees but was related through overlapping and coordinated staffs. Ibid.

33. Ibid.

34. Ibid.

35. Janis Williams, telephone interview by author, 11 February 1992.

36. During the long Colonial period, visitors arrived by boat to disembark in the central plaza, resulting in less north-south movement.

37. In 1997, counted visitors to the Castillo de San Marcos numbered 582,730. Doubling this figure would give a conservative estimate of 1,165,460 visitors per year. Based on figures from the Department of Revenue of total dollars spent, as determined from tax receipts from the tourism recreation aggregate of hotels, gift retail stores, and restaurants, the Saint Augustine Chamber of Commerce estimates the total number of visitors to Saint Augustine during 1997 to be 2.6 million.

38. Troy Bunch, interview by author, 10 January 1991, Saint Augustine, Fla.

39. Excavations one foot below grade must be monitored by a city archaeologist. Craig Thorn, interview by author, 9 January 1991, Saint Augustine, Fla.

FOURTEEN *Conclusion: Threats and Opportunities*

1. Department of Commerce 1997, 39. Long 1990, 6. These figures include the Great Lakes and St. Lawrence River but exclude Hawaii and Alaska. Culliton et al. 1990, 3–4.

2. Long 1990, 6.

3. *Wall Street Journal* 1996, 1.

4. Castine is the most remote, approximately 125 miles from Portland and 230 miles from Boston. Edgartown has frequent ferry connections to mainland Massachusetts, and Edenton is 70 miles from Norfolk and approximately 225 miles from Washington, D.C. The remaining six towns are more conveniently located to major cities and even more so to their suburbs.

5. Horton 1991, 34; Beatley 1994.

6. Edgerton 1991, 49–76.

7. Titus 1990, 149; Burby and May 1997.

8. Edgerton 1991, 17–20.

9. Titus 1991, 40.

10. Edgerton 1991, 24–39.

11. Beatley 1993, 26–30.

12. Ibid., 4.

13. Ibid., 3.

14. The public owns the beachfront areas up to the edge of the high water along tidal coasts, as defined by the "public trust doctrine" of English common law and by numerous state constitutions.

15. Fortunately, all nine Atlantic towns now have height restrictions, with maximums varying between thirty-five and fifty feet.

16. Daniels 1991, 422.

17. Titus 1990, 166.

References and Bibliography

Albion, Robert, et al. 1972. *New England and the Sea*. Middletown, Conn.: Wesleyan University Press.

Allaback, Sarah, ed. 1995. *Resorts and Recreation: An Historic Theme Study of the New Jersey Coastal Heritage Trail Route*. Mauricetown, N.J.: The Sandy Hook Foundation and National Park Service.

Allen, Everett S. 1982. *Martha's Vineyard: An Elegy*. Boston: Little, Brown.

Allis, Sam. 1989. "A Small Town Goes Prime-Time." *Time*, 9 January, 14, 18.

Antiques Magazine. 1979. "History in Town: Edenton, North Carolina." June, 1244–65.

Appleton's General Guide to the United States and Canada. 1879–1901. New York: D. Appleton.

Bachelder, Peter, and F. Schauffler. N.d. "The Mystique of Maine: Tourism in Vacationland." Pamphlet, Maine Coastal Program.

Bailey, Anthony. 1971. *In the Village*. New York: Knopf.

Ballance, Alton. 1989. *Ocracokers*. Chapel Hill, N.C.: University of North Carolina Press.

Banks, Charles Edward. [1911–25] 1966. *The History of Martha's Vineyard*. 3 vols. Reprint, Edgartown, Mass.: Dukes County Historical Society.

Barefoot, Daniel W. 1995. *Touring the Backroads of North Carolina's Lower Coast*. Winston-Salem, N.C.: John F. Blair.

———. 1995. *Touring the Backroads of North Carolina's Upper Coast*. Winston-Salem: John F. Blair.

Barker, James F., Michael J. Buono, and Henry P. Hildebrandt. 1981. *The Small Town Designbook*. Mississippi State, Miss.: Center for Small Town Research and Design, School of Architecture, Mississippi State University.

Beatley, Timothy. 1993. *Risk Allocation Policy in the Coastal Zone: The Current Framework and Future Directions*. Washington, D.C.: Prepared for the Office of Technology Assessment, U.S. Congress.

———. 1994. *Ethical Land Use: Principles of Policy and Planning*. Baltimore: Johns Hopkins University Press.

Beaufort County Joint Planning Commission. 1979. *City of Beaufort Development Plan*. Beaufort, S.C.

———. 1989. *City of Beaufort Development Plan*. Beaufort, S.C.

Bell, Malcolm, Jr. 1987. *Major Butler's Legacy: Five Generations of a Slaveholding Family*. Athens: University of Georgia Press.

Benjamin, S. G. W. 1878. "The Sea Islands." *Harper's Magazine* 57, no. 342:839–61.

Bird, Eric C. F. 1984. *An Introduction to Coastal Geomorphology*. Oxford: Basil Blackwell.

Bishir, Catherine W., and Michael T. Southern. 1996. *A Guide to the Historic Architecture of Eastern North Carolina*. Chapel Hill, N.C.: University of North Carolina Press.

Blake, Curtis Channing. 1976. "The Architecture of Carrère and Hastings." Ph.D. diss., Columbia University.

Bloomer, Kent C., and Charles W. Moore. 1977. *Body, Memory, and Architecture*. New Haven, Conn.: Yale University Press.

Blumenfeld, Hans. 1967. *The Modern Metropolis*. Cambridge, Mass.: MIT Press.

Bodo, Robin. 1994. "A Partial Survey of Rehoboth Beach." Delaware State Historic Preservation Office, Dover. Draft.

Bookchin, Murray. 1980. *Toward an Ecological Society*. Montreal: Black Rose Books.

Bourne, Russell. 1989. *The View from Front Street: Travels through New England's Historic Fishing Communities*. New York: W. W. Norton.

Boyce, W. Scott. 1916. *Economic and Social History of Chowan County, North Carolina, 1880–1915*. New York: Columbia University Studies in History, Economics, and Public Law, vol. 76, no. 1.

Bradbury, Charles. [1837] 1967. *History of Kennebunk Port*. Reprint, Kennebunkport: Durrel Publications.

Bradbury, Thomas E. 1986. "Growth in the Kennebunks: An Historical Perspective." *Village Gazette*, 20, 27 June and 4, 18 July.

Brewer, Richard, E. 1987. *Perspectives on Ocean Grove*. Ocean Grove, N.J.: Historical Society of Ocean Grove.

Bridenbaugh, Carl. 1964. *Cities in the Wilderness: The First Century of Urban Life in America*. New York: Capricorn Books.

Bridwell, Ronald E. 1982. " . . . *That We Should Have a Port . . .*" *A History of the Port of Georgetown, South Carolina, 1732–1865*. Georgetown: Georgetown Times.

Brooks, Noah. 1894. *Tales of the Maine Coast*. New York: Scribner's.

———. 1901. *A New England Village Boy*. New York: Scribner's.

Bucke, Emory Stevens, ed. 1964. *The History of American Methodism*. Vol. 2. New York: Abington Press.

Burby, Raymond J., and Peter J. May. 1997. *Making Governments Plan: State Experiments in Managing Land Use*. Baltimore: Johns Hopkins University Press.

Burroughs, Polly. 1988. *Guide to Martha's Vineyard*. Chester, Conn.: Globe Pequot Press.

Butchko, Thomas Russell. 1992. *Edenton: An Architectural Portrait*. Edenton, N.C.: Edenton's Woman's Club.

Butler, Joyce. 1980. *The Kennebunks—A Watering Place*. Kennebunk: Brick Store Museum.

———. 1984. *A Kennebunkport Album*. Kennebunk Landing: Rosemary House Press.

———. 1989. *Kennebunkport Scrapbook*, vol. 2. Kennebunk Landing: Rosemary House Press.

Candee, Richard M. 1992. *Building Portsmouth: The Neighborhoods and Architecture of New Hampshire's Oldest City*. Portsmouth: Portsmouth Advocates.

Castine Planning Board. 1979. *Castine Comprehensive Plan*. March.

Castine, Town of. 1941–1991. *Annual Reports for the Town of Castine, Maine*.

Chamberlain, Samuel. 1941. *Martha's Vineyard, a Camera Impression*. New York: Hastings House.

Chandler, David Leon. 1986. *Henry Flagler*. New York: Macmillan.

Chaney, Edward, and Kathleen A. Deagan. 1989. "St. Augustine and the La Florida Colony." In *First Encounters*, edited by Jerald Milanich and Susan Milbrath. Gainesville, Fla.: University of Florida Press.

Chatelain, Verne. 1946. *The Defenses of Spanish Florida, 1565–1763*. Carnegie Institution Publication 511, Washington, D.C.

Clayton, Barbara, and Kathleen Whitley. 1979. *Exploring Coastal New England*. New York: Dodd, Mead, and Co.

Colby, G. N. 1881. *Atlas of Hancock County, Maine*. Ellsworth, Maine: G. N. Colby.

Conkling, Philip W., ed. 1995. *From Cape Cod to the Bay of Fundy: An Environmental Atlas of the Gulf of Maine*. Cambridge, Mass.: MIT Press.

Conly, Robert. 1966. "St. Augustine, Nation's Oldest City, Turns 400." *National Geographic* 129, no. 2 (February): 196–229.

Cooch, Francis A. 1936. *Little Known History of Newark, Delaware, and Its Environs*. Newark: Press of Kells.

Cooper, Constance J. 1983. "A Town among Cities: New Castle, Delaware, 1780–1840." Ph.D. diss., University of Delaware.

Craig, Warren. 1987. "Asylum by the Sea." *New Jersey Reporter*, March, 8.

Crespo, Rafael A. 1987. "Florida's First Spanish Revival." vols. 1–3. Ph.D. diss., Harvard University.

Crouch, Dora P., Daniel J. Garr, and Axel I. Mundigo. 1982. *Spanish City Planning in North America*. Cambridge, Mass.: MIT Press.

Culliton, Thomas J., et al. 1990. *Fifty Years of Population Change along the Nation's Coasts, 1960–2010*. Rockville, Md.: U.S. Dept. of Commerce.

Curtis, Jane, Will Curtis, and Frank Lieberman. 1995. *Monhegan: The Artists' Island*. Camden, Maine: Down East Books.

Daniels, Thomas L. 1991. "The Purchase of Development Rights." *Journal of the American Planning Association* 57:421–31.

Davis, Claude G., and Robert Stutz. 1991. "Economy: A Final Look at Facts; Seasonal Citizens Need a Voice." *Vineyard Gazette* 9 August, 15.

Davison, Robert A. 1967. "Comment." In *The Growth of Seaport Cities: 1790–1825*, edited by David T. Gilchrist.

———. 1967. "New York Foreign Trade." In *The Growth of Seaport Cities: 1790–1825*, edited by David T. Gilchrist.

Delbonis, Paula. 1991. "Public Lands Protect a Balanced Future." *Vineyard Gazette* 10 May, A1.

Des Barres, Joseph F. W. [1780] 1966. *The Atlantic Neptune*. Reprint, Barre, Mass.: Barre Publishing.

Dibner, Martin, and George A. Tice. 1973. *Seacoast Maine: People and Places*. Garden City, N.Y.: Doubleday.

Dickey, John W. 1983. *Metropolitan Transportation Planning*. New York: McGraw-Hill.

Dodson Associates. 1989. "Upper Main Street Masterplan." Edgartown, Mass.: Edgartown Planning Board and Martha's Vineyard Commission.

Dolan, Robert, and Harry Lins. 1985. *The Outer Banks of North Carolina*. U.S. Geological Survey Professional Paper 1177-B. Washington, D.C.: U.S. Government Printing Office.

Dorfman, Joseph. 1967. "Economic Thought." In *The Growth of Seaport Cities: 1790–1825*, edited by David T. Gilchrist.

Dorsey, Rhoda M. 1967. "Comment." In *The Growth of Seaport Cities: 1790–1825*, edited by David T. Gilchrist.

Doudiet, Ellenore W. 1978. *Majabigwaduce*. Castine, Maine: Castine Scientific Society.

Douglas, Elisha P. 1967. "Speaker." In *The Growth of Seaport Cities: 1790–1825*, edited by David T. Gilchrist. Charlottesville, Va.: University Press of Virginia.

Drake, Samuel Adams. 1875. *Nooks and Corners of the New England Coast*. New York: Harper and Brothers.

Drosdick, Nan, and Mark Morris. 1995. *Atlantic Canada Handbook*. Chico, Calif.: Moon Publications.

Dullea, Georgia. 1989. "In Tents by the Sea, An Annual Revival of the Spirit." *New York Times*, 6 July, C1.

Dunlop, Beth. 1990. "Quixotic Saint Augustine: Remaking History for Commerce." Reprint. *Southern Accents*, July-August.

Edenton Board of Councilmen. 1976. *The Code of the Town of Edenton*. Charlottesville, Va.: Michie Company.

Edgartown Planning Board. 1990. *The Edgartown Master Plan*. Edgartown, Mass.

Edgerton, Lynne T. 1991. *The Rising Tide*. Washington, D.C.: Island Press.

Epstein, Jason, and Elizabeth Barlow. 1985. *East Hampton: A History and Guide*. New York: Random House.

Federal Writers' Project, Works Progress Administration. 1937. *The Intracoastal Waterway, Norfolk to Key West*. Washington, D.C.: U.S. Government Printing Office.

———. 1937. *Maine: A Guide "Down East."* Boston: Houghton Mifflin.

———. 1937. *Massachusetts: A Guide to Its Places and People*. Boston: Houghton Mifflin.

———. 1937. *Rhode Island: A Guide to the Smallest State*. Boston: Houghton Mifflin.

———. 1937. *Seeing St. Augustine*. St. Augustine, Fla.: City Commission.

———. 1938. *Beaufort and the Sea Islands*. Savannah, Ga.: Clover Club.

———. 1938. *Connecticut: A Guide to Its Roads, Lore, and People*. Boston: Houghton Mifflin.

———. 1938. *Delaware: A Guide to the First State*. New York: Viking Press.

———. 1938. *Ocean Highway: New Brunswick, New Jersey, to Jacksonville, Florida*. New York: Modern Age Books.

———. 1939. *Florida: A Guide to the Southernmost State*. New York: Oxford University Press.

———. 1939. *New Jersey, A Guide to Its Present and Past*. New York: Viking Press.

———. 1939. *North Carolina, A Guide to the Old North State*. Chapel Hill, N.C.: University of North Carolina Press.

———. 1940. *Georgia*. Athens: University of Georgia Press.

———. 1940. *Maryland: A Guide to the Old Line State*. New York: Oxford University Press.

———. 1941. *Virginia: A Guide to the Old Dominion*. New York: Oxford University Press.

———. 1955. *North Carolina Guide*. Edited by Blackwell P. Robinson. Chapel Hill, N.C.: University of North Carolina Press.

———. 1972. *U.S. One*. New York: Modern Age Books.

———. [1936] 1973. *New Castle on the Delaware*. Edited by Anthony Higgins. Reprint, Newark, N.J.: New Castle Historical Society.

———. [1941] 1978. *South Carolina: A Guide to the Palmetto State*. Reprint, St. Clair Shores, Mich.: Scholarly Press.

Fischer, David H. 1989. *Albion's Seed: Four British Folkways in America*. New York: Oxford University Press.

Fisher, Allan C., Jr. 1973. *America's Inland Waterway: Exploring the Atlantic Seaboard*. Washington, D.C.: National Geographic Society.

Funke, Lewis. 1990. "St. Augustine Celebrates 425 Years." *New York Times*, 13 May, 16.

Garland, Catherine A. 1988. *Nantucket Journeys*. Camden, Maine: Down East Books.

Garrow, David J. 1989. *St. Augustine, Florida, 1963–1964: Mass Protest and Racial Violence*. Brooklyn: Carlson.

Garvin, James L., and Nancy Merrill. 1971. "Exeter: Its Architectural Heritage." *New Hampshire Profiles* 20 (June), 33–51.

Gibbons, Richard. 1976. "Ocean Grove." In *History of Township of Neptune*. Neptune, N.J.: Township of Neptune.

Gilchrist, David T., ed. 1967. *The Growth of Seaport Cities, 1790–1825*. Charlottesville, Va.: University Press of Virginia.

Gill, Brendan. 1978. *Summer Places*. New York: Methuen.

Godschalk, David R., and Kathryn Cousins, eds. 1985. "Coastal Management: Planning on the Edge." *American Planning Association Journal* 51 (summer), no. 3:263–336.

Godschalk, David R., David J. Brower, and Timothy Beatley. 1989. *Catastrophic Coastal Storms: Hazard Mitigation and Development Management*. Durham, N.C.: Duke University Press.

Goldfield, David R. 1988. "Pearls on the Coast and Lights in the Forest: The Colonial South." In *The Making of Urban America*, edited by Raymond A. Mohl. Wilmington, Del.: Scholarly Resources.

Graham, Thomas. 1975. "Flagler's Magnificent Hotel Ponce De Leon." *Florida Historical Quarterly*, July.

———. 1978. *The Awakening of St. Augustine, the Anderson Family and the Oldest City: 1821–1924*. St. Augustine: St. Augustine Historical Society.

Griffin, Patricia C. 1983. "The Spanish Return: The People-Mix Period 1784–1821." In *The Oldest City*, edited by Jean Waterbury. St. Augustine: The St. Augustine Historical Society.

———. 1990. "Mullet on the Beach: The Minorcans of Florida, 1768–1788." *El Escribano, the St. Augustine Journal of History* 27:135–39.

Groves, George E. 1985. "Renovating the Oldest Street in North America." *Public Works* (June) no. 116:77–79.

Hand, Jill. 1986. "Ocean Grove Today." *Asbury Park Press,* 3 August, H1.

Harvey, Karen. 1980. *St. Augustine and St. Johns County: A Pictorial History*. Virginia Beach: Downing.

Hatch, Francis W. 1971. "Castine—Historic Gem of Penobscot Bay." *Down East*, July, 66–91.

Hatton, Hap. 1987. *Tropical Splendor: An Architectural History of Florida*. New York: Knopf.

Hawkins, Robert B., Jr. 1989. "Residential Community Associations: Private Governments in the Intergovernmental System?" Conference Sponsored by the Commission on Intergovernmental Relations. Washington, D.C.: Advisory Commission on Intergovernmental Relations.

Hay, John, and Peter Farb. 1966. *Human and Natural History from Long Island to Labrador*. New York: Harper and Row.

Haynes, William. [1957] 1969. "Horseshoe Nails to Squeeze Bottles." *Connecticut Antiquarian*. Essex, Conn.: Pequot Press, 3–11.

———. 1976. *The Stonington Chronology: 1649–1976*. Chester, Conn.: Pequot Press.

Heite, Louise B., and Edward R. Heite. 1986. "Town Plans as Artifacts: The Mid-Atlantic Experience." *Quarterly Bulletin, Archaeological Society of Virginia* 41 (3):142–59.

———. 1989. *Saving New Amstel*. New Castle: Trustees of the New Castle Common.

Herbers, John. 1986. *The New Heartland*. New York: Times Books.

Historic Beaufort Foundation. 1985. *A Guide to Historic Beaufort*. Beaufort, S.C.: Historic Beaufort Foundation.

Hoffecker, Carol E. 1983. *Corporate Capital: Wilmington in the Twentieth Century*. Philadelphia: Temple University Press.

Horton, Tom. 1991. *Turning the Tide: Saving the Chesapeake Bay*. Washington, D.C.: Island Press.

Hough, Henry Beetle. 1936. *Martha's Vineyard, Summer Resort, 1835–1935*. Rutland, Vt.: Tuttle Publishing Company.

Hough, Michael. 1990. *Out of Place*. New Haven, Conn.: Yale University Press.

Houston, Lawrence O. 1988. "Living Villages: Thoughts on the Future of the Village Form." *Small Town*, November-December, 14–25.

Hughes, George. 1873. *Days of Power in the Forest Temple*. Boston: John Bent.

Hunton, Gail, and Jennifer Boyd. 1989. *A Home Renovator's Guide to Historic Ocean Grove*. Ocean Grove, N.J.: Ocean Grove Home Owners Association.

Hutchins, John G. B. 1967. "Trade and Manufactures." In *The Growth of Seaport Cities: 1790–1825*, edited by David T. Gilchrist.

Huth, Hans. 1957. *Nature and the American: Three Centuries of Changing Attitudes*. Berkeley: University of California Press.

Immanuel Episcopal Church. 1989. *A Day in Old New Castle*. New Castle, Del.

Issac, Rhys. 1982. *The Transformation of Virginia: 1740–1790*. Chapel Hill: University of North Carolina Press.

Ivy, Robert A., Jr. 1985. "Building by the Sea: The Southeast." *Architecture* 74:70–85.

Jackson, John B. 1984. *Discovering the Vernacular Landscape*. New Haven, Conn.: Yale University Press.

James, Terry, and Bill Plaskett. 1996. *Buildings of Old Lunenburg*. Halifax: Nimbus Publishing.

Johanes, Jan H., Sr. 1976. *Yesterday's Reflections: Nassau County, Florida*. Callahan, Florida: Thomas Richardson.

John Milner Associates. 1979. *The Beaufort Preservation Manual*. West Chester, Pa.: John Milner Associates.

———. 1990. *The Beaufort Preservation Manual Supplement*. West Chester, Pa.: John Milner Associates.

Johnston, Frances B. 1947. *The Early Architecture of North Carolina*. Chapel Hill, N.C.: University of North Carolina Press.

Jones, Katherine. 1960. *Port Royal Under Six Flags*. New York: Bobbs-Merrill.

Jordan, Terry G. and Matti E. Kaups. 1989. *The American Backwoods Frontier: An Ethnic and Ecological Interpretation*. Baltimore: Johns Hopkins University Press.

Kennebunk Comprehensive Plan Committee. 1991. *Kennebunk Comprehensive Plan*. Kennebunk, Maine. Draft.

Kennebunkport. 1939–90. *Annual Reports*.

———. 1982. *Updated Comprehensive Plan*.

———. 1987. "Draft Report of Kennebunkport's Growth Planning Committee."

Kovacik, Charles F., and John J. Winberry. 1987. *South Carolina: A Geography*. Boulder, Colo.: Westview Press.

Kruse, Albert, and Gertrude Kruse. 1932. *New Castle Sketches*. Philadelphia: University of Pennsylvania Press.

Lane, Mills. 1985. *Architecture of the Old South: North Carolina*. Savannah, Ga.: Beehive Press.

———. 1984. *Architecture of the Old South: South Carolina*. Savannah, Ga.: Beehive Press.

LaRoue, Samuel D., and Ellen J. Uguccioni. 1988. *Coral Gables in Postcards: Scenes from Florida's Yesterday*. Miami, Fla.: Dade Heritage Trust.

Lee, Everett S. 1967. "Speaker." In *The Growth of Seaport Cities: 1790–1825*, edited by David T. Gilchrist.

Lefler, Hugh Talmage, and Albert Ray Newsome. 1973. *North Carolina: The History of a Southern State*. Chapel Hill, N.C.: The University of North Carolina Press.

Lengnick, Lena Wood. 1962. "Beaufort Memoirs." Pamphlet. Beaufort: Woman's Society of Christian Service of the Carteret Street Methodist Church.

Life Magazine. 1968. 6 September, 35.

Lingeman, Richard R. 1980. *Small Town America: A narrative history, 1620 to the Present*. New York: Putnam.

Long, Larry. 1990. "Population by the Sea." *Population Today*, April, 6–8.

Lovejoy, Kim E. 1985. "Preservation Plan for Kennebunk and Kennebunkport, Maine." Natick, Mass.: privately published report.

Lynch, Kevin. 1972. *What Time Is This Place?* Cambridge, Mass.: MIT Press.

——. 1981. *A Theory of Good City Form.* Cambridge, Mass.: MIT Press.

Lynch, Kevin, and Gary Hack. 1993. *Site Planning,* 3d ed. Cambridge, Mass: MIT Press

Mallory, Philip R. 1954. *Mystic Seaport.* New York: Newcomen Society.

Maneval, John R. 1990. "Urbana, Virginia: A Case Study of the Basis of Small Town Design." Unpublished paper, School of Architecture, University of Virginia.

Manucy, Albert. 1978. *The Houses of St. Augustine, 1565–1821.* St. Augustine: St. Augustine Historical Society.

——. 1982. "Changing Traditions in St. Augustine Architecture." *El Escribano* 19:1–28.

——. 1985. "The Physical Setting of Sixteenth Century St. Augustine." *Florida Anthropologist* 38, nos. 1–2, Part 1, (March-June):34–53.

Martha's Vineyard Commission. 1991. "Affordable Housing Policy."

——. 1989. "Preserving the Island's Most Valuable Resource: Open Space."

——. 1992. "Regional Island Plan."

Marvin, Robert E. 1989. *Urban Design Plan for the City of Beaufort, South Carolina.* Report, Walterboro, S.C.

Massachusetts Historical Commission. 1984. "Reconnaissance Survey Town Report, Provincetown." Boston.

——. 1985. "Reconnaissance Survey Town Report, Marblehead." Boston.

——. 1985. "Reconnaissance Survey Town Report, Rockport," Boston.

——. 1985. "Reconnaissance Survey Town Report, Wellfleet." Boston.

——. 1985. "Reconnaissance Survey Town Report, Yarmouth." Boston.

Mazer, Milton. 1976. *People and Predicaments.* Cambridge, Mass.: Harvard University Press.

McAlester, Virginia, and Lee McAlester. 1991. *A Field Guide to American Houses.* New York: Knopf.

McFadden, Grace Jordan. N.d. "Eyewitness to History, Penn School, 1862–1948." Pamphlet produced by the South Carolina State Museum and the Mann-Simons Cottage: Museum of African-American Culture.

McIntire, Nicholas S. 1986. *The Best of Behind the Times.* New Castle: New Castle Historical Society.

——. 1988. *A Brief History of the Trustees of New Castle Common.* New Castle: Trustees of New Castle Common.

Meinig, D. W. 1979. "Symbolic Landscapes." In *The Interpretations of Ordinary Landscapes,* edited by D. W. Meinig. New York: Oxford University Press.

——. 1986. *Atlantic America, 1492–1800.* New Haven, Conn.: Yale University Press.

Methot, June. 1988. *Up and Down the Beach.* Navesink, N.J.: Whip Publishers.

Miller, Henry M. 1986. *Discovering Maryland's First City.* St. Mary's City Archaeology Series, 2. St. Mary's City: St. Mary's City Commission.

Mohl, Raymond A., ed. 1988. *The Making of Urban America.* Wilmington, Del.: Scholarly Resources.

Moore, Edward C. 1965. *New Castle, Delaware, Comprehensive Planning Study.* Parts 1, 2. City of New Castle.

Moore, Elizabeth Vann. 1989. *Historic Edenton and Chowan County.* Edenton, N.C.: Edenton's Woman's Club.

Morgan, F. W. 1959. "Hinterlands." In *Readings in Urban Geography,* edited by Harold M. Mayer and Clyde F. Kohn. Chicago: University of Chicago Press.

Mundigo, Axel I., and Dora P. Crouch. 1997. "The City Planning Ordinances of the Laws of the Indies Revisited." *Town Planning Review* 48:247–68.

Nash, Gary B. 1979. *The Urban Crucible: Social Change, Political Consciousness, and the Origins of the American Revolution*. Cambridge, Mass.: Harvard University Press.

New Castle County. 1988. *Comprehensive Development Plan*. Final Draft. New Castle County, Del. Department of Planning.

New York State Office of Parks, Recreation, and Historic Preservation. N.d. "Historic and Natural Districts Inventory Form, Cold Spring Harbor." Historic Preservation Field Services Bureau, Waterford, N.Y.

——. 1986. "Southampton Village Historic District."

——. 1987. "East Hampton Village District Boundary Expansion."

New York Times. 1985. "An Historic Jersey Town Longs for the Old Days." 14 November.

Nichols, Frederick Doveton. 1957. *The Early Architecture of Georgia*. Chapel Hill, N.C.: University of North Carolina Press.

Nordheimer, Jon. 1992. "Shore Towns Dread Release of Mentally Ill," *New York Times*, 25 July, 25.

Ocean Grove Chamber of Commerce. N.d. *The Ocean Grove Story*. Ocean Grove, N.J.: Ocean Grove Chamber of Commerce.

Ocean Grove Home Owners Association. 1992. "A Community Response to the Department of Human Services." Report, May 5, Ocean Grove, N.J.

Palmer, Henry Robinson. 1913. *Stonington by the Sea*. Stonington, Conn.: Palmer Press.

Parnes, Brenda. 1980. "Ocean Grove: A Planned Leisure Environment." In *Planned Utopian Experiments: Four New Jersey Towns*, edited by Paul A. Stellhorn. Trenton, N.J.: New Jersey Historical Commission.

Parramore, Thomas C. 1967. *Cradle of the Colony: The History of Chowan County and Edenton, North Carolina*. Edenton, N.C.: Edenton Chamber of Commerce.

Parris Island Museum Exhibit, Marine Corps Recruit Depot, 1991.

Peattie, Roderick. 1940. *Geography in Human Destiny*. New York: G. W. Stewart.

Pepper, Adeline. 1965. *Tours of Historic New Jersey*. New Brunswick, N.J.: Rutgers University Press.

Pilkey, Orrin H., Jr., William J. Neal, and Orrin H. Pilkey, Sr. 1980. *From Currituck to Calabash: Living with North Carolina's Barrier Islands*. Durham, N.C.: Duke University Press.

Platt, Rutherford H., et al., eds. 1987. "Cities on the Beach: Management Issues of Developed Coastal Barriers." University of Chicago, Department of Geography, Research Paper No. 224.

Pratson, Frederick. 1973. *A Guide to Atlantic Canada*. Riverside, Conn.: Chatham Press.

Preston, Dickson J. 1984. *Oxford: The First Three Centuries*. Easton, Md.: Historical Society of Talbot County.

Price, Chester. 1963. "Place Names and Indian Lore of York County, Maine," New Hampshire Archaeology Society, Miscellaneous Papers no. 2, May.

Railton, Arthur R. 1988. "Walking Tour of Historic Edgartown." Edgartown, Mass.: Dukes County Historical Society.

Rees, Ronald. 1995. *St. Andrews and the Islands*. Halifax: Nimbus Publishing.

Reps, John W. 1965. *The Making of Urban America*. Princeton, N.J.: Princeton University Press.

——. 1969. *Town Planning in Frontier America*. Princeton, N.J.: Princeton University Press.

——. 1972. *Tidewater Towns: City Planning in Colonial Virginia and Maryland*. Williamsburg, Va.: Colonial Williamsburg Foundation.

Rhode Island Historical Preservation Commission. 1974. "Historic and Architectural Resources of East Greenwich, Rhode Island." Statewide Historical Preservation Report, Providence, R.I.

——. 1980. "The Southern Thames Street Neighborhood in Newport, Rhode Island." State-wide Historical Preservation Report, Providence, R.I.

——. 1990. "Historic and Architectural Resources of Bristol, Rhode Island." Statewide Historical Preservation Report, Providence, R.I.

Roberts, Kenneth Lewis. 1938. *Trending into Maine*. Boston: Little, Brown.

Robinson, William F. 1989. *Coastal New England*. Secaucus, N.J.: Wellfleet Press.

Rose, Willie Lee. 1964. *Rehearsal for Reconstruction: The Port Royal Experiment*. New York: Bobbs-Merrill.

Rosenfeld, Mary. 1986. "A Basic Guide to the Kennebunk River and its Tributaries." Friends of the Kennebunk River.

Rowland, Lawrence, Alexander Moore, and George C. Rogers, Jr. 1996. *The History of Beaufort County, South Carolina, vol. 1, 1514–1861*. Columbia, S.C.: University of South Carolina Press.

Rubbing, Juleps. 1967. "Urban Growth of the Seaport Cities, 1790–1825." In *The Growth of Seaport Cities: 1790–1825*, edited by David T. Gilchrist.

Rubin, Julius. 1967. "Urban Growth and Regional Development." In *The Growth of Seaport Cities: 1790–1825*, ed. David T. Gilchrist.

St. Augustine City Commission. 1989. "A Guide to Development in Historic Preservation Districts."

St. Augustine Historical Restoration and Preservation Commission. 1968. "San Agustin Antiguo: La Calle Real."

St. Augustine Institute of Science and Historical Society. 1913. *Pictorial History and Guide Book of Saint Augustine*. St. Augustine: W. J. Harris.

City of St. Augustine, Planning and Building Department. 1987. *Comprehensive Plan-Update, Future Land Use Element*.

——. 1989. "Architectural Guidelines for Historic Preservation."

Sale, Kirkpatrick. 1980. *Human Scale*. New York: Coward, McCann and Geohegan.

Sanborn Map Company, Pelham, N.Y. 1886. "Fire Insurance Maps of Stonington, Connecticut."

——. 1893. "Fire Insurance Maps of Edenton, North Carolina."

——. 1899. "Fire Insurance Maps of Beaufort, South Carolina."

——. 1904. "Fire Insurance Maps of St. Augustine, Florida."

——. 1911. "Fire Insurance Maps of Kennebunkport, Maine."

——. 1911, 1925. "Fire Insurance Maps of Castine, Maine."

——. 1912. "Fire Insurance Maps of New Castle, Delaware."

——. 1912. "Fire Insurance Maps of New Jersey Coast."

——. 1914. "Fire Insurance Maps of Edgartown, Massachusetts."

Sandbeck, Peter B. 1988. *The Historic Architecture of New Bern and Craven County, North Carolina*. New Bern, N.C.: Tryon Palace Commission.

Scardaville, Michael C. 1980. "Developmental History of St. Augustine," In *Historic Sites and Building Survey of Saint Augustine, Florida*. St. Augustine, Fla.: Historic Saint Augustine Preservation Board.

Schmidt, Henrietta. 1975. *Through the Years*, edited by Thomas E. Bradbury. Kennebunk, Maine: Star Press.

Schneider, Keith. 1991. "A Historic District in South Carolina Struggles to Preserve Black History." *New York Times*, 26 May, 22.

Schoenbaum, Thomas J. 1982. *Islands, Capes, and Sounds: The North Carolina Coast*. Winston-Salem: John F. Blair.

Sears, Joan Niles. 1979. *The First One Hundred Years of Town Planning in Georgia*. Atlanta: Cherokee Publishing Company.

Silverman, Jane. 1978. "The American Coastline: New Frontier of Planning." *AIA Journal* 67 (August): 46–53.

Simon, Anne W. 1973. *No Island Is an Island: The Ordeal of Martha's Vineyard*. Garden City, N.Y.: Doubleday.

Smith, H. M. Scott. 1990. *Historic Houses of Prince Edward Island*. Erin, Ontario: Boston Mills Press.

Snead, Rodman E. 1982. *Coastal Landforms and Surface Features*. Stroudsburg, Pa.: Hutchinson Ross.

Sprague, Laura F., ed. 1987. *Agreeable Situations: Society, Commerce, and Art in Southern Maine, 1780–1830*. Kennebunk, Maine: Brick Store Museum.

Stackhouse, H. H. 1979. "The Model Land Tract: The Development of a Residential Neighborhood." *El Escribano* 16: 25–32.

Stanislawski, Dan. 1947. "Early Spanish Town Planning in the New World," *Geographical Review* 37: 94–105.

Stephenson, Tray. 1973. "Beaufort, South Carolina: A Brief Historical and Architectural Summary." *Southern Antiques and Interiors* 2, no. 3 (fall): 3–12.

Stokes, E. H. 1875. *Summer by the Sea*. Philadelphia: Haddock and Son.

——. 1874. *Ocean Grove, Its Origins and Progress*. Ocean Grove, N.J.: Ocean Grove Camp Meeting Association.

Stonington, Borough of. 1991 "Report of the Historic District Study Committee."

Stonington Planning and Zoning Commission. 1978. "Stonington Plan of Development."

——. 1989. "Stonington Plan of Development."

Surowiecki, John, and David Tedone. 1982. *A History of Connecticut's Coast: 400 Years of Coastal Industry and Development*. Hartford: State of Connecticut.

Teal, Roger F., et al. 1976. "Tourist Traffic in Small Historic Cities." Washington, D.C.: U.S. Department of Transportation.

The Lowcountry Ledger. 1990. 11 July, 3.

Thomason and Associates. 1989. "An Update to 'A Preservation Plan for Historic Beaufort, South Carolina,'" Historical Preservation Consultants' Report, Nashville Tenn. March.

Thompson, Deborah. 1976. *Maine Forms of American Architecture*. Camden, Maine: Colby Museum of Art.

Thorndike, Joseph J. 1993. *The Coast: A Journey Down the Atlantic Shore*. New York: St. Martin's Press.

Titus, James G. 1990. "Greenhouse Effect, Sea Level Rise, and Coastal Zone Management." *Coastal Zone Management Journal* 14:147–71.

——. 1991. "Greenhouse Effect and Coastal Wetland Policy: How America Could Abandon An Area the Size of Massachusetts." *Environmental Management* 15, no. 1 (November/December): 39–58.

Torrey, E. Fuller. 1989. "Why Are There So Many Homeless Mentally Ill?" *Harvard Medical School Mental Health Letter* (August): 8.

Trask, John J. 1980. *Stonington Houses*. Old Saybrook, Conn.: Peregrine Press.

Trefil, James. 1984. *A Scientist at the Seashore*. New York: Scribner's.

Trewartha, Glenn T. 1943. "Types of Rural Settlement in Colonial America." *Geographical Review* 33: 568–80.

Tyler, David B. 1955. *Delaware*. Cambridge, Mass.: Cornell Maritime Press.

Upchurch, Frank D., ed. 1959. *St. Augustine Restoration Plan*. St. Augustine, Fla.: Florida Board of Parks and Historic Memorials.

Urry, John. 1990. *The Tourist Gaze*. London: Sage Publications.

U.S. Department of Commerce, Bureau of the Census. 1978. *Final Environmental Impact Statement: Maine's Coastal Program, 1978*.

———. 1997. *Statistical Abstract of the United States 1997*. Washington, D.C.: Government Printing Office.

U.S. Department of Commerce, National Oceanic and Atmospheric Administration. 1986. *United States Coast Pilot*. Vols. 2, 3. Washington, D.C.: Government Printing Office.

U.S. Department of Commerce, Tourism Administration. 1989. "A Strategic Look at the Travel and Tourism Industry." Washington, D.C.: Government Printing Office.

U.S. Department of the Interior, Environmental Protection Agency. 1989. *The Potential Effects of Global Climate Change on the United States*. Washington, D.C.: Government Printing Office.

U.S. Department of the Interior, National Park Service. 1969. "Historic Beaufort." Nomination form, National Register of Historic Places Inventory.

———. 1972. "Rockville, Village of, Historic District."

———. 1973. "Castine Historic District."

———. 1973. "Edenton Historic District."

———. 1974. "East Hampton Village District."

———. 1975. "Kennebunkport Historic District."

———. 1975. "Orient Historic District."

———. 1975. "New Castle."

———. 1976. "Cape May Historic District."

———. 1976. "Ocean Grove Camp Meeting Association."

———. 1978. "Greenport Village Historic District."

———. 1979. "Stonington Borough."

———. 1982. "Key West Historic District."

———. 1982. "McClellanville Historic District."

———. 1983. "Edgartown Village Historic District."

———. 1984. "Chestertown Historic District."

———. 1985. "Fernandina Beach Historic District."

———. 1986. "Lewes Historic District."

———. 1994. "Sag Harbor Village Historic District."

———. 1996. "Bluffton Historic District."

———. N.d. "Cambridge Historic District."

———. N.d. "St. Augustine Town Plan Historic District."

———. N.d. "St. Michaels Historic District."

Vanstory, Burnette. 1956. *Georgia's Land of the Golden Isles*. Athens, Ga.: University of Georgia Press.

Vineyard Open Land Foundation. 1973. "Looking at the Vineyard." West Tisbury, Mass.: Vineyard Open Land Foundation.

Wallace, Birgitta Linderoth. 1990. "L'Anse aux Meadows: Gateway to Vinland," *Acta Archaeologica* 61:166–97.

Wallace, David Duncan. 1951. *South Carolina: A Short History*. Chapel Hill, N.C.: University of North Carolina Press.

Wall Street Journal. 1996. 7 October, 1.

Ward, Larry, et al. 1989. *Living with the Chesapeake Bay and Virginia's Ocean Shores*. Durham, N.C.: Duke University Press.

Wasson, George S., and Lincoln Colcord. 1932. *Sailing Days on the Penobscot: The River and Bay as They Were in the Old Days*. Salem, Mass.: Marine Research Society.

Waterbury, Jean Parker, ed. 1983. *The Oldest City, St. Augustine: Saga of Survival*. St. Augustine, Fla.: St. Augustine Historical Society.

Weiss, Ellen. 1987. *City in the Woods: The Life and Design of an American Camp Meeting on Martha's Vineyard*. New York: Oxford University Press.

Wheeler, George Augustus. 1875. *History of Castine, Penobscot, and Brooksville, Maine*. Bangor, Maine: Burr and Robinson.

Wheeler, Richard Anson. 1900. *History of the Town of Stonington*. New London: Press of the Day Publishing Company.

Whipple, Joseph. 1816. *Geographical View of the District of Maine*. Bangor, Maine: Peter Edes.

Whitehill, Walter Muir. 1971. *Boston: A Topographical History*. Cambridge, Mass.: Belknap Press, Harvard University.

Whittlesey, Derwent. 1944. *The Earth and the State*. Washington, D.C.: published for the U.S. Armed Forces Institute by Henry Holt and Company.

Wilford, John Noble. 1996. "A Fort Lost and Found," *New York Times*, June 9, Section 4, 2.

Williams, Marshall H. 1965. "A Tree of Life, Frederick Harrison Williams." New Haven, Conn.: Yale University Press.

Wilmerding, John. 1988. *Paintings by Fitz Hugh Lane*. Washington, D.C.: National Gallery of Art; New York: Abrams.

Wilson Museum Bulletin. 1974. " 'Quality Avenue'—Upper Main Street, Castine." Castine Scientific Society, Castine, Maine. Vol. 1, no. 30 (spring).

——. 1990. "The 1920s." Castine Scientific Society, Castine, Maine. Vol. 3, no. 19 (spring).

Wojtas, Joe. 1991. "Rights of Way Paths to Borough's Past." *The Day* (New London), 7 October.

——. 1992. "Affordable Housing Law Takes Power from Hands of Borough." *The Day* (New London), 12 January, A1, A4.

Wooten, Bayard, and Anthony Higgins. 1939. *New Castle, Delaware, 1651–1939*. Boston: Houghton Mifflin.

Worley, William S. 1990. *J. C. Nichols and the Shaping of Kansas City*. Columbia, Mo.: University of Missouri Press.

Index

229; town silhouette of, 285; waterfront of, 12, 231, 233, 284; water-land configuration of, *6*; wood scrollwork in, 291–92

Edgartown, Mass., *26, 30,* 99–104, *100, 102, 108,* 115; adaptation to climate in, 8; bike path in, *291*; civic landscape of, *102*; doorways in, *103*; early settlement of, 104–6; as fashionable retreat, 108–11; international reputation of, 301 n. 2; limited growth of, 5; location of, 7; lot size in, 22; maps of, *100–101, 105, 107*; N. Water St. of, *21*; plan of, *104*; postwar development of, 111–15; public buildings in, 286; quantitative characteristics of scale in, 295; ship captains' residences in, 13; street section of, *96–97*; town plan of, 10, *11,* 105–6, *109, 110*; traditional patterns retained in, 287; Upper Main St. plans in, *288, 289*; and waterfront, 12; water-land configuration of *6, 101*; water's-edge parking lot in, *283*; whaling industry in, 99, 106, 108

Edison, Theodore, 37

Elizabeth City, N.C., 205–6

Elizabeth Islands, 42, *100–101*

Entrance corridors, 16, 290; in Beaufort, S.C., *254,* 255; in Castine, 17; in Stonington, 126

Erie Canal, 4

Essex, Conn., 48

Exeter, N.H., *26,* 38, *39*–40

Exploration, age of, 29

Fairfield, Conn., 48

Fall River, Mass., 3

Farmlands Preservation Program, of Suffolk County, 50

Federal style, 8; in Castine, 57, 63, 73; in Edenton, 223; in Exeter, N.H., 39; in Kennebunks' Port, 85; in Sag Harbor, 51

Feiss, Carl, 252

Fenwick, James, 142

Fernandina Beach, Fla., 214

Ferryland, Newfoundland, 31

Fishing areas, 28, 40

Flagler, Henry M., 201, 213, 214, 215, 216, 261, 267–71, 278

Flaring avenues, in Ocean Grove, 8, *160, 164,* 166, 168, 284

Florida, 200–201, 213–17; islands along, 199

Fort George, 57, 60, 64, 71

Fort Pownall, 60

Foursquare style, in Ocean Grove, 169

French and Indian Wars, 29, 144

Gentrification, in New Castle, 191–94

Georgetown, Prince Edward Island, 34

Georgetown, S.C., *198, 210*

Georgia, 211–13

Georgian style, in Edenton, 223

Gilded Age, and Newport, R.I., 45

Glaciers: and Cape Cod, 41; and drumlins, 40;

and islands off Cape Cod, 42; and Long Island, 48; and North Atlantic region, 27, 28

Gloucester, Mass., 40

Gosnold, Bartholomew, 105

Gothic or Gothic Revival style: in Bluffton, S.C., 211; in Edenton, 223; in McClellanville, 210; in Ocean Grove, 169; in Plymouth, N.C., 206; in Stonington, 130; in Tappahannock, Va., 151

Grand Bank, Newfoundland, 31–32

Granville, earl of, 226

Greek Revival style: in Castine, 57, 63; in Edenton, 223; in Edgartown, 106; in Kennebunks' Port, 85, *85*; in Nantucket, Mass., 43; in Sag Harbor, 51; in Stonington, 130, *130, 131*

Greenport, N.Y., 51

Greenwich, N.J., 142

Greenbelts, 8, 20, 179, *180,* 234

Grid configurations, 10; in St. Andrews-by-the-Sea, New Brunswick, 35; in Edenton, 223, 226; in Edgartown, *109*; in Fernandina Beach, 214; in Georgetown, S.C., 210; in New Castle, 179; in Ocean Grove, 167; in Rehoboth Beach, Del., 145; in Virginia towns, 150

Griffin, Patricia, 264–65

Guilford, Conn., 48

Gulf of Maine, 28

Gulf Stream, 28, 34, 41, 48, 99

Guzy, Pierre du, 29

Halifax, Nova Scotia, *26,* 33

Harbors, 11–12

Hassam, Childe, 47, 49

Hastings, Thomas, 267, 268, *269,* 270

Hatteras, N.C., 204

Hatteras Woods, 203

Henri, Robert, 37

Hertford, N.C., 206

Hewes, Joseph, 228

Hilton, William, 209

Historic American coastal towns. *See* Coastal towns

Homeowners' associations, 173

Homer, Winslow, 49

Hopper, Edward, 37

Horton, John S., *266*

House location or size, and social class, 13–15, 63, 86, 125, 239

Hudson, Henry, 142, 143

Human scale of towns, 20–23; of Beaufort park, 253; in Castine, 59–60; in Noank, Conn., 47

Hutchins, John G. B., 2

Industrialization, 4; and Delaware River region, 140; and English colonial policy, 303 n. 2; in New Castle, 190, 191; in Stonington, 122, 124–26

About the Author

Warren Boeschenstein grew up in St. Louis near the Mississippi River but has lived for the past twenty-five years in Charlottesville, Virginia, a convenient base from which to explore the nooks and crannies of the Atlantic coast. A graduate of Amherst College, Washington University, and Harvard University, he is a professor of architecture at the University of Virginia. His current professional work, which has been recognized with national design awards, focuses on the planning and design of compact communities served not by oceangoing vessels but by contemporary mass transit systems.

Library of Congress Cataloging-in-Publication Data

Boeschenstein, Warren.
    Historic American towns along the Atlantic coast / Warren
Boeschenstein.
       p.   cm.
    Includes bibliographical references (p.   ) and index.
    ISBN 0-8018-6144-6 (alk. paper)
    1. Atlantic Coast (U.S.)—History, Local.   2. Cities and
towns—Atlantic Coast (U.S.)   3. Historic sites—Atlantic Coast
(U.S.)   I. Title.
F106.B66   1999
974—dc21   99-10668
                                         CIP